BOUNDLESS

An Adventure Beyond Limits

BOUNDLESS

AN ADVENTURE BEYOND LIMITS

by Karen Darke

Boundless

An Adventure Beyond Limits

First published in 2012 by Akreative
www.akreative.com

ISBN 978-1-904207-66-5

CONTENTS

For Mum and Dad. Thank you for teaching me to 'walk' so well.

INTRODUCTION

A few people have commented after reading *Boundless* that they would like to know more about my background and accident. That's the story in my first book, *If You Fall* ... but for those of you who haven't read it, here's a brief bit of context which is also built on in the first chapter.

I had a fairly easy going childhood. I was born in Halifax – "Alifax" to locals – and grew up in the village of Mytholmroyd in West Yorkshire. My childhood memories are of happy and loving times spent with my Mum, Dad and brother Simon. My parents were both teachers and outside of work, my Dad rode his bike whenever he could (apart from getting into a brief stint of clog-dancing!) and my Mum rushed about supporting and keeping us all going.

My parents instilled into us a sense of adventure, although when they dragged us out for Sunday walks my brother and I usually resisted. There's no walk in West Yorkshire that doesn't involve a very steep hill. On one of these walks, my brother sat down on a stone in protest only to realise that it was a cow-pat in disguise – the laughs made the walk well worthwhile. Despite grumbling about going out, we usually came home with smiles. Somewhere in the pain and strain of walking as a youngster over hills and mountains – basted in mud or drenched in rain – was an experience to remember. Somewhere in my childhood I got hooked.

Every summer was spent camping in France and making the most of the long school holidays. People used to ask how we could afford to have six weeks of holiday but we weren't rich and there was no extravagance. We ate out once each holiday – a special treat that we usually saved until the final week – and were allowed a maximum of one 'treat' a day, be that a drink or an ice-cream. I guess I learnt early how to have adventures without needing a lot of money. People ask me now how I've afforded to enjoy the adventures

I've had and that I write about in this book, but if you're wild-camping and eating porridge it's cheaper to be away than at home. Besides, in the kinds of wilderness places I end up there's usually nothing to spend any money on!

At sixteen, I saw an advert on the wall at school. It was a poster from the 'Yorkshire Schools Exploring Society'. They were seeking young people interested in joining an expedition to China. It would cost two thousand pounds. I instantly excluded myself. Our family couldn't afford that and China was the other side of the world, a far and distant place way beyond my reach. A few weeks later though, a friend convinced me that I should apply to go on the selection weekend – 'you may as well go just to see what happens' he said. I joined tens to hundreds of other Yorkshire teenagers for a sleepless, wet and muddy weekend in the Yorkshire Dales. I forever remember getting home and collapsing on the sofa, utterly exhausted yet strangely elated after two days of carrying planks and barrels over mountains, across rivers and into caves.

I was full of excitement when offered a place on the expedition but also trepidation about how to raise two thousand pounds, not to mention getting fit. I chose to be part of the mountain biking group and my first go on the bike was one lap of the field behind my parents house. After one tough circuit around the field it felt like my lungs were ripping through my chest but I kept going. Each time it got a little easier, and eventually I started riding further. The year that followed was transformational for me. I worked various jobs to raise funds for the expedition – waitressing, picture framing, selling linen at house parties (like I was an expert on the quality of sheets and towels!) and organised special fundraising events with another pupil from school who'd also been selected to go. I trained every day to get fitter and once a month, our small team of twelve met up in the Yorkshire Dales for a training weekend. We cycled uphill and down dale, most often in Yorkshire rain, camping and carrying all our gear.

The process of getting to China taught me so much. We so often set things out of our reach (I nearly didn't apply to go) and with commitment and hard work, surprising things become possible - I never thought I could get fit enough to cycle as far as we did without chest burn and a sore bum!

The experience of that year got me hooked, so by my late teens I was rock-climbing, mountain biking, running and pursuing any activity that gave me a reason to be outside. I went to Leeds University and joined clubs and met people with similar interests and that led to spending two summers in the Alps climbing icy mountains, constantly pushing myself to climb higher and harder.

I didn't set out to climb the iconic mountains of the Alps, but somehow in my first 'season' out there I ended up climbing Mt Blanc and the Matterhorn. It seemed impossible not to go up them, their great summits dominating their respective patches of the Alps somehow calling me to climb. I was lucky of course to have friends there to venture up with and whilst we climbed successfully and stayed safe, it was kind of crazy to use a postcard as a route guide for the Matterhorn. Then again, it was busier than an English shopping centre up there so no danger of getting lost. Twenty-four hours later as we limped back down, exhausted from queueing at abseils in the middle of the night, I found my sleeping and bivvy bag had been stolen so had to keep staggering on down to the valley through the night to stay warm. The Matterhorn might be the icon of good chocolate, but it's the worst climbing experience I ever had.

My first and only boyfriend back then was a climber, now a mountain guide, and our life together was dominated by climbing, running, orienteering and mountain-biking (in the days before suspension and fancy forks). We ran mountain marathons – not together as he was way too fast for me – and usually spent our holidays wet, muddy and in a tent. We were both up for anything as long as it was active and outdoors, but where he was focused primarily on climbing, I liked variety. He would stay in the Alps every student summer from the end of one term to the very start of the next, whereas I had other plans too – one year I mountain biked around Corsica, and then next year Iceland doing fieldwork and collecting rock samples for my geology studies. I worked a job picture framing in the other holidays for the luxury of long summers of freedom, and whilst I was near broke (plain pasta for tea, hitch hiking for transport), they were summers I would never trade for anything.

After three years as a student in Leeds, I struggled to find a job, but was offered a postgrad position at Aberdeen University. So, I moved north to do a PhD in geology, the whole wilderness of Scotland a new and giant playground.

The weekend of my accident was innocuous enough – there was no terrible weather or storm or excuse for things going wrong. We set off from Aberdeen – a small group of student friends and me – and headed for the village of Cove, just south of the city. I should have let Mark, my climbing partner, lead the climb – he was a strong guy. I was ambitious though, and thought I could lead the climb without too much trouble.

The rock was overhanging and slippery smooth and I remember struggling up the first part of the climb. Instead of coming down, I pushed on to traverse beneath an overhang. My arm strength couldn't hold out and I watched my fingers peel from the rock. I fell ten metres, landing on a shelf of rock just above the waves. In those few moments my life changed forever. I woke up in intensive care with a broken back, neck, skull, wrist, elbow, ribs...the injuries went on. I was left with no sensation or movement below armpit level. Paralysed from the chest down, I began a journey into a whole new life on wheels.

It probably isn't surprising in retrospect that I fell off the cliff, my exposure to danger ever-increasing as my penchant for adventure developed. At the time it felt like my life had come to an end. The night before the accident I'd been out with friends and bizarrely, we'd ended up talking about the prospect of being paralysed.

"I'd rather be dead than paralysed" were my exact words.

I couldn't imagine anything worse.

What did I know? I was young. I was immature. I didn't know the strength that resides within the human spirit.

I didn't know that the community where I grew up would rally around and raise funds for my first lightweight wheelchair, and for a racing wheelchair too. I didn't know that with the help of friends I hadn't even met yet, I would be back in the mountains learning to ski in the Alps. I had no idea that even though I couldn't at first get into the racing wheelchair, I would be racing the London Marathon within the year. I could only hope that the University would have me back and support me to continue the geology PhD and the fieldwork for it in Bolivia. I couldn't have imagined that I would be able to cycle again, let alone visit the mountains I'd always dreamt of climbing in – the Himalaya – and cross them on a handbike. I would never have believed it if someone told me I'd sea kayak from Canada all the way to Alaska.

I was naive to what was possible without the use of my legs. I was yet to learn just what lay ahead – the good friends and good strangers that would help to bring even my most far-fetched dreams to life.

Boundless tells the stories of three adventures that I've been lucky to have – crossing the wilderness of the Greenland icecap, sea kayaking around Corsica, and climbing the kilometre high overhanging mountain face of El Capitan.

These adventures seemed wild and impossible to me at the time, especially thinking back to the early days of paralysis when just sitting up and getting out of bed seemed almost too big a challenge to overcome.

People sometimes tell me that the things I've done are 'an inspiration' but I feel awkward and embarrassed when they say this. What has made everything possible is the inspiration I've gained from many people: friends, family, and others I've met along the way who have begged me to ask the question 'Is that possible?' and supported me to find out. The question awakened in me the realisation that we can chase a dream and make surprising things happen no matter how impossible it might at first seem.

There is a pleasure in the pathless woods,
There is a rapture on the lonely shore,
There is a society where none intrudes,
By the deep Sea, and music in its roar:
I love not man the less, but Nature more,
From these our interviews, in which I steal
From all I may be, or have been before,
To mingle with the Universe, and feel
What I can ne'er express, yet cannot all conceal.

~ Lord Byron

1. THE LIGHT

"*I'd rather be dead than paralysed.*"

That's what I'd said, the night before my accident, talking about a friend who had fallen from his bike and ended up in a wheelchair. Those words haunted me, as I lay for half a year – body smashed – looking up at the ceiling tiles of the hospital ward.

"*I'd rather be dead than paralysed.*"

That's what I'd said to my friends as we cycled home from the pub, the night before we went climbing on the sea cliffs just outside Aberdeen, life so full of energy and movement that I meant every word.

"*I'd rather be dead than paralysed.*"

At twenty-one, if I couldn't dance on the rock, step along the high ridges, pound across the moors, venture into the high places, then what kind of life would it be? I would rather be dead.

Yet in less than a day from speaking those prophetic words I lay in a coma, my arms, ribs, neck, skull and spine all broken, my body torn to pieces by gravity and the sharp rocks which caught my long fall.

I was paralysed.

I was almost dead.

When I awoke after three days – arms in plaster, head bolted into a metal cage, feeling nothing below my chest – I knew that although the turn of events was almost too much to bear, I had been wrong.

Falling was the beginning of an entirely new life; different, harder, but perhaps richer, one sculpted without design by my strange determination to push harder all the time, as if I needed someone to say 'Well done. Look what you've done.' Perhaps my determination set out to prove that this was not the end, the end of life or of dreams. Only a small percentage of my body could move, but I knew that determination, not flexing muscle, lay at the heart of success.

Perhaps it was in my blood to push, something I had done since being a little girl. Life and its possibilities had always excited, my eyes wide at the adventures to be had.

My first summer to climb in the Alps, I stumbled weary off the coach from London, and strained my neck to look upwards, awed by the ridges and gullies that stretched up to the sky, my eagerness to be up there more intense than a teenager's first sexual encounter. I couldn't wait to be up high, feel the crisp air sting my cheeks, have the rope slung over my shoulder, strap the crampons around my new plastic boots, and feel like the climber I aspired to be.

Like many tourists, I fell in love with the Matterhorn at first sight, it's Toblerone pyramid highlighted by snow against the blue summer sky; but unlike most tourists, I had the equipment and the boldness of youth to climb it. With no money and no guidebook, a picture postcard with a line marking the Hornli route seemed perfectly adequate to begin the climb. I seemed un-intimidated by the hoards of climbers from around the world who'd arrived to climb it with decades of ambition. So we began, at midnight, to climb, and even when a boulder the size of an armchair whistled down just inches from my ear, we carried on.

Years later, in my new life, I stared at a photo of myself on the summit of the Matterhorn, and saw something I hadn't seen before. I was age nineteen, slim, worn looking from the climb, dressed in fleecy dungarees and a tie-dyed T-shirt. I had a one-handed 'thumbs-up' pose, a hint of triumph in my stance, an expression so cocky that I hardly recognised it as me. Not the 'me' I thought of myself as. The look on my face made me uncomfortable, as if it showed a part of me I didn't like. I never liked that picture. I hid it in preference for those where I looked more excited, or elated, or tired – those things you were 'supposed' to feel at the summit – anything but proud or cocky. I buried it so deep I still can't find it. That image had captured a part of me in glossy ink. I know with hindsight it was that part of me which drove me up the life-changing cliff, when really I should have backed off.

It had been an ordinary Sunday, the early spring sunshine warm on weathered granite, a sea cliff just outside Aberdeen. I squeezed my toes into the cold suede and rubber of my too-tight climbing shoes, pulled the webbing of my

Setting off to climb the Matterhorn, summer 1992. PETE ROUND

harness up over my hips and the waist belt tight at the buckle. They were sensations I still found thrilling even five years after my first teenage climb. How could I have known it would be the last time I'd feel my toes nip together, or the cold of the metal gear clipped to my harness penetrating through my leggings? How could I have known that in a few short minutes, my world would burn to the ground?

My climbing partner had a physique like a condom stuffed full of walnuts, rippled shoulder muscles that would have made pulling through the overhanging section look as easy as climbing a ladder. Yet I had insisted on going first and started off up the cliff. The rope dragged behind me and became heavier the higher I climbed, the lack of secure placements in the rock raising a hint of alarm that I chose to ignore. Higher it got steeper, but I stuck in, determined, ignoring the trembling in my muscles, the beads of sweat on my forehead, the screaming signs that it was too hard for me and I should go back down. I didn't seem to acknowledge fear; I just refused to recognise its signs – those necessary primal signals that exist to protect us from harm – because I knew better, and I could do it. Like with everything back then, I gambled everything to climb higher or further. I was invincible.

Except I wasn't. That day my grip failed and I watched my fingers uncurl from the rock, the sweat of fear easing them off further until I was falling.

The rope didn't hold.

I fell ten metres, head first into the rock below.

If only I'd learnt sooner the art of giving in. If only I'd not allowed that confident cocky streak of youth in me to ruin it all.

I've thought a lot since then about why I did it – climbed mountains that is – and I've always thought my reasons were simple; because I love being outdoors, discovering new places, climbing high to get a view. I grew up with mud and sweat and fresh air, so it was just how life had always been. That's why I did it. That's why I still do those sorts of things. Yet that picture on the Matterhorn, that bit of my personality that stopped me from backing off the sea cliff revealed something else; something deeper that I'd be lucky ever to understand.

It was my friend Will who inspired me forward from the early gloom of life in a wheelchair. Will and the banana lady.

Will wasn't my best friend, he wasn't even a particularly close friend, but we had shared climbs, runs and geology stories together. The previous summer he took time out from geology fieldwork in the Alps and drove us in his beaten Astra to Eldorado slabs, stunning drapes of granite that glistened with damp streaks and lit up like a rainbow as the morning sun caught them. The granite had giant crystals just large enough to pinch between your fingers and balance with or even to creep upwards. We hung around on ledges to breath-taking views, ate peanuts and giggled the day away, while my boyfriend Al did all the scary stuff high above us. We began and ended in the dark, stumbling back along boulder-strewn paths to the fairy lights of a star-crammed sky and the dim glow of our head-torches. The tumble of glacial streams roared above the crunch of our footsteps and occasional chat, and the experiences of the day, of our friendships, the adventure and the clear mountain air painted an unforgettable canvas in my memory.

When I landed up in hospital, Will came to see me every day. In three months he became the best friend you could ever wish for. When both my arms were in plaster, he cleaned my teeth. When I felt helpless he brought his old beat up car to the hospital and had me paint over the rusty patches and I felt useful again. When I could venture beyond the pale glossy hospital walls he took me out for muddy wheelchair walks and curry.

For three months, he gave me some life.

Then he lost his.

He fell from a cliff while descending from a climb. He damaged his head and died in the rescue helicopter. It was a devastating loss for everyone he'd known and very hard to accept. He had died and I was alive – if ever I needed a kick up the arse to make something of my new situation, Will's death gave it to me.

Soon after his death was the banana lady. I don't even know her name or remember her face. I'm not even sure we ever spoke. She had broken her neck, lost dexterity in her fingers and strength in her arms. For months and months, she had been trying to peel a banana for herself. Day after day she had persevered, flexing her wrist to contract her fingers, to find the action that would break the end and peel back the skin. It was only through overhearing a small but raucous celebration in the wings of the hospital ward that I learned her story. And then it struck me. If she could keep persevering, failing time and again but pick the banana back up the next day to try again, then so could I.

I didn't need to peel a banana – that was easy for me with full use of my hands – but I did need to learn how to sit up without the use of stomach muscles, a task I'd been labouring and crying over for weeks. I did need to accept being in a wheelchair, rather than hiding under the baby blue blanket of my hospital bed before anyone arrived to visit. There was a lot I needed to do. I needed to get my life back, however different it might be. Will didn't have his anymore and I felt compelled to make the most of the fact that I did.

So it began; months of hard work, in physio, in the gym, gripping lumps of iron like they held the key to my future. I wasn't alone. The camaraderie of the diverse bunch of strangers we each found ourselves amongst was a pillar of support. We had nothing in common besides spinal cord injury and a desire to get out and get on but that was enough to keep us going and the warped humour enough to keep us laughing.

A spinal-unit 'escapee' was reported to the police, last seen heading east along the nearby canal bank! It could have been me. I longed to be out, pushing and exploring to see anything in the world more interesting than polystyrene ceiling tiles, or the views through the mirror strategically angled above my bed, of hairy nostrils, or worse, private hair beneath bunched-up sheets as the man opposite fumbled to pee into a cardboard bottle. When it was my turn to venture out, I began with the hospital grounds, and took the bored young girl who was my bed neighbour along too, thinking she'd enjoy getting out. Both with poor wheelchair skills, we got stuck at a large curb. She boldly went for it, then landed in a heap in the car park and wet herself and I was chastised for leading her astray. It wasn't long though before I got further afield, and pushed the heavy tank of a wheelchair around paths, canal banks and lanes until my arms would take me no further, or until I got stuck in a cattle grid.

My first big trip away from concrete and tarmac had been to the Orkney Isles, to the island of Hoy. It had seemed such a great adventure, the long drive north, a ferry, more driving, another ferry, and then just wild hills and a single lonely lane twisting like black ribbon through heather and grass. I'd been excited to be out, to be with friends, to see what I saw and smell what I smelt. My friend Liz walked with me as I pushed the heavy national health chair up and over the lane, towards a lonely bay called Rackwick. I shed tears at the sight of the heathery hills, at raw and painful memories of days that were gone. I imagined my feet pounding over hollow peat until I'd cried so much there were no tears left. After six miles, the lane petered out into grass and mud, then sand dunes and to the bothy where we'd spend the night.

Rackwick Bay bothy is an old stone croft positioned end on for protection from the storm-battered beach. It's perched at the brow of a steep, boulder beach and surrounded by rainbow cliffs of Old Red Sandstone. After a cold evening amongst the boulders watching the waves hammer the shore, we slept. But in the morning as the others rose and left for a walk to the 'Old Man of Hoy', a spectacular sea stack that is a climbing icon, I lay on the hard flagstone floor of the bothy, cold and suffocated. My sense of suffocation wasn't only down to wood-smoke from the unruly morning fire that was now only embers – embers which reminded me of my life. Nearly extinguished, struggling to stay alight.

Despite the inspiration from Will and the banana lady to get on with a new life, it was a challenge. Liz stayed with me in the bothy, nursed my sadness and worked hard to make me smile. Back in the environment I loved so much, with memories so vivid, it was all too easy to focus on what I couldn't do anymore rather than what I could.

Going to Rackwick had opened a window into my old life, one I wasn't sure whether to confront or flee. I wondered for a while whether it would be easier to leave places like that behind, to create a new life in the manmade world and lock away the memory of who I was.

But I was still the same person. Why should dreams change just because you can't walk?

When we're in the thick of the difficult stuff in life, it's like our windows are blackened and it's hard to see out. The future only seems bleak. 'This too will pass' is a saying that helped me through. Nothing is forever. When we're down at rock bottom things might even get worse but eventually, as sure as the sun will shine after weeks of rain, things will look up.

That's all true but in the darkest moments, the future was nothing but black. Sometimes just being in the dark and accepting fate was the only thing I could do.

After more trips to the mountains, I learned a trick of my imagination. I would take myself into the land around me by visualising an imaginary hand that belonged to me. With this large hand on a long arm, I could reach up into the mountains around. I could run my fingertips over the skyline and explore the contours. My fingers sank into the folds of valleys, felt the creases and ripples of rock, the spikes and tips of the summits. Whilst my eyes picked out the features; scree, vegetation, large boulders or glistening slabs, my hand could feel their textures, rough like sandpaper, or silky smooth, bracken, heather, moss.

It was a silly mind-game but one that transformed me into a gentle giant, crouched over the mountains enjoying them as if they were a toy.

Incredibly, I felt in those moments that I was there.

I could never have known what lay in store. Lying there in the early days broken and sad for a life I'd lost, it was impossible to imagine what the future held.

Looking forward, I knew I wasn't destined to be an armchair adventurer. I'd never be satisfied to live vicariously through the exploits of others or even just with my imaginary hand. I had a deep longing to feel the elements weather me, to be wet and cold then appreciate the heat of a fire, to be deprived and hungry then find the most basic and simple food delicious, to keep going to the point of exhaustion then lie and feel blood seep into my muscles and revive me.

Gradually, I dared to dream of more daring things, of journeys far and wild, of adventures like I'd once known and still hungered for.

If someone had told me then that I'd be happy again, and that life would become filled with adventure once more, I wouldn't have believed them.

But many things lay in store.

They would challenge me.

They would teach me.

They would destroy any sadness left within.

They would bring me back into the light.

GREENLAND

2. PIGGING

It all began in the Arctic circle with three important lessons I chose to ignore. The first was that minus thirty degrees Celsius is very cold – so cold it makes your eye lids stick together and any warm parts of you soon turn black and drop off if you're not careful. I hate the cold – always have – but now having no real control over my internal body's thermostat, the cold has become my worst enemy yet constant companion. My hot water bottle is my best friend – summer or winter – in bed or at work. I'm always freezing, and the thought of being somewhere that was also always cold – and REALLY cold – well it was never going to be a good holiday destination was it? You expect it to be cold in the Arctic, but when you face real cold, real skin freezing, lung burning cold, you realise that such a thing is abstract until you feel it for real – as different as luke warm bath water from the boiling water of a spilled pan on your skin.

Lesson one: The Arctic was no place for me.

My second lesson was that cross country skiing – the only way to travel in the Arctic on foot – is hard work, and doubly so when you're almost frozen solid by lesson number one, your skis stuck to the super frozen ground. This difficulty of gliding like a nomadic reindeer herder is further compounded by not being able to walk and having to sit on a pair of skis with all the whoosh of a shopping trolley stuck in mud, trying to move yourself just an inch with your puny arms alone.

Lesson two: Cross country skiing sucked, and I sucked at it as well.

Lesson number three was really just the realisation that by combining lesson one (me and minus thirty degrees Celsius didn't get on) and lesson two (that for me cross country skiing was like bringing the mountain to Mohammed) that me cross county skiing in Arctic Lapland in winter was a really bad idea, but I think I already knew that before boarding the plane to Finland.

Anna was a friend from my student days, a super fit woman who excelled at ultra distance events and adventure racing, always very able, organised and confident; the type of woman who gets things done. She had met Pasi during an adventure race somewhere exotic, as solid a man you could ever wish to meet, super athlete, ex-Commando and martial arts expert. He was from Finland. They got married in mid-winter inside a Sami hut in traditional Lappish-style, an unconventional wedding of down jackets rather than strappy backless dresses. I hadn't been able to go but a year later they invited my partner Suresh and I to join them in the cold, dark, special place of their wedding to celebrate New Year in Lapland. Pasi told me over the phone in his deep solid voice that it was the perfect place for cross-country skiing. It was a sport I'd only tried briefly once before, by which I mean I'd used every ounce of energy I had to push myself two hundred metres along a track until I could slide downhill – the result of which left me totally knackered and wrapped around a tree.

We left the UK on a bright winter's morning and landed in the black starlit darkness of the Arctic – and it wasn't a long flight. It was only a day after Christmas and fittingly, a layer of frozen snow crunched beneath us as Pasi helped us across the car park and into the van. We followed a road north – Pasi telling us it was hard to get lost as there was only one road – white and squeaking as we drove. Driving along I looked out of the window into the nothingness – just a never ending dark band of forest lined the white strip of road that ploughed onwards for miles on end. The idea of being out there in the cold was terrifying.

After two hours of nothing but snow cast on endless trees I spotted lights twinkled through the camouflage of forest and we turned into the outdoor centre that would be our home for the week, the stars shining brighter than I'd ever seen. My fingers instantly stuck to the metal rims of my wheels as soon as I transferred from the van.

I had never been anywhere so cold.

We didn't wake until late. The sky still coal black at midday, body clocks confused by the barely-ending darkness. Lunch was breakfast, long and slow as we searched for some enthusiasm to venture outside. Minus thirty just didn't entice. It was colder than a domestic freezer by a good twenty degrees, and even Pasi's van needed its own electric heater to stop the diesel from freezing overnight.

It took me most of an hour to get dressed, wrestling at layer after layer of clothing that I hoped would stave off hypothermia or frostbite. I thought of Ranulph Fiennes chopping off his own frostbitten fingers in his garden shed and stuffed an extra pair of gloves in my pocket. After much delaying we squeezed from the apartment in our puffy padded outfits, out into the twilight. In the first breath the hairs in my nose froze solid, followed by my eye lashes, making me wish I'd taken my hot water bottle along. Pasi stood in lycra and told us how we had a few hours until darkness – even though the sun had only just lazily popped up behind a horizon of trees. It wouldn't be long before the sky smudged black again and if we were lucky the lasers of the northern lights would play above the frozen landscape.

It was my first real attempt at cross-country skiing, and Pasi borrowed a special sit-ski, designed for someone like me to use: a little metal seat bolted to two skis via short legs. With my bulging clothes it didn't fit well. We worked to improve it, improvising with duct tape, rope and a kid's plastic sledge that made it look more like an eccentric travellers trolley of junk than a hi-tech piece of sports equipment. It needed to fit me snugly like a glove so I could plant my ski poles just ahead and pull down on them to propel me forward, but we couldn't get the fit, or maybe it was just me that wasn't fit enough.

"No problem" said Pasi, which didn't really help, and we set off anyway, but without my abdominals I flopped around like a rag doll at every twist in the trail.

The snow seemed extra sticky, impossible to glide on. I wondered if my skis had the wrong sort of wax for such extreme cold, the pressure of a ski usually turning the ice crystals to water, creating the glide. But not there. Either they didn't have wax on or more depressingly my arms were simply too weak, barely able to move me more than a few inches at a time and that was on the flat.

On the uphill, every inch I gained forward I slid back further and I couldn't make progress without a tow or a push. Worse, every uphill went down again and as I mounted each crest and picked up speed, I went flying along a narrow trail like some rally-driving computer game. Warning sounds reverberated through my arms, my skull, my brain. Trees, ditches and protruding spikes threatened to stop me, spear me, maybe even kill me.

Pasi was ultra fit, an accomplished adventure racer, used to undertaking multi-day marathons. He was so at ease on skis he would chat on his mobile, gliding gracefully whilst the rest of us stumbled. We crept around a five kilometre loop of groomed track that undulated through the forest. Pasi could have zoomed ahead and lapped me before I'd moved just a hundred metres, but he didn't. He, Anna, and Suresh patiently waited, helped me, encouraged me, picked me up when I fell down – every few metres – and so, I kept trying. It's what I'd grown good at.

My fists tightened around my ski poles as we stopped at a crest where the trail fell downhill. It looked a very long, steep way down. A man of few words, Pasi unclipped the tow-rope he'd pulled me up with.

"I will ski behind you and hold on."

"Uh, is that safe do you think?" I asked, feeling like a car with no brakes.

"Do not worry."

When Pasi said that you believed him.

We skied down the hill in the darkness, slowly first, then faster, the snow changing from soft and slowing to icy and fast, pole and ski edges losing any grip as we accelerated down, unable to brake.

Faster and faster I went, wobbling with the speed, up on one ski, then the other, out of control towards a wall of trees, until with a bone jarring crash, the ski hit the deep powder at the trail edge and catapulted me into the snow.

I lay there feeling frustrated, wondering where Pasi was, then like a drunk snowman he appeared beside me. He had been with me all the way. Without a word he pulled me up.

We dusted down and went on again.

At the end of the day, as we shuffled back, I felt wearied and bruised, frustrated and beaten. Cross-country skiing scared me, not to mention the pain of defrosting fingers and I was glad for once that I couldn't feel my feet, but also a little fearful I'd pull off my thick boots only to see a couple of black toes fall onto the carpet.

Back inside we thawed ourselves with hot drinks and fatty food. The others would warm up quickly, whilst for hours I shivered, my toes like ice pops, as my dysfunctional thermostat tried to work out what was going on. All I could do was hug my faithful hot water bottle while sitting in the sauna wearing thermal underwear until, at last, the heat worked its way through and I finally felt warm.

Later in the week, sat around the kitchen table one evening, me sat next to the stove as usual, a friend of Pasi's called round, another Finnish hard-man, only she was a woman. Pasi introduced us and told her about my efforts at learning to ski, to which she replied that she was also learning, which seemed odd seeing as she looked as if she'd been skiing long before she could walk. "Wait" she said, seeing my surprise that she was a beginner, and pulled off her big winter boots. Where her toes should have been there were only stumps. She wasn't learning to ski, but relearning, having lost all her toes attempting to ski solo and unassisted to the North Pole. Part-way there, she had fallen into the ice, got badly frostbitten and had to be rescued. I looked at this superwoman and wondered just how tough – or crazy – you'd have to be to venture out into the cold like that?

"I am leaving again next month. To try again" she told us.

I thought she was brave, and I thought she was foolish, and I wished that I could try something like that too.

We were almost prunes as the week drew to an end, over indulged in bone-warming saunas and a toasty apartment. My skiing had improved very little, but I'd developed a fondness for the place, found something magical in the frozen landscape. I still feared the cold, but I knew each night that soon I would be back warm in the house – well eventually anyway. The Scandinavians call this warm feeling in the winter 'hoogli'; that feeling of being warm, cosy, full of good food, having happy chat with friends. It was the last night of our holiday, and we were having a hoogli moment. Until Pasi dropped a suggestion. He was a man of few words, so I knew he had been thinking about what he had to say for a while.

"That was a very good week. Now we should all ski across Greenland."

"What?!" I blurted, incredulous at the idea, unsure how far such a trip was, but it was up there with skiing to the Poles.

It seemed an outrageous suggestion. I couldn't ski. I couldn't keep warm. How would we ever do that with me, wobbling along, struggling to make my ski move?

Everyone burst out laughing, and I felt a little embarrassed at Pasi pulling my leg – making fun of my terrible skiing. It was like suggesting I take up ballroom dancing.

Pasi wasn't laughing.

"No" he said in his deep voice "I am not joking."

"No" I said, the outrageous suggestion rattling in my head.

Pasi raised an eyebrow and nodded.

"No" I said again while an excited voice in my head began whispering something dark and troubling: "Yes, yes, yes!"

I suddenly wondered if the awkward game of cross-country skiing could be a key to a great adventure.

On the flight home I read Pasi's book on Greenland and the first crossing of the ice cap by the Norwegian, Fridtjof Nansen, in 1888, an adventure that was as bold and 'out there' as the moon landings a century later.

Nansen and his team had no room for error, no chance of rescue, and had to be totally self sufficient, being dropped off near the east coast by a sealing ship, then making the crossing to the west side.

Newspaper articles of the day showed that many had criticised his plan, considering it 'to be absolutely good for nothing'. The idea of abandoning a ship's firm deck and 'creeping like a polar bear from one rocking ice-floe to another on his way to the shore' was acclaimed to be too reckless to criticise it seriously. Nansen was blamed for deciding to leave himself without a way of retreat. Opinion was that a good leader shouldn't do that, otherwise he wouldn't deserve the trust of his companions. But Nansen was convinced that the possibility of retreat would be an obstacle for achievement of the goal.

Nansen was daring to do what others dared not, risking failure for the prize of success. He had to withstand the ridicule poured on his planned exploits – one article about the forthcoming expedition showed a drawing of a dead young man covered in snow – and stay determined in his goal. The more I read, the less ridiculous I felt when I considered my chances of making the crossing myself, but inspiration from Nansen permeated my doubts and fears. I knew I had to adopt a Nansen attitude and not let doubt stand in the way – either from without or within. It would be better to fail than never to try. It had been this attitude that got Nansen and his team across, making it to safety on the west coast after forty-nine days.

I put the book down and grinned at the thought of skiing over miles of sparkling ice, to experience an other-worldly place, the wild space, the cold beauty. To ski across Greenland. But then I would see the ice crystals forming up along the edge of the plane's thick window, think about the cold outside, the cold of the ice cap, and my smile would fade. The beauty disappeared leaving only the obstacles that might stand in the away of such an adventure. Behind my enthusiasm hid that gremlin of disbelief, the gremlin that hides in us all, the dull gremlin of reality; the stealer of dreams.

I shiver in a British summer – how will I keep warm, and my feet, what about frostbite? What about going to the toilet? I can't squat – maybe my bum will freeze it takes me so long. If I have to change my catheter on the icecap, what will I do if it goes wrong and even worse if I wet myself and I freeze in my own pee? Will the catheters just snap in the cold? What if anything goes wrong in the other department....?

I looked out of the window, past the ice and the cold, to the clouds, to the horizon.

Think positively, I told myself, but wondered what that really meant. Maybe the gremlin of self doubt was really the angel of self preservation, that me skiing across Greenland was just as foolhardy as going solo to the Pole.

Anything I'd read about positive thinking seemed to suggest only allowing yourself happy, successful thoughts. 'Jump and the net will appear' they say. But what if it doesn't? What if I'd just been lucky so far? Skiing across Greenland would take more than blind optimism.

I sat there making a mental list of all the 'whats' and the 'ifs'.

First the big one. Forget being able to ski five hundred and fifty kilometres in temperatures down to minus forty, but how would I go to the toilet? A very basic question for anyone, but especially for me.

If you've ever wondered about such things then read on. If not then skip this bit. First off I have to wee via a catheter, a tube that goes into my bladder. Sounds horrible, but that's how it has to be. So would it freeze, lose its flexibility and snap in the cold? It was only twentieth century warfare that changed things, brought social and medical developments that meant people could survive trauma and live with disabilities. Plastic, silicone and rubber revolutionised the world of catheters and the quality of life for people in my position. Before that there were only reeds, the hollow leaves of onion plants or later rigid catheters of bronze, silver and gold if you were loaded. I wondered if anyone had tested modern catheters in conditions as cold as minus thirty or forty? I guessed it was a little outside of their design spec. I decided when I got home I'd experiment, I'd deep-freeze some catheters and test what happened. It wouldn't be an exact science, but it would ease my mind if they didn't snap.

I also worried about my catheter blocking. In the urology trade I'm what is known as a 'blocker', prone to choking the plastic plumbing with sediment and calcium deposits. I either drink like a fish or risk the trauma of clogging the tube to the point of useless, then wetting myself. On the icecap, staying hydrated would be a challenge, every drop of water needing valuable fuel to melt ice and hours patiently tending the stove. Nansen wrote about the importance of staying dry in the Arctic – how it's vital to strip down when working hard to avoid sweat that will freeze as soon as you stop. He didn't mention weeing your pants – which at minus forty could be more than just embarrassing.

There'd also be the bladder washes, the bulky sachets of acidic solution I used each day to dissolve the offending clog, but probably they would freeze and I pondered how I'd keep them liquid in the cold temperatures on the ice.

Then there was going to toilet in the other way. Let's just say it's not easy, takes a long time, and the thought of sitting out in the cold for an hour with my bum to the wind was the biggest obstacle of all.

But if I had learnt one thing in all my trips away it's that no obstacle is insurmountable. The same questions came up before I hand biked over the Himalaya, with many saying there was no way I could do it, that medically it was impossible. In the end I ignored their advice – none of them being in a wheelchair or having crossed the Himalaya, and just took a wheelbarrow inner tube to sit on as a toilet. Sure it wasn't perfect, and yes it did explode and dump me into an open toilet in Pakistan, but such is the price of adventure. After all isn't a true adventure just a series of seemingly insurmountable obstacles?

By the time we touched down I'd convinced myself that Greenland would be my goal.

I got into specifics and picked off my fears and worries one by one. For each, I made a plan, and listed possible solutions no matter how odd they might seem, in the hope I could reduce the chances of things going wrong, and help my mind rest easy. There was also that 'minor' issue of me not being able to ski cross-country, or having any equipment.

I took a leap of faith that if other paraplegics can cross-country ski, then I'd figure it out too. I googled and trawled through pages of adaptive sports equipment, looking for something that might be up to the job. There was endless information about manufacturers, retailers and clubs, mostly

American, who always seem to be a step ahead with disability innovation. I became a geek of adaptive snow sport, found sit-skis, bi-skis, tri-skis, and over-engineered buggies with articulation, suspension, anodised paint jobs and eyebrow raising price tags.

That old saying about a poor workman blaming his tools is totally negated when it comes to disability sport. Equipment is everything. The right fit, an extra strap in just the right place, can make all the difference between being a wobbling no-hoper or a high performing athlete.

I came full circle, back to Europe, to an Austrian company I knew made good downhill skis. I had an idea in my mind of what might work. I needed a seat with straps that would fit me like a glove and move with me as I lunged forward without slicing me in half. The seat needed to be warm and padded to protect me from cold and pressure sores, and the frame needed to be strong, robust and reliable. Eventually, I placed an order. A one-off combination of a cross-country sit-ski with a carbon-fibre moulded seat, the kind usually fitted on downhill sit-skis. The seat was articulated, but the frame was surprisingly basic, just a rigid construction with two skis fixed in parallel positions, with no articulation or any of the fancy features I'd found in the American designs. 'Less is more' I told myself, 'simple is good'.

I hoped it would work.

I didn't have huge faith that the sit-ski would be up to the job, and decided to go to Norway, where cross-country skiing is to them like football to the Brits. An annual disabled ski festival in the heart of Norway's mountains sounded like a good place to learn some skills. Intrigued and hopeful, I arrived in Beitostolen, and entered the world of sit-skiing. The Norwegians call it 'pigging', but the disabled athletes I saw gliding fast along forest tracks made that a disingenuous term, and certainly none of them were grunting. I wanted to know their secrets, how they sped along the cut-tracks, lunging arms and torso in such a seamless graceful motion.

I climbed awkwardly into my new sit-ski, and began, very slowly, to follow the ski tracks uphill, the effort heavy on my lungs, sweat beading on my forehead, my triceps quickly burning. The trail flattened – relief – but then began downhill, quickly getting steeper. Like a runaway train I descended at the mercy of the tracks, wobbling, lurching, hoping I'd make the bend, then popped out and tumbled over.

"Use your knuckles" a grey-haired lady skied up behind me, skilfully hopped out of the tracks and gave me her arm to help me up. "Do it like this."

She began ahead of me, her chest crouched over her knees, hands as fists, knuckles scraping the hard snow, ski poles pointing skyward behind her.

I followed, happy for a way to dampen my speed but still wishing for more control over which direction I sped in, and for a thicker pair of gloves.

I thanked the lady for her help and later discovered she was a legend in Norway. Raghnild was a serial winter Paralympic gold medallist. An easy day for her would be a fifty or more kilometre ski over the hills and mountains of Norway. Her back was a glorious pattern of muscular prowess, like a Braille storyboard of winter journeys. I wished I'd been on those mountains too.

I gaped at the international teams, lean and fast in lycra. The way they flew by. The Japanese, lithe and so very light. We exchanged friendly smiles and I asked if I could try one of their sit-skis, wondering if I'd ordered the wrong thing for Greenland as speed would be important. The largest of the men hopped out of his ski and into his wheelchair. With a lot less style and the bulk of my puffy warm pants, I tried to fumble myself into his ski seat. Like a square peg into a round hole my child-bearing hips weren't going. With impeccable manners and a wry smile he accepted his ski back whilst I struggled out with the grace of an elephant and shrugged with disappointment.

I stuck to my own ski and learnt more skills as the week progressed, my enjoyment rising as the number of tumbles I took got less.

Training for skiing would be difficult back home, where the chances of cross-country skiing were less than 1 in 365. I asked around, wondering how the athletes trained for their sport in summer and one of the Canadian team described bolting the frame and seat of her sit-ski on to a mountain board. When the winter ended she told me she 'pigged' on dirt tracks, the dirt more akin to snow than tarmac. Incidentally she told me she was struggling to use the facilities in her lodging, her hips so tiny she said she couldn't sit on the toilet without falling down it. The story fuelled my doubt further about my ability to cross-country sit-ski, reminding me of my weight, height and large bones that all needed hauling uphill.

Later Raghnild explained that she trained in summer in her regular wheelchair, strapping her abdomen to its back so as not to lose balance then poling along with tungsten-tipped ski poles that bit the tarmac. It seemed slightly more feasible. Slightly less suicidal than an out-of-control mountain board with no brakes.

There's a joke about stopping a Scandinavian in the street and asking if they know where the railway station is, and them replying 'Yes'. Raghnild had none of this reserve and invited me to join her and the Norwegian Paralympic ski team in the spring for a training weekend, so that I could learn their techniques for asphalt training.

It was a weekend of madness. The blind skiers hurtled on roller-skis downhill to a dead-end car park and a precipice into the forest, each with a guide whose voice they had to distinguish from all the other guides shouting at them to turn or stop. Watching them, my shoulders tensed, my face muscles winced and I breathed out relief every time one of them made the turn, which they always did. I followed Raghnild and the others in wheelchairs. They tightened up their small front wheels, to stop the speed wobbles, strapped abdominal supports around the wheelchair backs, and zoomed along miles of road, tracks and even canal paths.

From then on, I pigged every day. I poled mile after mile, in light and dark, wet and dry, working until my triceps burned and my hands were sore from gripping. We had five hundred and fifty kilometres of Greenlandic ice to ski, and I needed to believe I had it in me. Poling would help me find that belief.

Learning to master the sit-ski near Anna and Pasi's house in Finnish Lapland. PASI IKONEN

3. SHOULDERS OF A GIANT

I lay in bed alone, Suresh long gone to work, my shoulders so sore and stiff I doubted I could get up. I looked sideways at my wheelchair, sat like an obedient pet beside the bed.

Waiting.

Always waiting.

Its once shiny alloy tubing was battered and scratched, deep dints and dings where it had been used 'inappropriately'. It had drawn the short straw in the showroom, being wheeled out for me to try, my last chair having broken – the metal fatigued and cracked, then welded in an Aberdeen offshore engineering place – then broken again for good.

I reached out my sore arm to stretch it, touching the cold metal of the chair with my rough fingers.

I hated that chair.

I loved that chair.

I couldn't live without it.

We were bound together.

The tyres were dirty from pigging down the lanes, mile after mile after mile. On and on. I stretched my arm out onto the other side of the bed, the soreness of pigging abating a little with the stretch.

I had to get up. I had to get out and start pigging before work. I had to. It gave more reason. More reason to get out of bed. More reason to get in my chair.

Greenland I thought, pushing back the duvet, my leg and stomach muscles spasming as I started to move and throwing me back flat again.

Greenland I thought, as I half rolled onto my side by grabbing the mattress and winced as my sore shoulders rebelled.

Greenland I thought as I pushed myself upright and began pulling my fleecy trousers on.

Greenland I thought as I yanked the chair forward, and transferred my body across.

Greenland I thought. *There will be times much harder than this in Greenland.*

Perhaps it was the promise of hard times that got me through my days. Something to look forward to.

The dream of crossing Greenland took on a life of its own, pushed on through the wax and wain of emails and lists, until its momentum was unstoppable. It was one of those situations where you're in waist deep, but you only ever meant to dip your toes in to see how it felt – one of those things, like signing up for the London Marathon – when you suddenly say 'blimey – I'm actually going to have to do it now!' unsure if you even can. Emails were zipping between Anna, Pasi, Suresh and me. A plan was taking shape – slowly – to cross Greenland from east to west. The route was five hundred and fifty kilometres, almost a straight line, across an ocean of nothingness – no mountains – no glaciers – nothing but unending flat ice. Flat ice would be an advantage as I had a better chance on level ground, although there wouldn't be a nicely prepared track to follow, just the tracks of the team. The only landmark on the map was a slight deviation in the middle to a place called DYE 2, a mysterious cold-war US radar station and the only mark in the midst of the blank white map. DYE 2 was a historical landmark but more importantly it gave us something to aim for. If we reached it we'd be more than half the distance across the ice.

I searched for information and any maps or photos, anything to tell me a little more about this blank white space. Google Earth flashed a pixelated white screen – either it had no coverage, or the satellite had coincided with a snowstorm – and images I found from space showed ice torn apart, a serrated collage of crevasses and ridges that appeared impossible to navigate by ski. I began to hear of Greenland horror stories and I heard of countless failures, rescues and retreats. Instead of building our confidence, our search for knowledge just added to our intimidation and left us wondering how anyone had managed to cross the void.

For a while I kept our plan quiet. I was unsure that we would ever actually begin, let alone make it across. There seemed so many obstacles to overcome and I lay awake at night worrying about them.

Each one of us took responsibility for some small part of the complex jigsaw. It took months to work through the list of problems to solve. We knew our goal clear enough, though how we would get there – practically, financially and for me emotionally – we had little idea; but that's adventure – a journey with an unknown outcome – and that was the lure that pulled us all.

When the whole idea felt finally for real, we muttered our plan to friends and family. Some were excited for us and seemed to show no doubt, whereas others forecast failure and had no qualms about telling us we were plain mad. The mixed responses mirrored my own feelings about it, a cocktail of fear and hope. One thing that gave me strength was knowing that Nansen had shared similar doubts and he too had to overcome both his own negative thoughts and those of people around him. I knew too that a void would appear if this dream – this overriding focus of my everyday life – this thing that got me up out of bed – was to just disappear from life. In my most doubtful moments I'd thought about bailing out, and other people thought that would be for the best too. They doubted we could do it. But why should I not go just because people who knew less about it than we did said we couldn't do it? This is what I told myself when people looked concerned, my strength and determination rebelling against their doubt. They were the same kind of people who said I'd die in the Himalaya or drown in Alaska or break my neck skiing down the Valle Blanche.

But with hindsight these people didn't really doubt. They cared too much. They wanted to keep me safe from harm.

The hardest judgments to take came from those who knew what they were talking about.

"What if you fall in a crevasse?" said an expert at the extreme clothing conference in the Lake District, a conference Anna had recommended as a place to get some ideas about how to stay warm.

"If you can't feel your legs then how will you know if you have frostbitten feet or that your skin is freezing?" carried on the 'expert', Anna's friend who was speaking at the conference, a mountaineer called Andy Kirkpatrick.

"If you piss yourself – which I'm guessing is a possibility – then how would you dry your pants at minus forty?" he carried on, bluntly.

All of a sudden his doubts were added to mine. But what did he know about icecaps and paraplegia anyway? He looked more like a rugby player that spent too much time in the bar than a mountaineer.

"Don't worry though – don't let anything like that stop you" he said smiling. "Its just details. No reason not to."

I smiled again at this 'expert' giving me the thumbs up.

Anna gave a knowing look. She'd said he'd be a good man to help. She asked about what clothes I should wear, discussed the idea that big puffy down trousers would be a good plan, and that a company had offered to make some.

"Down isn't warm when its compressed so you'd be better with fleece under your bum and down on top. What you need is some baby push chair technology, just a half sleeping bag to sit in."

"Maybe you should come with us" Anna suggested, looking at him.

"Nah – its only failed climbers that do polar stuff" he said. "And posh wankers."

~

Skiing across Greenland was far from the frontiers of exploration it once had been, with commercial expeditions and independent teams like our own attempting the ice every season, but we'd never heard of anyone doing it sitting down – well, apart from some Spanish people who skied the long way across Greenland, north to south, using a giant kite and a kind of sofa on a sledge. There's always someone out there doing something a little bit more mad than yourself. Although the crossing was straightforward, there seemed to be many failures and rescues. Our team faced the same challenges as any team: storms, fatigue, just putting one foot in front of another, as well as the extra challenges I brought: perhaps moving more slowly, not being able to tow a pulk plus a whole raft of medical and physical unknowns. Not being able to pull a pulk frustrated me as I always want to take my share of the burden, but towing a pulk – the name of the sledges pulled with a harness – weighing seventy kilos or more was just not going to happen. We were four, Anna, Pasi, Suresh and me. We calculated a team of six would be optimum for towing gear and yet still be a manageable sized team, but how to find anyone stupid enough to join us was another headache. Most people didn't have the inclination and six weeks to spare for such a trip, and even if they did, they might be unwilling to jeopardise their slim chance of making it across by having me along in the team. I'd be slow. Then of course there was the cost. The trip would mean six weeks away from earning, though the four of us were self-employed and would manage to juggle things, working hard before and after to make up for the time away. Whilst it would cost next to nothing once we were there, we were busy finding companies and organisations who might consider sponsoring the flights, freight and equipment involved.

Every day I would look at the line that was drawn on the map of Greenland on my computer, a line labeled 'Ordinary Crossing', knowing that it was going to be anything but that. It was uncharted territory. Or at least that's what I thought.

'You may as well stop your expedition now' said the email from a friend who had a friend, who had a friend, who had read a book. Their email sounded concerned.

Why? I wondered as I read on, already feeling a bit irritated by what I imagined to be another concerned email telling me we shouldn't do it.

'You won't be the first Karen – a Russian beat you to it!'

What?

'A Russian in a wheelchair has skied across Greenland already – I have read his book!'

The book arrived in the post a week later, the cover a bold image of a bulky-shouldered man in a sit-ski, poling over ice – poling over Greenland! She was right, I wouldn't be the first paralysed person to have made the crossing. I devoured its pages.

In 2000, a Russian polar explorer, Matvey Shparo had the idea to organise a ski expedition across Greenland with a disabled team member. Unlike Nansen, Matvey had a positive response from his leader – Vladimir Putin.

'Your idea is a stroke of pure genius. How marvellous, audacious – poetic even. To cross the endless, white expanse of Greenland with a unique team. One member, a fellow bound to a special chair on skis. He propels himself forward, absolutely independently, by plunging ski poles into the snow and uses a rope to pull himself up steep slopes'.

Matvey wrote he had no doubts it was possible, but that he'd wondered if there was anybody out there on earth who could grasp the idea.

'I feared that such a person did not exist. We had a real conundrum

on our hands – a great idea, not a crazy or shadowy one, one that could be executed. We were quite confident of this, our past experience proved it'.

If I'd known in 2000, I would have been daft enough to volunteer. Matvey and his companion Boris Smolin set about to find the disabled person with the belief and the will to pursue the idea. They found their man in a Russian Paralympic weight-lifting champion, Igor Kuznetsov, a triangular shaped man with shoulders twice my size. With a combination of Kuznetsov's strength and stamina and Matvey's belief and vision, the three of them crossed Greenland.

As I flicked through the glossy pictures – blue sky, white ice, stark beauty, seeing the pain and the joy – my excitement was polished and my doubts dulled.

It was an impressive feat, one that I could hardly comprehend even though I was about to attempt the same thing; to propel myself with only my arms over miles of ice. They had crossed the icecap in forty-three days. We had planned for thirty-five. Maybe we'd planned too little time, but as a larger team to share the load, perhaps we would move faster.

At the end of the book were letters and telegrams of congratulations from mayors, governors and chairmen of state across the Soviet Union. Like Nansen, they had become national heroes. Even president Putin wrote to them.

'Please accept my most sincere greetings on your victory! Rigorous Greenland has bowed to you. For the first time, a Russian team has conquered the snow-filled wasteland of the largest island on earth. For the first time, a disabled person, who uses a wheelchair in his everyday life, has participated in this difficult quest. More importantly the success of the expedition opens new horizons and possibilities for people with disabilities'.

To some it may have come as a shock or a disappointment that they were no longer 'the first' disabled person to plan on skiing across Greenland. But being first has never been of interest to me. Nor has being in the limelight. Perhaps I'm selfish but the things I do I don't do for world records, acclaim or to be 'an inspiration' to others, but simply because it's what I like to do. The fact that the Russians had done it made the idea seem less crazy and gave inspiration in doubt-filled moments. If they could do it, so could we. We still had so far to go to get to Greenland. We still had to find our team and I still had to get strong enough to make it across and make it all worthwhile. Yet from that moment on, every morning no matter how sore I felt, there would be no avoiding hard work. Now there was just training. Hard training. Now it wasn't just me on those dark lanes, mile after mile after mile, on and on and on. Now I was standing, well sitting, on the shoulders of giants like Igor Kuznetsov.

4. SYRINX

I held the baby in my arms. Tiny grasping fingers, magnetic eyes sparkling blue, head soft with downy hair that I brushed with my cheek as I held it close. A perfect baby. A baby I gave back to my best friend.

Once I hit thirty, the busy period of being invited to weddings seemed to subside, and soon was replaced by a steady stream of babies. As my friends reproduced, I happily jogged their babies on my lap, had my hair pulled and fingers squeezed by their vice-like grip and flatteringly agreed to be a Godmother twice, even though neither set of parents seemed to believe in God. Conversations changed from tales of wild parties, crazy stunts and hot-blooded adventures, to discussions on the merits of different buggies, sleep strategies for tired mums and the consistency and colour of 'babies' nappy. Their baby was the most important thing in their world of course, and I watched friends pour themselves into their offspring, letting go voluntarily, often with gusto, of the trappings of what they now saw as an empty selfish life. They had grown up and left thoughts of freedom and sleep behind.

The world became a world of babies and it was a world I felt excluded from.

Part of me wanted to be in the club and waited for my own hormones to kick in, to find myself looking longingly into the windows of Mothercare or wandering down the baby-wear aisles in a trance of blue and pink. It never happened.

"We've got a mini-Darke on the way. Due in July." My brother, loud and clear from the other side of the world – he lived in Sydney – was having a baby too. I was thrilled for them, for us, at the prospect of being an aunty, that my Mum and Dad would at last be grandparents. But my excitement was tainted with sadness that my brother and his family were a long-haul flight away and I wondered how well we'd ever know the baby that would be born.

The news naturally lifted the lid off the issue. It was a topic that had been bubbling for a while between Suresh and me.

"What about us Karen? I'd really like to start a family." Suresh was keen – very keen.

"Maybe." I was less keen – a lot less keen.

"What does that mean?"

Suresh and I had been together for three years. We'd met in London through Anna, Suresh a talented designer. He'd proposed to me on a trip to Iceland and I suppose I was flattered that anyone would want me. We got married a year later, me in a wedding dress – of sorts – I never thought I'd ever wear, my family and friends around us beside Loch An Eilean in the Cairngorm Mountains.

"I mean I'm not sure. There are lots of things I worry about, like managing to get around with a big bump. It would stop me from being able to lean forward so I wouldn't be able to push up hills or wheelie up kerbs."

"Well that would only be for a couple of months."

"I suppose so, but then there are the practicalities of looking after a tiny baby, pushing a pram around, getting out and about."

"So you don't want a family then?"

"I didn't say that. I just need some time to get used to the idea and work a few things out."

"Okay, but I just can't imagine a future without a family. It makes me wonder what the point is if we don't have kids."

It sounded like a threat – not overt – but a threat to the simple happiness we had. I felt like a football had been kicked into my gut. I thought there was a lot of point.

Perhaps that was the moment – those words – where I pushed him away.

Instead of avoiding the topic, I had to at least consider it. I watched my own mum worrying about us, caring for us no matter what and fussing after me when I went home to visit. When her first grandson was born I saw the photographs printed from emails get carefully framed and mounted around the house, the love shining out of each one. I wanted to tell her that we were having a baby too, that she would have a grandchild to love and nurture closer to home. I hoped that one day soon my maternal desire would be aroused enough to bring the good news.

The growing number of babies appearing in our circle of friends offered a starting point to grow into the idea of motherhood. Two sets of Suresh's close friends had baby girls. We visited them and immersed ourselves in the goo and ga of a happy family weekend.

In between feeds and sleeps, we prepared for a walk. It was like a mini-expedition getting ready to go, prams and all the necessary accessories, waterproofs and sun cream just in case of either extreme, lunch and all the paraphernalia. Eventually we wandered along a quiet lane to the sounds of summer, birds singing and planes droning overhead.

"Can you see daddy yet?" The baby of course couldn't answer but someone else did.

"Not yet. But there's a plane taking off just now. Maybe he's in that one."

One of the dads was into skydiving. He had no legs, blown off by a coffee-jar bomb in Northern Ireland, and had since become addicted to throwing himself out of planes. I thought how he seemed to be making it work – piecing together disability, family and adventure. If he could, maybe I could too.

The little wheels on the front of my chair rattled over the rough tarmac, together with the pram wheels. The two mums were pushing their babies and I was wheeling beside them. I wondered how I'd manage to push a pram myself.

I could see headlines, 'Baby dies in runaway pram'. I'd be trying to wheel myself and a buggy with baby downhill, at least two sets of wheels to control with only one set of hands. Speed or steering, one would have to give. Either me, the baby, or both would end up off the kerb mangled with a car or crash-landed in the bushes. I'd have to tie the pram to me and shunt it around, either like a supermarket shopping trolley in front or an articulated lorry behind. We'd be in a different league to one of those yummy mums jogging behind their all terrain buggy.

As if reading my thoughts, Suresh made a suggestion, "Why don't we try and tie the buggy to your wheelchair Karen, just to experiment."

"Errrr, yeah, okay." I tried to sound keen but I doubted my voice hid how I felt. Reluctant. I didn't like facing the topic head on.

I played along but it felt like a game and I felt sorry for Suresh that I couldn't take it more seriously. I knew that adding an extra pair of wheels to my daily equation had always been a recipe for disaster.

Years earlier, in a last indulgence of job-less freedom, I'd gone to France handcycling for a month on my own. There was no room on my bike for panniers or camping kit, not to mention my wheelchair so I had a kind of tow bar contraption made in an engineering workshop in Aberdeen's docklands. The gruff, broad northeast engineer was obviously thinking I was mad as he handed me the contraption with oily hands. The plan was to tow my wheelchair behind the handbike and carry all the camping gear in the chair, something that even to a man used to dealing with the high risk world of North Sea platforms seemed rather on the dangerous side. He waved me off with a "You be careful now lassie." As it turned out, his doubts were well founded.

Dumped on the platform in Avignon I began to wish I'd tested this new device, as I fiddled awkwardly with nuts and bolts, attaching one part to my bike and a smaller coupling system to the footplate of my chair. A blue-clad station master who looked like he was fossilising with the station helped me hook the system up. He looked pleased with himself when it was done, only to raise his eye brows in alarm when I pointed at the mountain of camping kit that then needed loading on board. Feeling free at last I cautiously began pedalling out of the station towards the road, excited it was actually working, imagining all the roads of adventure that it opened up.

I cycled past a square: smiling, old men stopping their game of boules, mouths open as I pedalled by, past the patisserie where I wished I could easily pop in for an afternoon treat without having to de-articulate. The woman swatting wasps in the window looking at me as if I was piloting a UFO.

I headed for the river, where with my rusty French, I understood I'd find a campsite. The extra weight of the camping gear and chair soon had my arms straining, increasing my feeling of vulnerability as cars and lorries with wheels much bigger than mine sped past. I somehow manoeuvred into the right lane of the four-lane bridge without being flattened, my triceps burning as I pushed the cranks hard, dragging the load up the rise and wishing I'd brought a few less things, until, towards the crest of the bridge, a view of the city opened up for the first time. It was beautiful. I knew all the faff had been worth it for that.

My optimistic mood increased as I stretched my neck tall to see more over the stone wall, tasting freedom at the sight of the wide river beneath, suddenly feeling lighter, more energised, the load almost effortless.

Then I realised why.

My wheelchair, like a rickshaw piled high with bags, overtook me in the fast lane.

The chair sped past as I braked in surprise but within a split second I pedalled madly after it, only to watch in horror as it careered in front of me. It wobbled precariously then hit the kerb, span, and spilled all its contents into the road ahead of me.

I looked at my possessions scattered around the bridge and at my battered wheelchair and imagined if that had been my baby.

I just couldn't imagine being a mum, but then I wondered, can anyone? Is it just something that happens and you go with it, reluctant but willing to enter a new phase of life?

∼

Later that year and as a very late 'honeymoon', we went on a trip to India. We were treated by family to a spa experience, in a fancy hotel on the downstream banks of the Ganges. It wasn't our usual style and Suresh had once paddled a canoe down the Ganges so was more used to a tent with dirty water and dead bodies floating by. It was a luxury and we indulged in the lavishness on offer. In the yoga room with its floor-to-ceiling window and a view of a hazy polluted sunset, Suresh had a yoga lesson and I sat cross-legged, stretching and attempting my own form of yoga. One of my knees dropped slightly and made a gentle clicking sound. I thought the cross-legged yoga pose was doing me some good, settling tendons and muscles into better places, but back at home a few weeks later I felt tingly, noticed goose bumps on my legs and a light sweat. They were signs that something was wrong, though I couldn't feel what. I went to hospital for an X-ray.

"Everything's fine" I was told. "No need to investigate further." But a few days later, I returned, virtually begging for an X-ray.

"But everything seems fine" repeated the doctor, no doubt placing me in the 'trouble' category of patient. "There's no sign of bruising or swelling. We don't think you've broken anything."

He knew more about broken bones than me but I knew something was wrong.

"Please." I insisted.

The X-ray revealed a broken femur.

It was shocking news. I knew that if you were paralysed and didn't stay active or use a standing frame to put some weight through the legs, then over the years your leg bones could become like those of an old lady. Weak, brittle and prone to breaking. I'd done everything I could to prevent it. I drank lots of milk, stood up fairly often, and exercised like a demon.

The doctors decided not to operate and not to pin the hip.

"With your osteoporosis, it's unlikely that a pin would hold your bone successfully." The consultant smiled at me. "Floating hips are quite common, especially in countries with less medical resources. People walk around with them and have no problems, although usually the broken hip results in shortening of the leg so a built up shoe is sometimes needed."

He produced a measuring tape and a pen and I felt like part of a house being measured up for a new fitting.

My right leg was already four centimetres shorter.

The doctor looked at me seriously, speaking in his best doctor voice "A broken femur is a very serious break. It probably won't fuse, so we need to give it time to settle, so it's best that you try and avoid any kind of impacts or bumps, okay?"

I nodded and was discharged. A few weeks later I saw the doctor again, only the white walls of the hospital were swapped for the snow white ski slopes above Aberdeen. I slid out of the mist in my ski chair.

"Well fancy meeting you here Karen. Shouldn't you be taking it easy?" he said lowering his ski goggles at me.

"Er, maybe, but I figured that the sit-ski seat is so tight it's like a brace for my hips."

"Mmmmm" he said, looking at the battered sit ski, rock marks and tufts of turf betraying that fact I'd strayed from the easiest runs.

We both knew I was a hopeless case. He raised his eyebrows, I felt embarrassed, blushed, and we skied on our separate ways.

As predicted I was left with a 'floating hip', the ball of the hip joint detached from the femur with just muscles and tendons holding everything in the right place. Often when moving around it grinds, the sound indescribably horrible like fingernails on a blackboard, grating through my body, reminding me of my injury and worse still my obvious frailty.

Even harder was the fact that Suresh seemed to imagine I could shatter at any moment, and perhaps he too began to have doubts about babies, and worse still – Greenland.

I began to see that I was making a list of 'reasons not to' when it came to a baby, my broken hip the latest addition. The thing was that my 'reasons not to' – like not having enough energy to look after a baby – didn't quite measure up given that I would go out pigging for hours around the lanes and that I was planning to ski across Greenland. The whole baby thing had me thinking in a way that was completely opposed to my usual approach to life's many challenges. But as my list of reasons 'not to' grew, I felt no satisfaction – only sadness that I didn't feel the same euphoric longing that had gripped my friends. I would often wish that I could simply say 'I can't have kids', four words that would stop any probing or self doubt stone dead.

But I couldn't.

Instead I had to find the courage to say 'I don't want kids'.

Both to my friends, to Suresh and to myself.

Something was wrong with me – with us, and I knew it was something that needed sorting but instead I just ploughed on planning for Greenland. Greenland offered an escape, putting off any conclusions on having babies. Maybe going to Greenland would help, maybe crossing Greenland together would make Suresh see that babies were not for me and that what he'd loved about me was enough.

Beyond my to-do-lists I kept on training, often glad to get out of the house, swapping my desk for the lanes, just pigging along, mile after mile. These training runs were never without incident, with the odd tumble as a ski pole got caught in a wheel, or the police stopping me to tell me a member of the public had complained about me being a 'road hazard'. The most embarrassing accident was getting stuck in a cattle grid, wheels caught down the metal grates, stranded until a passing motorist could fish me out.

But as my training increased, and I put more and more strain on my body – by which I mean the twenty percent that works, I began to feel not right. Little signs – tingling fingers – feeling sick – just not right. When you're paralysed, any stimulus to the sensation-less parts of your body causes messages to be sent to the brain, but they can't get through. Instead they 'short-circuit' at the spinal injury, and often this creates muscle contractions, or spasms. These muscle-spasms began to increase. My leg and hip muscles jumped, twitched and pulled me into awkward positions. Wheelchair manoeuvres that had been difficult at the beginning of paralysed life but had become simple everyday normalities, became harder than ever again. Pushing up a gentle ramp became an art of fighting my muscles to prevent being somersaulted sideways or back-flipped onto the concrete, and that happened a few times. I might not have used my leg muscles for over ten years, but they still had a powerful kick. Only a few months earlier, they booted a chiropodist in the chin. Involuntary muscles spasm was normal for me but now my karate kicks had more force than ever.

During the night, my leg and trunk muscles would contract so hard that I'd wake up with a start, winded, my stomach muscles rigid like a board as if reacting to a hard punch. I was worn out with lack of sleep and so once again I returned to hospital.

The consultant suggested a series of Botox injections and I wondered if I'd taken a wrong corridor to the plastic surgery department. I didn't think I was too wrinkled and my lips seemed fine enough, but he looked blankly at my jokes and explained that the Botox reduced wrinkles by relaxing muscles and that it might work well on my hip muscles to make daily getting around more manageable again. So, one of the biggest needles I'd ever seen was sunk into the bright white long-Scottish-winter flesh of my hip, and I enjoyed telling friends I'd had Botox.

But months later, back in the consultant's office, the Botox having made little difference, I felt frustrated and wanted so hard for my hip to never have been broken. Instead of wishing I could walk again, I was simply wishing that life sitting down could be as easy as it had been. My other option was to fill my veins with muscle-relaxing drugs, but drugs with the label 'May cause drowsiness, do not operate machinery' may as well have read 'Poison' to me. I didn't want to dull my brain or become any less than fully alert. Instead, I settled on an MRI scan.

"It'll help us check for anything else that might be causing your increase in spasm" the consultant informed me. I stripped myself of metal, including my wheels, and was transferred into the MRI room in a plastic wheelchair. The technicians pressed buttons as I prepared myself to be slid into the giant machine, and lying there, headphones feeding me Radio 4 as a supposed distraction, my face only inches from the confines of the white coffin, I began to wonder what that 'anything' might possibly be.

I slid out again.

I was referred to the neurological consultant.

"I'm afraid to say the scan has shown that you have a Syringomyelia" she said, looking at a file, as if this 'thing' was as well known as hay fever or a migraine.

"Oh" I said, thinking the 'syringe' bit of the word could only mean it wasn't a good thing.

"That's a spinal syrinx" she said, looking at me now, probably imagining that talking in 'layman's terms' would make more sense.

"Oh" I repeated, feeling a cold terror creep through me without really knowing why.

"It's a bubble of fluid inside your spinal cord." she said. "It's a rather large one I'm afraid – extending from your brain stem to your sacrum."

There was a long silence.

"What does that mean?" I said, unsure I really wanted the answer, knowing that her next words could change my life.

"It means that at some point you will most likely lose function in your hands and arms."

The austere Germanic consultant held back no punches.

"The fluid will put pressure on the nerves that feed the part of your body you can feel. If you ever experience tingling in your hands...?"

I felt dizzy, my mind flashing to the tingling hands I got every night, that I'd put down to sleeping in a bad position.

"If you do then you must call us straight away. Come in for the operation. In the procedure we'd put a small drain from the inside of your spinal cord into your lung cavity, to drain any excess pressure within your cord."

I felt sick.

"Maybe you'd like to book in for it immediately?" she said, as if I was planning on a new hair style, not a spinal tap.

I wished she didn't look so stern.

It didn't make it any easier.

No sugar to sweeten this pill.

But then she wasn't telling me anything to smile about.

I thought about what the loss of function of my hands, my arms, would mean. What would I have left?

"No" I faltered. "No thanks." What would be the advantage of an operation now, given that my hands and arms seem fine at the moment?

"Think about it."

I left the hospital and sat in the park thinking about this news, watching people wandering by, joggers enjoying a clear spring afternoon, kids playing on the swings. I used to feel envious of people who could walk, tormented by the unfairness of being paraplegic. At the gym, I would lie on the weights bench lifting dumb-bells but through the corner of my eye, watch thigh muscles flexing and shiny around me, in wonder at their movement, so perfect and in wonder at what one small sever of the spinal cord could do. I wondered why people didn't use their legs all the time, why they would want to sit on sofas and never walk further than the fridge or car. It seemed to me they had the world at their feet and weren't even running with it. I had the world at my arms and was gripping it as tight as I possibly could. Life isn't fair, but what is fair? Life just is but I refused to accept that my situation could wind up another notch to a place where I'd feel envy of people pushing themselves in wheelchairs.

It would be so unjust.

But who said life was just.

Suresh took it hard. He treated me with kid gloves, like I would stop moving any moment – especially when I told him the bit about how sudden exertion or holding my breath too long might cause the worst to happen. Out kayaking, he was fearful I'd capsize or remind me to be careful when I swam underwater at the pool or anytime I lifted something heavy.

His fear grew oppressive.

There was enough to deal with in my own nightmare, without doubling it.

I wanted to run away from the truth, for someone to wipe my memory of it, even for a moment but for Suresh it was a nightmare we shared, and he seemed convinced I would lose the use of my arms any day.

I tried to ignore the reality by throwing myself into the headlights of my fear: hand-cycling more miles than ever before, swimming length after length, moving weights in the gym until my poor elbows felt as if they would break. There was no way I could go to Greenland, but at that moment I felt it was all I had.

Suresh said he wasn't sure about going to Greenland anymore. He said he didn't feel fit enough but looking back I wonder if it was because he thought I shouldn't ignore the syrinx and didn't think it was a good idea to push myself physically like Greenland would inevitably demand. Maybe it was an effort to dissuade me but he decided he wouldn't come.

I'm not good in a corner.

I said fine.

I was going – even if it was the last thing I would ever do.

Suresh immersed himself deeper in his work. When he got home late or from a few weeks away, he would watch TV or disappear into the shed.

Both of us stood at the edge of something terrible. I had never been in a relationship so long before. It looked as if maybe this would be my high water mark. Perhaps I pushed people away, and instead of facing up to truths just buried my head in adventures. But all I wanted was for him to hold my hand and tell me it would all be okay, not to worry, our combined denial enough to keep this terrible thing from our door.

At least until the door was smashed down.

Instead he shared my deepest fear and so I pushed him away.

It was too much to bear.

Instead I embraced Greenland.

Our first view of the Greenland coast and the sea ice breaking up as our plane circled in towards the village of Ammassalik, from where we would begin our crossing. ANDY KIRKPATRICK

5. THE RED HOUSE

As our plane slowly circled into Ammassalik, I peered through the tiny scratched window at the frozen black and white landscape below, ice choking the sea, mountains leaping black and white from the snow covered tundra.

My eyes filled with tears.

Greenland at last.

The plane dropped down with lurching jumps, the wind coming off the icecap battering the coast line, a petrified scene. Dark cracks in the pack-ice, fissures of water in the shattered pane of sea. Unadulterated whiteness stretching inland to glacial summits scarred with black rock.

I peered at the colourful roofs of the town below as we circled the dirt airstrip, the village clinging to the country's rim, splintered sea for miles before it. It was forbidding in its beauty, like nothing I'd seen before. At that moment it all seemed worth it. Two years of organising, the hours and days phoning and planning and packing. I was glad of it all.

We sat with big grins on our faces, even Pasi who seemed good at hiding his emotions. I smiled at Anna but felt choked to say words. I knew we'd never have made it so far without her.

Across the aisle of the plane sat the other three members of the team, people I'd only met less than twenty four hours before in London. Our only introduction was a brief drink in the pub before heading back to finish packing.

Harvey wasn't a stranger but I'd not seem him since university days as he'd moved to Norway to work for the Polar institute. He was fit, capable and all the time he'd spent in the Arctic added more experience to our team.

Jacek was our oldest recruit, a polish car salesman and the dad of one of Anna's adventure racing team mates. His white beard and well worn face made him look very much like a polar explorer. The only problem was that at age sixty and with less experience than the others, there were a few doubts about how it would work out.

Lastly there was our mountaineering expert Andy, who through some badgering from Anna had agreed to hang his climbing boots up for a few months, join the team and in his words, become a 'Polar Wanker'!

Looking along at the five of them: Commando, Adventure racer, Polar Expert, Mountaineer, Car Salesmen, it did look like an incongruent bunch, but then if I added 'me – paraplegic' to that list I felt that maybe I was the most out of place of the lot.

The plane dropped again and the engine changed pitch. The wheels hit the dirt strip and rumbled to a stop, the props slowing until there was only the sound of the wind battering the fuselage.

I suddenly felt terrified.

The Inuit first settled in the icy expanse thousands of years ago, living along the coast, fishing and hunting in small groups, moving by dog sled and kayak. The next to discover Greenland's frozen coasts were Vikings, blown off course travelling from Norway to Iceland in the tenth century. The Vikings had tried to settle there as well but found the land too harsh, far tougher then Iceland, and many early settlers starved to death during the long winters. After a tumultuous history of trading and isolation, the Danes claimed sovereignty over Greenland in the 1600s and Greenland became autonomous in 1979, though still closely tied to Denmark.

From the air it was easy to see that there was nothing green about Greenland. It was in fact far icier than Iceland. The white land's name originates from white man, an attempt to make its frozen expanses more attractive to settlers. It was all a huge real estate scam. Greenland's population at around sixty thousand is ninety percent Inuit, spread in small towns around its rocky edge. The climate is harsh and the sea frozen for all but a few months of the year. Old ways of living and surviving have been lost and for many, alcohol has filled a void. It seemed the land of ice wasn't as pristine as it looked.

One by one, everyone filed off the plane. I waited until my wheelchair could be found in the hold and Andy came and sat next to me to wait too. "I've never met anyone in a wheelchair before" he said. "It's a right pain in the arse isn't it?"

I'd begun to wonder if his bluntness had something to do with Tourette's syndrome or maybe he just felt awkward around someone with a disability – I'd realised over the years that plenty of people did – and didn't quite know what to say.

"I mean flying, having to wait for your chair like now, that's a pain in the arse" he continued.

As we sat waiting for my wheels to appear I asked Andy why he'd changed his mind about coming on the trip.

"It was a free holiday" he said smiling. Then his smiled faded. "Actually Anna told me about your spine thingy and that maybe this was going to be your last trip."

The joy of being there suddenly faded like his smile and I felt bothered if that's what had got him there. Hell! What if that's why they were all there?! I hadn't mentioned it to any of them so the jungle drums must have been beating. I didn't know what to say but I felt humiliated, like I was a charity case. I didn't want to be some unfortunate cripple that people felt sorry for.

My wheelchair arrived outside the plane.

Andy piggy-backed me out.

I didn't want Greenland to be like that.

The airport was perched on an island, just a large Portakabin really. As we made our way across to passport control, we got our first sight of real Greenlanders, leaving the terminal and boarding the plane. They were all wrapped up tight against the wind, looking solid and capable. Before planning for the trip I might have called them Eskimos but now I knew that would be insulting and they were Inuit, meaning 'the people'.

We went into the terminal and had our passports checked, just a man in a police uniform casually looking at each one, no x-ray machine in sight.

"It is much easier that we don't have a gun" said Pasi, as the man looked at our bags, no doubt used to mountains of expedition baggage.

We'd made the decision not to bring a gun as only Pasi could use one and the rest of us were so incompetent in such things that we'd only end up shooting each other by accident. We'd been told by a Greenland expert that guns were not needed on the ice, so we took his advice. We knew there were polar bears around but they were more likely close to the sea.

"Look at the size of that monster" said Andy, pointing into the small waiting room to a Polar bear skin pinned on the wall. It must have been nine feet high.

We all walked over and marvelled at it, thinking how it could have killed the lot of us in an instant, each paw about the size of a dustbin lid.

"Maybe we should buy a gun" said Jacek.

"Don't worry Jacek" said Anna, "there aren't any polar bears around town or on the ice."

I looked at the small plaque screwed beneath its massive claws: 'Shot in 2001, Ammassalik Airport Runway'.

After our passports had been checked we went back out again and squeezed into a helicopter for a five minute flight across the bay to Ammassalik, our last village before being airlifted onto the icecap in a few days time – when the weather allowed.

Pasi lifted me into my seat whilst the rest packed bags in around me, the small cabin chock-a-block with kit and pulks and rucksacks, the rest of our gear awaiting us at the helipad in the village.

"I hope we have enough strength to pull all this crap across Greenland" said Harvey, half buried under a pulk.

Everyone laughed and the pilot turned and put a thumb up as the rotors got up to speed. Anna smiled at me – my head just poking out from behind my wheelchair – and I felt a little better. Anna had used the syrinx not to make people feel sorry for me but to make this all happen. It didn't matter what people thought or why they came. It only mattered that we could get ourselves over the ice.

The flight was short. The view from the plane was even more impressive than before as we swooped down and out across the ice filled bay. The town's tiny coloured houses grew nearer, enclosed in a ring of mountains. The helicopter touched down and we climbed out, dragging our luggage out with us, the cold air cutting our cheeks as the rotor blades came to a stop. We surveyed the weather-tattered buildings that faced out to the frozen sea. Wooden houses, faded bold colours, red, blue, with paint peeling like old skin. It looked a bit messy and dirty but there was no doubt – looking at the dogs tied to the houses, chewing on bones that looked like they might have been seals – that we were somewhere special.

There was a ton of bags to unload and barrels of pre-sent freight to locate. Anna set about getting the blokes into action, everyone smiling with the excitement of finally getting the trip underway, happy to do their bit and get everything shifted, sorted and eventually packed and ready for the ice. She checked with the pilot who'd brought us in, who confirmed he would try to fly us onto the ice in two days time but only if the wind died down a little. In the meantime we would stay at the Red House, a hostel up the hill.

At last with everything sorted and in grey twilight, we headed through tired winter streets with soggy rubbish and disinterested huskies to a rickety flight of stairs that led us into the baking warmth of the Red House.

We stacked our luggage, then drank tea and chatted, beginning to get to know each other, finally starting to relax.

"First things first" said Andy "I'd just like to point out that if we see a polar bear I think we should let it eat Karen – survival of the fittest and all."

Everyone laughed – maybe a little uncomfortably. I was starting to wonder if Andy was a bit of an arse but he smiled enough and looked like a cuddly teddy bear which helped him get away with it – kind of.

"As long as it only eats your bottom half you'll be fine" he went on.

No-one laughed.

Jacek sat quietly, a white beard hiding his weathered brown face, his leather skin creasing into a late smile as he caught up with Andy's humour.

"I always wanted to ski across Greenland," he began with his heavy Polish accent, "after I joined a commercial expedition to the North Pole. I enjoyed it a lot but I thought I was getting too old. Then when I heard about this from Macek, my son – he adventure races with Anna – I wanted to come." We nodded. "Well, I thought if you can do it Karen, I can do it."

"How old are you?" Anna joined in.

"Sixty. The old guy."

We burst open a bag of biscuits and loaded in some calories against the deprivation that lay ahead.

"At least you know how to use a pair of skis Jacek. Andy's never even tried backcountry skis before." Pasi crinkled his forehead in mock surprise.

"Well, it can't be that difficult can it?" Andy teased.

An accomplished climber from Sheffield, Andy was quickly turning into our team joker and brought along some useful alpinism skills. With his wide stocky build, legs solid like tree trunks, unkempt mop of black hair, and heavy-rimmed glasses held together with duct tape, he gave the impression of indestructibility but also chaos. Wherever he went a trail of gear was left behind, his bags exploding all over the floor.

Jacek was our team elder and with his generous white beard could have been a great Father Christmas if he wasn't so slim and athletic in appearance.

Instead he kind of resembled a garden gnome. Years of selling Toyotas for work and flying planes for a hobby would have been useful skills if we'd had any engines with us, but his supply of Polish sausage would keep our human engines going instead.

Harvey was our second source of ice expertise after Pasi, a Brit turned Norwegian after years as a researcher for the Norwegian Polar Institute. Spending at least half his year in Antarctica, in Svalbard and other polar climes, he'd developed the bushy look and hurdy-gurdy accent. He brought a wealth of mountaineering and cold place skills. With his compact athletic build and fetish for fishnet style underwear (supposedly great for trapping warm air against the skin), he became labelled the gay porn star by Andy!

After tea, as the others fiddled with gear and dragged the skis and pulks up into the big hallway to pack, Anna and I wrote our first blog. We were working with Careers Scotland, on the "Hands and Feet Across Greenland" project, linked in with two primary and two secondary schools. The young people were to set themselves personal challenges to work on at the same time as we skied across the icecap. Many of their challenges seemed harder than ours. We hoped to hear from some of them via the satellite phone whilst on the ice.

Poking through the mess of kit on the floor I suddenly spied something odd and out of place, a tiny figure with a yellow beard, red hat and fishing rod. "Erm If you don't mind me asking, why have we got a gnome?"

Harvey looked up from his packing – "It's our lucky mascot – he goes on all my trips."

"I guess if you're not going to be the first person in a wheelchair to ski across, we may as well go for the first gnome instead" Andy shouted from across the room.

The two days went by in a flash. There was a lot to do: bags and barrels of equipment to sort; meals and snacks to divide into day packs; communication gadgetry to figure out; an inspection from the Greenlandic police; things to buy; bodies to fuel and our minds to focus.

We went to bed late but woke fresh and ready for action, each of us knowing that very soon we'd be saying goodbye to central heating and warm beds.

At the Red House, we sifted through all of the food and packed it into ration packs for the coming weeks – peanuts, raisins, more peanuts and bags of dehydrated food. We'd need close to five thousand calories each per day, adding packets of palm oil to bring the total up. Most of the food we'd freighted from home months in advance by air from Heathrow, too late to send it by sea before the winter freeze (there's only a tiny weather window each year when ships can get through the ice to Ammassalik). Apparently the shelves of a Greenlandic supermarket were sparse with frozen food and biscuits, the stock only as reliable as the last shipment from Denmark. By early Spring there'd be little left.

It seemed ironic to buy peanuts at twenty-five pence, then to pay two pounds per bag to freight them. We didn't like to think of our carbon footprint. I wished we could live like the Inuit, spearing seals through ice holes and preserving the meat to carry with us, but peanuts sounded more appealing than old seal meat and even the locals had mostly lost the traditional hunting skills.

Pasi and Andy played at connecting the tangle of widgets, wires and plugs to the solar panel. It was a traumatic attempt, with a plume of smoke, molten wires and gadget meltdown; followed by a search for anyone with a transformer that we could beg, borrow or buy to help us in our quest for power. We would rely on our satellite phone for weather reports, to send updates and link back home. Without power the risks were increased. I thought of Nansen, pre-satellite, no communication and the even deeper adventure it must have been. It had been stressed to us that the further we went out into the ice the harder it would be to be rescued and that rescue would only take place in perfect weather. Bad weather was going to be the main cause for a rescue, with a tent blown to bits or valuable equipment blown away by hundred mile an hour winds. It was the same with most rescues – when you didn't want one you could have one and when you did, well you were on your own. Here the rescue could only pick up the pieces, if they could find the pieces that is!

Besides the phone were our digital cameras, video cameras, a GPS and a laptop for blogging, though it was more like a lead brick. All would add kilos to the load. I would be light without towing a heavy burden behind me but with our growing mountain of baggage, I wondered if the others could get the pulks to budge.

We had a special permit for the icecap, issued by the Danish Polar Centre, but before being allowed onto the ice we had to be inspected. The Ammassalik police arrived full of officialdom, to check our equipment and insurance documents met the requirements. They surveyed the floor of the Red House which was almost invisible beneath the orderly piles of food and gear: such a big collection of kit, we couldn't possibly be missing anything. We showed them our EPIRB (our last ditch mayday device that would send our location), our sat phone, our 'we'll rescue you from anywhere' insurance documents, and everything else they asked to see. As they checked through the stuff they kept looking at me. I wondered about disabilities in Inuit culture – there was a distinct lack of ramps or blue parking badges on skidoos around town! I'd heard that in the past that when the old people's teeth were worn down to nothing by chewing seal hides to make clothing, they were seen to be of no value anymore and so would be asked to walk out into the cold to die. I wondered what they'd have thought about me setting off across the ice.

The inspection finished, the police stamped our official form and we were approved to go.

It was an intense few days and although I had my wheelchair, which I'd soon have to say goodbye to for a month, it was almost impossible to leave the Red House. Six weeks was the longest I'd gone without wheels before and it had been hard. We'd kayaked from Vancouver to Juneau in Alaska, a ten-week epic, sea kayaking all day and sleeping on beaches. Two of us were paralysed and there was no room aboard for wheelchairs. So we'd posted them up the coast hoping to meet them every few weeks, but something had gone wrong with our logistics and meant six wheel-less weeks.

The love and hate I felt for my wheelchair.

I'd hated the sight of a wheelchair in the early days of being paralysed for it represented a life I didn't want. But now it gave me mobility and independence. It would be hard to leave it, difficult to entrust it to Air Greenland to deliver safely to the other side of the icecap. It was far more than a bunch of metal tubing and wheels and I felt an anxious pang about being separated from all that it gave.

By the end of two days packing and preparing, our mood was weighed on by the challenge ahead. The hostel's polished floor boards and big rooms were an accessible island in the midst of Ammassalik. I only left the Red House once. Down its wobbly wooden stairs, to steep narrow paths of slush, streams that emerged from beneath dense old snow and the black dirt tracks that led to the town centre. It all discouraged me from venturing out and when we dragged ourselves away after days of packing, going down town was an expedition in itself. It demanded piggy-backs, ropes, wheelies and stunts I'd never pulled before, all for the excitement of going to the shop, the shelves sparse: biscuits, tins, a shrivelled lemon and a tired cabbage.

In the main street we sat on people sized blocks of roadside stone, eating Danish pastries that looked lonely in the bakery and watched life go by. Kids with hoods and hats kicking ball, mums rushing by with prams that sounded as squeaky as my wheelchair, piles of blankets hiding babies. The harsh climate seemed etched in the people who moved purposefully from one peeling building to another, the bright old paint the most colourful thing. I wondered how different it was when spring arrived, how much green there would be in the black and white scene.

There was nothing easy about exploring Ammassalik. My gloves were sodden and gritty from pushing through dirty snow, my hands cold and chapped beneath. Steep uneven streets meant I needed shoving and pulling to get anywhere. There was an eerie sound of wailing huskies and that with the cold sent shivers through me despite all the layers of fleece and down. We explored a bit further past the post office, the bank and then the cake shop again, before making our way back uphill to the Red House. It was a struggle to manoeuvre my chair around frozen obstacles and lumps of ice and up the final flight of slippery wooden stairs to our temporary home perched high above town.

We prepared for our last supper, appreciating the running water, the electric kettle, the instant flame of the gas stove, things we'd soon be without. With only a bag of frozen meatballs, one of mixed veg, and a pan of stodgy rice, it wasn't an inspiring spread, but one we devoured anyway.

We ate dinner with another Red House guest, an Icelandic mountain guide, there to record the ways of the local Inuit. He'd spent the last months hunting on the sea ice with a wizened group of local men, the last still using indigenous skills. Most others were unemployed, maybe alcoholic, traditions destroyed by modern ways. He was filming their life on the ice and would share it with Icelandic schools, to sustain the knowledge of traditional ways.

He seemed a kind man who was concerned for our safety and he told us tales full of caution. Due to failed equipment and bad weather, no team had successfully crossed the ice yet that year. The Namibians were rescued with frostbite; another team flattened by a Piteraq storm. I'd never heard of a Piteraq, but it turned out to be a hundred mile an hour wind storm that could appear as if from nowhere; it would be almost as unpleasant as meeting a polar bear on the ice. We asked him about polar bears and he said how a

British team, just returned from a climbing expedition on the icecap, had a polar bear stick its head into the tent whilst they played Trivial Pursuit. They'd scared it off by banging pots and pans through the night until they were air lifted to safety the next day.

It was unusual to get polar bears far up on the ice away from the food of the sea, but we questioned our decision not to bring a gun – but it was too late and we'd have to hope that flares would do.

The others had joked that it would be survival of the fittest. If we met a hungry polar bear it would eat me first. I'd lost sleep over polar bear nightmares so when I heard they don't like loud noises, I'd bought a rape alarm.

"A bloody rape alarm" said Andy "I think they'd rather eat you than shag you!"

I knew it was a feeble attempt at self-defence but it made me feel just a bit better. If we met a bear, at least I had something I could do instead of feeling helpless.

After the Icelandic mountain guides tales of warning, I felt more terrified about what lay ahead than ever. My confidence wasn't helped by the team motto Pasi seemed to have adopted.

"We're all gonna die" he teased in his deep serious voice. I joined in the laughing, but his words jabbed. It was very possible we might.

I wondered just how dangerous this really was, how much of the fear was real fear of death, not just failure. Pasi's friend Dominick Arduin, whom I'd met at his house, had no doubt faced similar fears, balancing the rational and irrational fear of the worst. But Dominick had made the judgement – even though she had lost all her toes – to go back to the Arctic. When I'd asked Pasi how she had got on he just said she never came back. No body. No sign. Just swallowed up by the Arctic.

Dead in pursuit of adventure.

I didn't want that to be us.

I'd come too close once already.

A friend suggested that if I hadn't been paralysed, I'd probably be dead now, as it was in my personality to always push things too far.

The question was, was crossing Greenland just the same as climbing up that sea cliff in Scotland; out of my depth but pushing on regardless? The mountain guide looked at me across the table, straight into my eyes. It felt as if he knew what I was thinking, could see all my insecurity and worry. Maybe that's what mountain guides do.

"I don't think you can do it" he said, his voice serious. "I don't think you can cross Greenland."

I didn't argue.

We went to bed and I shivered in the warmth of the bunk.

What lay in store?

No-one had succeeded yet this year, so why should we? We were a bunch of souls united in a goal, but we knew little of each other's strengths, weaknesses, or motivations. After just three days together, we were already a clunky team. Little things that were annoying would soon be magnified on the ice. Within twenty-four hours we would be there. I felt the odds were stacked against us. I felt fear like I'd never felt before. Was it too late to turn back? Perhaps for the good of the others I should stay behind. It had taken two years of planning to get us there, but what would be the point if I messed it up for them, if some of their motivation was to help me cross too.

My mind was racing.

What to do.

For the best.

For the worst.

The evening's motto echoed through me, Pasi's deep voice, over and over again, suggesting we could all die.

The helicopter lifts off. Now we were really on our own. ANDY KIRKPATRICK

6. RED, WHITE AND BLUE

It came from the east, just a dot at first, way out over the ice, then grew larger, the low rattle of its rotor blades growing in volume as the sounds echoed back and forth across the hills. I sat at the edge of the helipad feeling my head beat fast in time with the rhythm of the rotors, the blades deafening as the shiny red helicopter came in to land. I put my hands over my ears to shut out the noise but then I realised I couldn't push myself towards the edge of the helipad with the others, so I kept moving and bowed my head as if that would lessen the racket, the whole time my heart beating fast – because I knew this was it.

Spirals of dirt whipped around until the rotor slowed, the doors slid open and people clambered from the back seats – two figures, dressed in bright colours, their postures kinked with the weight of heavy kit bags. There was something familiar about one of them; a tall and lanky body topped with a shock of black hair, his gait a kind of lollop.

"You're kidding me!" I shouted over the din of the helicopter as he looked up, head clear of the chopping rotors, the man's mouth agape with the shock of recognising me too.

It was Al – the first boyfriend I ever had.

Al was a mountain guide now, but when I knew him, when he'd been my boyfriend, he'd just been a super fit Leeds student. He was the only person I'd been out with before my accident – as it happens we split up only a few days before. As he walked closer an image flashed through my mind of my Mum actually thanking him in the raw weeks following my accident, for sharing sexual encounters with me, the thought making me blush. I mean, how embarrassing does it get for someone to be thanked for that by their ex-girlfriend's mother.

It felt a little awkward for a moment, then he gave me a hug, introducing me to his mate, who was also a client, the two of them heading for the cold peaks north of Ammassalik. I felt envious that they would travel on by dog sled, but later when I heard the loud eerie echo of the huskies and realised that they shit all over the sled ropes, I changed my mind. I wanted to stop and chat but we only had time for a quick conversation before wishing each other good luck and parting as quickly as we'd met.

"I heard you were going to ski across Greenland" he said, bending down to shout into my ear as if we were talking in a noisy pub.

"I'm going to try" I said back again.

He put his hand on my shoulder and gave it a squeeze, saying "If anyone's stubborn enough to do it, it's you."

"Thank you" I replied giving him a smile, glad of some positivity from another mountain guide "I'll try my best."

I could tell both of us were a little unsure what to say, so I just said "Better get in the chopper – hopefully see you again somewhere as random as this" and Al dragged his stuff off, the both of us a bit knocked sideways by our chance encounter.

With no time to dwell on such things, we set about carrying the kit to the helicopter, time precious and the commotion of getting our gear on board in full swing.

Flying onto the ice seemed a far more remote prospect than my only previous helicopter ride (to a rig in the North Sea) and this time there were none of the safety procedures. There was a weight limit though and it soon appeared we were over it; a months fuel and food for six, along with our personal gear came in at five hundred kilos before taking into account the weight of us all. We were way over the limit so we had to split into two groups for the twenty minute hop onto the ice. We frantically started dividing the kit, conscious that if for any reason the second flight didn't make it back, the first team would need enough stuff to survive up there. It was chaos whilst we tried to repack and I wondered how we'd missed it in the planning. I didn't dare think about what it meant for budget. We'd been lucky to find some sponsors but we'd also all saved to put personal money in. An extra helicopter ride could break the bank.

Andy, Pasi and Jacek took off first and we watched the helicopter lift, then move slowly off into the West.

Now there was silence again, except for the wind.

Once again I felt doubtful and uncertain about our ambitious plan.

I had butterflies.

I sat with Anna, glad it was just me and her, a last normal moment before we went into the deep end.

"I don't feel fit enough for this" she said, looking genuinely worried. "I've spent so long getting this trip together I've totally neglected training for it."

"You'll be okay" I said, knowing she was the toughest woman I'd ever met, with an incredible level of drive and determination combined with a seemingly limitless pain threshold.

"I really hope so" she said, the sound of the helicopter returning for us just audible.

Hearing Anna speak it struck me for the first time that I wasn't the only one having major wobbles, not the only one worried about how I would perform. It wasn't me and five hard adventurers, but just six people, each with their strengths and weaknesses and all of us would be tested.

The helicopter slowed, hovered and landed and before I knew what was happening I was waving good-bye to my wheelchair, donning my earphones, buckling up and we were off. I looked down at the helipad and at my wheelchair. It felt as if I was leaving a vital part of myself behind. It was only a web of metal tubes but my wheelchair was freedom and to leave it felt strange. From there on I would depend on the sit-ski and help from the others to get around. I wouldn't see it again until the other side and I hoped Air Greenland would deliver it safely.

The noise of the journey killed conversation but so did the sight below. We leaned with our noses pressed to the windows and eyes wide like children, mesmerised by the beautiful sparkling expanse of ice and frozen sea. The knot in my stomach tightened and I knew it wouldn't loosen until we reached the other side but at the same time I felt a zing of excitement, knowing just how lucky I was to be there looking at that view.

The sea gave way to mountains, the peaks looking close enough to touch as we slowly glided past, until one by one the mountains disappeared into the edges of the ice cap, a seemingly endless sheet of white nothingness.

It was as if we were at the edge of a world unmade.

Nothing there, apart from a few red dots that grew into Andy, Harvey and Jacek.

We landed softly.

Anna and Pasi pushed the bags out and Harvey pushed my ski up to the door. With a little help I slid into the sit-ski and was pulled away.

Andy slid the door shut and Pasi gave a thumbs up to the pilot, who signalled back and put on the power, the wheels lifting up off the snow, everyone holding the kit down as the chopper took off.

The wind died.

So did the sound of the rotors.

Everyone was silent as the chopper grew smaller and smaller until it was no more.

I looked around to get my bearings. On one side were the coastal mountains, on the other the ice cap, a horizon so empty we imagined we could see the curvature of the earth. The sky was almost flawless, except for the scars of planes, trails of cloud mapping flight paths from Europe to America. I watched one crawl above us, like an ant over a ceiling, so slow in such a vast space. To it we were as small as molecules.

The day had happened so fast, the pace picked up by the pressure of helicopter slots, and now, so still and silent, the ice had arrived. Rows and columns of gear surrounded us and we stared and wondered what critical thing we might have forgotten. One vital thing missing could mean the difference between comfort and pain or life and death.

We started making camp. I tried to help put the tents up but the sit-ski was hard to manoeuvre in anything but a straight line. I practiced techniques to turn it; a sharp nudge of the shoulders in the direction I wanted to go combined with a push on the poles to encourage the turn. It was hard, sometimes only changing direction by a few degrees, then other times I'd suddenly spin and find myself facing the opposite direction. I tried to read the ground and to time my nudging with the top of a bump to help the turn but the results were unpredictable.

"So how do you do this then?" I heard Andy ask no-one in particular, and I tried to turn and watch his first attempt at cross-country skiing. But as I turned my skis caught an edge and tipped me over, flicking my head on the ground and sending icy dribbles down my neck. From my horizontal angle, I saw Andy had fallen too. I was helpless to get up and needed the others to grab my hand and pull me upright with a foot jammed against the base

Dropped by the helicopter on the edge of the icecap, we were about to begin our long journey West. It all finally felt very real and remote, and we hoped we hadn't forgotten a vital bit of equipment. PASI IKONEN

of my sit-ski to stop it sliding sideways. We laughed, but again I wondered about our sense and our chances of success. We weren't even off the starting block, with five hundred and fifty kilometres ahead and four bad skiers in our team. We had a long journey in store.

We cooked tea and began eating outside, Andy's bowl a cut-down pop bottle and the dimples in its base the wrong shape for the spoon. The sun got low and we got cold and so we retreated into our two red tents noting not to bother with outdoor dining again. It wasn't barbecue country.

Inside three of us would sleep side by side, laying first on a big oblong of foam, then using two mats on top of this. Pasi and Anna and I were in one tent, and the boys in the other tent, the idea to rotate as we went on – not that it happened.

I pulled out my huge down sleeping bag, stuffed with a kilo of the best feathers money could buy – reassuringly massive. If too much warmth had been sacrificed for weight one would be in for a very grim time as it was at night that you really escaped from the unending chill, and the body and mind recovered.

I blew up my foam mat and slid into my sleeping bag wearing every stitch of clothing, as well as my equally high-loft down jacket, knowing that night would be the first test.

The forbidding sense of the previous night in the hostel had passed and now after two years of planning we were finally here. At last I felt the full and unhindered surge of pure excitement. The adventure had begun.

I sat up and watched the sun sink low through the open flap of the tent door as the steam rose from a pan of melting snow, Pasi dropping in big chunks of ice. My sit-ski became a silhouette against a red horizon, the sky above glowing colourfully like the embers of a fire.

I felt privileged to be there.

We woke early with the sun blazing red through the skin of our tent. We took forever to get ready spending hours melting ice for drinking and then more time puzzling over how to get all the gear into the pulks. There was no doubt we had too much stuff but it was too late now. We didn't want to leave anything behind and spoil the pristine landscape, though yellow snow, the odd bit of brown and tea bags could hardly count as no trace. We burnt our toilet roll and dug the rest down into the snow, but the shovelled snow was still a scar and I wondered how many years our debris would take before it ground to powder deep in the ice.

I sat in the tent waiting for the pulks to be packed and for the other tent to be broken down and packed too, putting off going out until the last moment, a system that came from necessity. Hanging around in my sit ski for even five minutes would be enough to make me so cold we'd have to put the tents back up again.

The pulks ready Pasi pushed the sit-ski directly into the big porch of the tent, and with Anna's help got me off the ground and strapped in, pulling me out to my waiting ski poles.

The rest of the team stood waiting.

I passed Anna my down jacket – feeling naked without it, while Pasi collapsed the tent, rolled it up, and clipped it along the length of his pulk.

At last we were ready.

I leaned on my poles and pushed.

"This pulk is a monster!" Andy exclaimed and I watched everyone struggle to get them moving. I didn't have anything to pull but within minutes my arms burned with effort.

We stopped.

We'd moved only a hundred metres. If that.

How would we ever cross the ice? My arms felt fit to explode already.

After another hundred metres we paused again. I looked up ahead and saw in the big blue sky two vapour trails of cloud crossing each other, forming a giant cross.

"Hallelujah, it's a sign" someone shouted and inside me something whispered that it would all be okay. None of us were religious but it's hard to be in wilderness and not sense something bigger than yourself. (From then on, no-one said "We're all gonna die." We remarked instead that it was better to fail than never to have tried, although it seemed a bit premature after only two-hundred metres!).

I pulled my arms on the poles – so heavy – and seemed to move a disproportionately small amount for the level of effort involved. As I pulled again my body lunged forward. As the ski moved through I was more upright and could see the way ahead. Just a huge expanse of unspoiled whiteness stretched away into the infinite distance. I thought of my excitement as a kid at seeing a field of virgin snow, unscarred by footprints or other kids sledging, but this was in another league, a galaxy of virgin snow and ice. Each lunge forward seemed to suck my arms of all their strength and I paused regularly to shake my arms out and catch my breath. I glanced over my shoulder and was glad for something to see, my eyes appreciating the rocky outcrops we were leaving behind. At least they were a feature to focus on but ahead was a blank canvas save for the horizon. Wherever on earth we were heading, it didn't look or feel like earth. There was absolutely nothing to distract from the effort of each movement, the tightness that screamed through my shoulder muscles and the overwhelming realisation of how hard it all was.

It felt like the hardest physical work I'd ever done.

We'd move another hundred metres.

"Are we nearly there yet?" asked Andy, looking very much like a man who'd never skied before.

On our first day skiing, we saw that vapour trails from planes flying across had formed this cross in the sky. Whilst not religious we imagined it was a kind of sign that everything would be okay! ANDY KIRKPATRICK

We paused and in spite of the cold put on sun-cream and pulled out hats with flaps to cover our necks, conscious of the burning sun. Andy crafted a triangular nose-piece from a roll of tape and hung it from his glasses. My nose was spattered with freckles already and I pulled my neck scarf up for cover, glad of the warmth from my breath against it and for protection from the harsh air. I imagined trekking across a desert instead and it made me glad of snow instead of sand and for cold instead of heat.

We skied another hundred metres.

We were stopping every five or ten minutes for someone to adjust a strap, drink water, fiddle with a buckle, take a photograph or do something. There were endless excuses for a brief rest.

"We'll never cover the distance if we stop so much" Pasi reminded us.

When Pasi spoke we all listened.

The next time we broke through our hundred metre record, we kept on going.

We'd already planned our strategy to ski for fifty-five minutes, then break for five. Each hour like that we called a 'leg' and there would be a minimum of eight legs a day, with a longer break for lunch. That way we'd be sure to cover the twenty kilometres each day that we needed to and make it over the ice before our rations were used.

"We need to save anything that needs adjusting for the end of each leg." said Pasi.

Again we all listened.

His discipline was needed, and we skied on, clock-watching as if we had boring factory jobs and couldn't wait to escape the conveyor belt. My Dad had a job in a cake factory when he was younger, putting glazed cherries on iced cakes. I thought of him standing there licking his fingers between cakes. I'd give anything then for a line of cherry-topped cakes to march past us instead of just endless white icing. Mmmmmm. Icing, that would be tasty.

Finally our fifty-five minutes was up. Time to rest.

The time it took to detach the pulks, make yellow snow, find peanuts, search for other more interesting snacks, eat, drink and try to be merry always took more than five minutes. Eventually with Pasi's permission, we changed our strategy to fifty minutes skiing and a ten minute break. It was a more achievable plan and avoided the disappointment of always running behind schedule.

Not that time mattered or really existed anymore in such a changeless place.

With each slide forward our skis sank into a depth of powder that covered the ice. Being the first to break the trail was hard work, losing energy to the compacting snow. It would have been luxurious to ski side by side and to break the intensity of our effort with light talk, but it would also be mad not to conserve our energy. So we skied in single-file concentrating only on each leg moving forward and not bumping into the pulk in front. We were silent in our line, the effort of shouted conversation too great to bother.

It was still. Soundless except for our breathing lungs and scraping skis.

I imagined looking down from one of the planes that flew above, seeing our red line marching slowly across the ice like ants. I expected we'd be too small to see and wondered how a plane finds anyone in a rescue. The thought made me feel vulnerable. I remembered our flares and emergency EPIRB and was thankful for satellite technology.

Not too slowly the monotony dawned on us. We had to ski in a line, one behind the other, as it was hard work breaking a new trail at the front. With the length of a pulk between each of us it was difficult to talk and by the end of each leg we were hungry for both food and conversation. We had a bag each for every day, full of nuts, raisins, oatcakes, chocolate and malt loaf. I wished we'd been more extravagant when we'd planned our food, though could only blame myself given I'd organised all the rations back in Scotland and posted them to Greenland. Anna complained there was no Haribo, Andy that he couldn't stand raisins and Pasi was silent as he ripped through a malt loaf. Harvey would have been happy with anything and Jacek had some extra Polish treats. I ate more peanuts and dreamt of cheese.

It was leg five and Harvey broke trail while the rest of us marched behind him, concentrating intently on the rhythm. I tried to shut out the pain of exertion but every now and then my mind spilled black thoughts like a pool of ink and I'd focus on how far it was, how impossible it seemed and how sore my hands were from gripping the poles.

My fingers were numb from gripping so tightly and the pain begged at me to stop.

It was way harder than pigging down the lanes at home had been.

My gloves and big mitts made it difficult to get purchase and my sweaty

Skiing in line like this meant that conversation was difficult. We would ski in silence, lost in our own thoughts. ANDY KIRKPATRICK

palms and the creases of mitt fabric didn't help. More than once I pulled on the poles and my hands slid out to leave the mitts hanging in the fabric wrist straps. I adjusted the straps and consoled myself that sweaty hands were better than frost bite.

My fingers ached with effort, their small tendons so painful it felt they'd rip from the bones.

We'd only done five legs but it seemed like we'd run a marathon. Adding to my sense of gloom, the GPS told us we'd only done nine kilometres so not even half our planned distance. We'd climbed quite a bit so that might explain our slow progress but it had looked flatter than a calm ocean all the way.

I felt we'd been there an eternity yet we were only halfway through day one.

There was no such thing as lunch, though lunchtime represented half a day of effort. The only sign that it was different from the other breaks was that Jacek drank cup-a-soup, ate Polish sausage and handed chewing gum around afterwards. Otherwise it was peanuts and raisins as usual, spiced up with an oatcake, a bite of malt loaf or a piece of chocolate.

Fed and watered, we began our procession again and the game of counting legs. I counted so hard that I lost count, sure that we'd done seven legs, deflated to discover we'd only done six.

I didn't think my arms could take me any further.

Legs six to eight passed in a blur. My body was exhausted and my mind worn out from thinking about what to think about. The last ten minutes of the last leg seemed to take forever, the softer snow of late afternoon heavy to move through and with nothing to aim for. The only thing that marked the end of our first day's skiing was the tick of our watches.

"That's fifty" someone shouted from behind. It was only forty-seven minutes on my watch, but I was happy for it to end.

We ground to a halt.

We looked around for a campsite as if a water feature or tree might appear and identify an obvious place to put our tents. There was only a blank canvas. All the same, it seemed right to make camp to the side of our tracks rather than right on them as if they marked a major thoroughfare. I thought of Ice Truckers, a TV programme about drivers taking trucks full of oil production machinery across the ice fields in Alaska. They have to keep driving fast so they don't break through the ice. Maybe it wasn't such a bad idea to camp off our tracks, just in case a juggernaut came along and flattened us.

Inside the tent, warm and snug, we ate dehydrated rations to the watercolour hues of late evening: kind of soft sunset as it never went dark. I peered into the foil bag while mixing the boiled water and powder. Raisins lurked in there (they were in everything, much to Andy's dismay) and after a few mouthfuls I thought how it didn't taste of the Moroccan couscous it advertised on the packet. I was hungry enough though to devour every last raisin and scrape into the deepest corners of the foil in search of more.

"Anyone for palm fat?" Pasi offered some foil packets to Anna and I.

The thought of forcing a dehydrated ration of palm fat down was enough to make me gag. I knew it was important to keep our fat intake up, but I reckoned I had enough reserves to see me a good way through the month ahead.

"No thanks. Got enough of that on me" I replied.

"Me too" agreed Anna.

Pasi went for a double portion, and I suddenly doubted my decision. What was good for Pasi was good for me – he was an Arctic expert.

At last, hours of cooking, water melting and faffing later, I laid back in my down jacket onto a down sleeping bag, on a down-filled mat, and sank as if the floor was hydraulic into a blissful horizontal world.

Day one was over.

Poling along independently was difficult even without towing a pulk. I had a small bag attached to the back of my sit-ski with essentials for the day. When the snow was very deep or sticky, I had to short-rope to the back of one of the other's pulks to help keep my momentum going. PASI IKONEN

7. GRIND

I plant my poles – handles in front – tips behind.
　　I lean forward in the ski – my head bowed to Greenland.
　　I pull down on the poles.
　　Nothing.
　　I pull hard on the poles.
　　Nothing.
　　I pull harder on the poles, wrist loops digging into my skin.
　　The ski moves another foot.
　　The ski stops.
　　I begin again.
　　I must not dwell on this.

I closed my eyes and felt my body throb with exhaustion. Gone was the excitement of a journey finally underway. Gone was the exotic nothingness of new surroundings. Gone was the spring of muscles eager to work after a week of packing and travelling. Even only a day in, there was only one thing left, something that I felt as soon as I woke, that I felt over every metre of the day, and at night laying exhausted in my sleeping bag. It was the 'grind' of it all, and the grind of what was to come.

I woke on the morning of the second day with muscles tight and sore, shoulders stiff, hands swollen. Pigging had seemed so hard at home, tough training for a tough trip. Perfect training, but I had never had to try *so* hard, or for *so* long, or for *so* far. I had no doubt that it would only get harder.

But we had to keep going. We only had rations for thirty four days more.

～

Day three was worse.

> *I plant my poles.*
> *I lean forward.*
> *I pull.*
> *The ski moves another foot.*
> *I think about those first days.*

Day one. Day two. Day three. Gone were the smiles and the laughter. It felt more like a march or a retreat. The others commented that the hundred kilo pulks that had seemed fine to pull a hundred metres, felt to be growing heavier by the hour. We were all so exhausted that in the evenings the atmosphere was tense, both in and between the tents. Sarcastic and frustrated comments buzzed through the air. The stress of getting there was replaced by the stress of being there.

Anna, Pasi and I had done a lot of work behind the scenes. There had been two years of planning to make the trip happen. It often happens that part of a team has more history, perhaps more invested, and that responsibilities get confused as they get shared. As a result, Anna hadn't done her tax return and Pasi hadn't submitted a magazine editorial that was overdue, both of which were creating stress in our tent.

Instead of resting each evening, Anna's worn out brick of a laptop whirred to life, its inner workings clicking in the same way as our numbed brains. Pasi pulled glossy outdoor magazines from his pulk that he needed to reference for his article. It was no wonder his pulk was extra heavy though Anna said they'd had no time to pack properly with all the other stuff there had been to sort out. None of it was helped by the trip falling in the midst of them moving house from England to Finland, so their gear was scattered in various boxes and storerooms in a trail between the two locations.

How any of us had managed to find six weeks in our hectic lives for a journey like this was a wonder.

> *I plant my poles.*
> *I lean forward.*
> *I pull.*
> *Head bowed again to the ice.*

I sat in the front of the tent getting the stove ready to melt water for tea while Pasi busily typed away. Unable to pull a pulk I felt guilty about not pulling my weight – well, double my weight, and so melting water was becoming something I looked forward to, something useful.

The job was the same each night, filling the fuel bottle from the big plastic petrol cans on the pulk. Priming the stove with a little fuel, lighting it so that the liquid fuel would vaporise as it whooshed out of the nozzle, the yellow flame warm against my face. Once the stove was roaring came the pan filled with snow, which would slowly melt into a small puddle to which more snow would be added. The job was slow and laborious, but the heat from the stove would quickly warm up the tent. A moment of bliss. The trouble was that soon after the ice began to melt, the stove would tip and spill the water out of the pan.

Jacek had been tasked with sorting out wooden boards to go under the stoves so that they didn't melt into the snow, but instead of wood he'd brought a dedicated metal stand. With the stove going, the metal stands heated up and the snow underneath would melt and shift. Then the stove would topple over, spilling the essential water we'd nursed. Every gram of fuel had to be pulled across the ice, and the water hydrated both us and our food, and so every drop was as precious as fine wine. Anna was persistently frustrated about the stove base and Jacek was receiving the brunt of the blame, even though the bases were designed for just our kind of trip. Although Jacek had skied the last degree to the North pole before, that had been a commercial trip and such details had been sorted by the guide. What made matters worse was that Harvey had brought his own mega Arctic pan set up, along with a wooden board which never fell over. It was a mistake that needed to be buried but Anna kept gnawing. I wondered if the stove base was a scapegoat for her feeling that her organisational efforts were unappreciated. But the fact was, she'd been our mover and shaker. She had kicked ass to make things happen. Without her determined work it was doubtful we'd ever have got ourselves to Greenland. The tension was never explicit but just seemed to sit there under the surface.

Looking back from my pan of snow I could see Anna treating her feet, the blisters so deep and large they looked more like a job for accident and emergency than a first aid kit. Years of blisters caused by ultra distance running and adventure racing had given Anna skin like paper.

I couldn't imagine just how much pain she was in, every step utter misery. It went a long way to explain how she had been since we'd started on the ice.

The bickering increased with each day we spent together. Little things that at home would have been funny quickly irritated others. The wrong word. The wrong action. Even just skiing a little bit too fast. Harvey had discovered

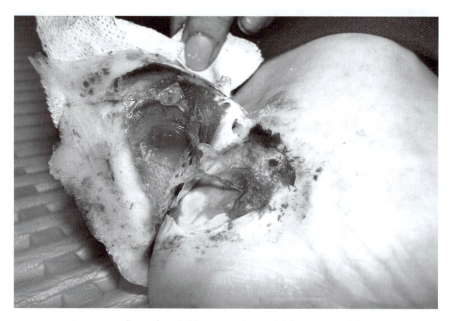

Anna was plagued with blisters and painful feet. We could only sympathise and wince at how sore they looked. PASI IKONEN

that he couldn't use his jacket pocket because Anna had stitched it up with a sponsor's badge. Andy left tea bags scattered on the snow. Jacek had his own more tasty lunch supplies. Pasi and Harvey competed in opinions about how things should be done. I was too slow. Pasi was too fast. Anna's feet were scarred in blisters so painful they took an hour to dress each evening. Andy was using up the satellite phone minutes calling home (but then his kids were only four and seven and missing him like crazy). Pasi still hadn't finished his article. It was everyone else's fault that Anna would be fined for a late tax return. Stress, stress, stress. And then there was the stove falling over.

I dropped another dollop of snow into the pan, the edges balanced with our flasks in order to avoid any spills. I hate confrontation and didn't want bad feeling amongst my friends, old or new, but I'd been on enough trips to know that the biggest hurdles often come from inside, not from the environment. I also knew that such things didn't stem from bad people but good people under tremendous pressure. All I could hope was that the pressure would eventually bring us together.

> *I plant my poles.*
> *I lean forward.*
> *I pull.*
> *The ski moves another foot.*
> *I reset my poles.*
> *I lean forward.*
> *I pull.*
> *The ski moves another foot.*
> *I feel to be skiing through sand.*

Resting at break time, a bag of peanuts in my lap, I looked up at the aeroplane moving slowly across the sky, it's vapour trail like ours only ten thousand metres higher, both heading West. I imagined passengers drinking gin and tonic, eating cocktail nuts and envied their luxuries: the films and the drinks, though nuts I'd had enough of. What I'd have given for a good film.

> *I reset my poles.*
> *I lean forward.*
> *I pull.*
> *The ski moves another foot.*
> *'Twenty kilometres, that's only twelve miles' I reason to myself,*
> *thinking about our daily target, the target we have to hit to avoid*
> *running out of fuel. 'That is less than an hour on my bike.' It's a short*
> *distance yet it feels like such hard work. It will take us at least nine*
> *hours instead of one.*

Although the ice ahead of us looked the same from a distance, it changed all the time. In the morning there was fresh or windblown snow on the surface and it was super cold and hard to get any glide on the skis. It felt like skiing on glue. If the sun shone, the surface warmed up enough to melt a thin layer beneath our skis and help us glide along. By late afternoon though, it was tough going again with the temperature drop and the cold sticky ice that came with it.

Much to my surprise the clothing I had on, including my kiddie's half sleeping bag for my body, worked amazingly well and kept me warm and toasty no matter how cold or grim. At the start, hands had been inserted every few hours to check if my feet where still warm, or even just still alive, but each time the answer was the same 'very warm'. After the third day people stopped checking.

> *I plant my poles.*
> *I lean forward.*
> *I pull.*
> *The ski moves another foot.*

Day four. Day five. The plot of what we had done on the GPS still looked pathetic, making all of us doubt we would make it to the other side. We stared at the horizon in expectation of a great oasis appearing before us as if we were in a desert. I'd never thought of an icecap as a desert but barely any rain falls there and the landscape is similar. A desolate, wind-sculpted place.

One day, I saw a black speck not far ahead. I called to the group, mildly excited that there was something other than white to look at. It gave us something to aim for and for the next ten minutes we skied towards it.

It turned out to be a dead bird.

> *I plant my poles.*
> *I lean forward.*
> *I pull.*
> *The ski moves another foot.*
> *I really feel to be skiing through glue.*

Each morning I woke with my hands like claws and would wait for them to come back to life. Once the numbness went then there would just be the pain. Pain in my hands. Pain in my forearms. Pain in my shoulders. Pain in my back. What kept me going was the knowledge that I wasn't alone. Everyone was feeling it, and although we grumbled about many things: the peanuts, the stove, the lack of a view, we rarely grumbled about the pain. Also I thought about Igor Kuznetsov and how he had found it tough, this superman. I owed it to all of them to keep pushing on.

I reset my poles.
I lean forward.
I pull.
The view is always the same.

Our minds searched for something to clutch hold of, unaccustomed to freedom from busy days with so many things to do and think about. Life had been reduced from a hectic schedule of doing, to the four simple actions of skiing, eating, sleeping and pooing. Surviving was all that mattered and although it wasn't easy it seemed simple next to the complexity of life at home.

"Let's sing," Anna suggested one day, and launched straight in.

"Pack up your troubles in your old kit bag and smile, smile, smile…"

Vera Lynn might have worked in wartime gloom but it wasn't doing it for me on the ice. Half-heartedly we sang along but within minutes our voices trailed and quiet fell again.

It felt like we'd scarred the silence.

"Maybe we can just sing in our heads" I suggested.

I tried it for a while but realised I didn't know the full lyrics to any song except American Pie. When it got to the chorus and the line about 'this'll be the day that I die…' I decided to stop.

I reset my poles.
I lean forward.
I pull.
The ski is stuck.
I pull harder.
The ski moves again.

We sat in a line, everyone resting on their pulks, all facing west apart from Anna, who faced east. I wanted to turn around and join her, to show some solidarity for my friend who I knew felt isolated and lonely. Only I didn't have the energy to turn myself around.

"Anyone want to trade a Mars Bars for a malt loaf?" I asked, craving a chunk of the sticky fruit loaf.

"Yes! How many Mars Bars is a malt loaf worth?" Andy jumped in, keen to trade away anything with raisins in.

"Two" I suggested.

"How about three?"

"It's a deal."

Bartering our snacks brought entertainment to our ten minute breaks. I was after malt loaf, Andy in search of Mars Bars and Harvey was eager for packets of oatcakes even though they were dry and crumbled.

"I've got a good strategy" Andy piped up, cheered with chocolate. "For one whole leg of skiing, have a topic to think about. I just did one on 'past lives that might have been' and I thought about all the things that might be different if I'd changed a few choices along the way. I'm gonna do 'friends and family' next."

I tried Andy's strategy of having a 'thinking theme' for a leg. My mind drifted to my Dad's voice telling me as a kid to always 'work hard and play hard'. He meant it – he'd never sold out his life to a career and I thought about how happy he'd seemed when I'd been offered a 'proper' job at last.

My Dad had called it a 'job for life'. He seemed pleased that all my years of being a student had paid off.

The office block was a pyramid of golden glass with air conditioning wafting through automatic doors. There was a sea of computer screens and a large empty desk just for me. It was an unfamiliar world. Uniformed penguins held handrails whilst they carried piles of documents or plastic cups of tea. Everyone spoke quietly in respect of the open plan office and busily went about their work. Crinkled foreheads staring at computer screens, hunched shoulders bent over piles of paper, concentrating and serious. It was the world of business.

Busy-ness.

I was grateful for the opportunity to do something with all that I'd learnt. I was a geologist only it didn't seem like much of what I knew applied, as the job was so different from the subject. I was grateful for the opportunity to travel, for swanky hotel rooms and three course dinners. But another 5am alarm, another modern hotel that seemed much like the last and the menu listing salmon, sea bass, and chicken a la something didn't rouse my appetite like it should.

Gradually things had become monochrome. I saw myself in black and white scenes, I scolded myself for not being able to paint things in bright colour and bring it all alive. Why did my eyelids want to close? Why was I so sleepy? Why was it so hard to find energy?

Lists filled my mind of things to do, things to finish, things to start, people to phone, email, meet. I'd wake in the night my head bursting with 'things' and I began keeping a pad bedside the bed to write them down. The busy-ness was wearing me down. The alarm was always rude and always too early. Money that once hadn't mattered much at all became a necessity; the mortgage, bills, shopping, car, the higher cost of convenience. When did everything get so expensive?

So slowly that I hardly noticed, my posture got a little more slumped. My shoulders felt stiffer and my old trousers got too tight around the waist. My spark got less sparkly. I didn't feel great but I didn't understand why. How could I feel so bad when I had so much? I'd done what I understood was best. I'd worked hard and played hard but now it seemed that the work, even though it wasn't harder sucked the marrow out of my bones.

I crashed into the back of the pulk in front. It snapped me from my daydream briefly, until the rhythm of skiing resumed.

To escape the monochrome world of office life, I'd begun to plan another adventure. I was in search of feelings I'd known but almost lost. I needed a journey, some mountains and simplicity; these were the things I craved and that would I hoped, put the heart back into my life.

Three months of unpaid leave seemed the perfect opportunity. So I hatched a plan to cycle from the island of Hokkaido in the north of Japan to Okinawa, a speck of land far away in the South China Sea. To cycle one hundred kilometres a day for three months was totally unrealistic for me but I wasn't looking for realism.

I could feel the creak and flex of the bike beneath me as if I was sat in it again, but it was only the creak of my sit-ski. The force of pedalling up the steep hills of Japan had caused some strain to the bike and my arms. "Up-u-down-u" a man had told me about the road that hugged the coastline of

Honshu Island, up and down, twisting and turning with each crinkle of the shore. The journey wore me out. A hundred kilometres a day of serious hills was just too much to sustain. We'd pedalled long and hard, detouring erupting volcanoes and roads lined with walls of snow, but then the snow had fallen fast and deep, freezing both our limbs and gears as we ground our way through mountain passes.

I'd felt exhausted yet oddly elated. A bit like being there on the ice.

Rioko was a TV producer, part of the team following us on our wheeled adventure through Japan. She cycled beside me on a foldable bike rigged with a camera and picked me apart with probing questions.

"What drives you Karen? I mean, why are you doing this?"

"I just like it."

"But what are you searching for?" she persisted.

"I don't really know. I just like being outside. I like cycling. I like exploring new places."

She crinkled her forehead, bewildered and frustrated as if she was sure there was more.

"But it's like you're searching for a missing jigsaw piece. What is it?"

I didn't know.

I liked being outside, I liked cycling, I liked exploring, I liked having direction.

Her questions made me wonder. Was it all a quick fix for something I was missing? Was I trying to prove something to myself? Was I avoiding something by keeping moving?

In the beginning, soon after I'd fallen off the cliff and put myself in a wheelchair, maybe then I'd had something to prove and something to avoid. I'd needed to know I could live independently and have an active life, still get outdoors to laugh and play. I'd needed distraction. That was a long time ago. It wasn't like that anymore.

So why did I do it? Why did I put myself through hours of monotony until my muscles ached and my tendons screamed? Perhaps it was just an escape, one that staved off a fear of life being mundane, routine, rigid and known. Maybe an adventure is like driving a car – sometimes you have a destination and sometimes you just invent one, to get away. Is it all hedonism or masochism or a kind of addiction, each experience a fix that only generates an ever-increasing desire for the next?

Or maybe it didn't matter.

> *I reset my poles.*
> *I lean forward.*
> *I wait before I pull.*
> *A micro rest.*
> *I pull.*
> *Today the ice feels like honey.*

With my arms pumping like pistons and ski poles rhythmically punching the ice, I'd still found no answers and thinking began to feel like patting my head and rubbing my tummy at the same time. The action was hypnotic and my thoughts gradually emptied on the trail behind until there were none left, only the thud of ski poles, the crackle of jackets and the sliding of skis and pulks.

> *I reset my poles.*
> *I lean forward.*
> *I pull.*
> *The pulk moves a foot.*
> *How long have I been doing this?*

"Pasi, that's fifty seven minutes!" Anna shouted from the rear, the exasperation clear in her voice. Her blisters probably needed respite. She was at the back of our line, practicing the art of skiing whilst reading as an antidote to the heights of her boredom and pain. She clasped a thick orange novel in her hand, something about matadors in Mexico and I wondered if reading about a hot climate gave her some kind of escape.

We stopped instantly at the realisation we were seven minutes over our leg time. I watched the others unclip their pulks, fumbling clumsily through their gloves and thought how they looked like giant over-flowing baths. I was grateful not to be pulling one. Everyone rummaged for snacks, and rested.

"Is that six?" Jacek asked, stirring a late afternoon cup-a-soup, sounding as exhausted as I felt.

"No that's seven" Harvey thought. It should have been easy to count to eight, but every day we lost track. It was a cloudy day, the horizon hidden, the ice indistinguishable from the swirling white. Each leg of the day had felt longer and my mind seemed as fogged as the weather. I wanted the day to end, to crawl into our red flapping homes, to feel warmth creep back into my bones, to escape from the opaque white.

"Anyone want to trade me some plain chocolate for milk?" Andy fussed.

"I would if I could." I shook my snack bag but could only see peanuts, raisins and more peanuts.

"We should keep moving," Pasi prompted us to get going. We had two more legs to do, as he'd counted only six.

I reset my poles.
I lean forward.
I pull.
The ski moves a foot.
The pulk in front moves.
I move again.

Jacek had a giant icicle extending from his beard. He led the way with the compass and we followed closely in the white out. We wore masks for protection from the cold and wind but our breath condensed and dribbled down until we all had long icy spikes protruding from our chins. They made us look like aliens.

I plant my poles.
I lean forward.
I pull....

In a near hypnotic state, I noticed that something seemed wrong. The wind was on the opposite cheek to normal.

We checked the compass. Its needle was lined up with the direction arrow but the pointer was a hundred and eighty degrees out.

We'd been skiing backwards.

Our previous ski tracks were invisible in the white out.

We turned around and retraced our steps, unsure how far we'd gone the wrong way. We quickly found virgin ice again and luckily we'd only lost a few hundred metres but our mistake added to our layers of stress and we fell quiet for the rest of the leg.

I reset my poles.
I lean forward.
I pull.
The ski moves a foot.
I lift my head and look into the sad eyes of the gnome strapped to
the back of Andy's pulk.

Theory says that teams go through four stages of development as they tackle something together: forming, storming, norming and performing. Forming is when everyone is being super nice to each other, enthusiastic about the task and trying to make a good initial impression. Storming happens when people start getting frustrated and discover clashes of personality and differences of opinion or approach. Norming is when people start to get over their differences and find their niche and role in the team. After all that, 'performing' should finally happen – when the team gets into a place of working really well together.

I felt like we'd been stuck in the storming stage for most of the journey so far.

I hoped it would pass soon and skied along wondering if I should do something to help improve things. I didn't know what and doing something seemed harder than doing nothing. I didn't dare risk making things worse.

I reset my poles.
I lean forward.
I pull.
The ski moves a foot.
I stop. The pulk in front has stopped.
Everyone has stopped.
They undo their harnesses for the eighth time that day, for the fifty
sixth time since we started.

We have skied for seven days.
We are a quarter of the way across.

I wonder if I have it in me to make it.
Maybe we actually stand a chance of making it to the other side.

The fact we'd survived a week seemed nothing short of a miracle.

Jacek and his giant icicle! Skiing into a cold wind we had to wear
full face masks for protection but condensed breath dribbled down
to form icicles. PASI IKONEN

8. EPIRB

The tiny LED display read minus 30°C, the ambient temperature inside our hastily pitched tent. The thermometer was designed for a fish tank with two sensors and two digital read outs. One of them read the air temperature and one of them the temperature of my foot. The wires led down my leg to my foot and the idea was to help me avoid getting frostbitten toes. It seemed funny to trust my life to a fish tank thermometer.

I shivered and pulled my neck scarf up to cover the ice-cream tip of my nose. I was sat in the front of the tent still wearing the oversized baby push chair sleeping bag bottoms and my down jacket. All I wanted to do was slide into my sleeping bag and recover from the long hard day of skiing across the unrelenting ice but first I needed to check my feet were okay. Then begin the cooking. Sleep was still hours of snow-melting away but I knew from experience that to neglect such things would always lead to trouble. It's an unwritten rule in such trips that everyone looks after themselves. It sounds harsh but there's no room for weakness. Every ounce of energy is spoken for.

I pushed the rubber button on the thermometer for news from down below, from the tip of the wire that ran down to my left foot.

Twelve degrees.

That was too cold for my immobile feet. I had to do something about it.

I looked over at Anna sorting her own feet out, Pasi outside digging a snow wall around the tent. The easy thing to do would be to ask for a hand, maybe even the loan of her stomach for me to stick my feet on for warmth. But I didn't.

I pulled my leg around and slid off my boots and socks – all five pairs, and started rubbing.

I sat there with my ice cold feet and considered the seriousness of our undertaking. There were so many things that could go wrong, so many small pieces of equipment we depended on. If our stoves were to break we'd have no way of melting ice, no water to drink and no warm food. The list of potential problems was long. It was early icecap-season in Greenland and two teams had already been rescued. I remembered an Inuit man in Kangerlussuaq telling us that we wouldn't make it, that no-one had made it across the ice yet this year. Some had been lucky to make it back. His words felt more real now, huddled in our small tent, the temperature dropping rapidly as night approached. Would I be able to manage the cold any better than them?

We were only ten days into the journey but I had to believe I could carry on for at least twenty-five days more.

I shuffled around and grabbed a heat pad already stashed in the pocket of the huge down jacket as my team mates hurried around outside, keen like me to get into the tent before the sun dropped beneath the white horizon. I ripped open the plastic packet of the heat pad so I could shake it in the air and feel the warmth of the chemical reaction seep through my fingers. It would warm my feet nicely. I grabbed my legs and pulled on them to get myself into a sitting position (oh how much easier it would be with stomach muscles that worked) and fumbled the heat pad into my thick woolly socks. My leg muscles spasmed and knocked me off balance. They were also cold, something which seemed to create more muscle spasm than usual. I felt a flare of anger towards my legs for making life so difficult but I knew how ridiculous it was to blame them and felt childish for feeling that way. After all it was me who had brought them here, not vice versa.

As I moved around the tent I brushed against its fabric and thin scabs of ice formed from condensed and frozen breath on the inside of the tent, tickled down the back of my neck. My back muscles tensed as the cold wetness ran down the track of my spine and over the border to a place I couldn't feel. I shivered again and zipped up my down jacket, grateful to all the geese that were plucked for it.

My foot no longer felt like dead meat.

I pulled my left leg around and began again on my other foot.

I thought about my wheelchair. Where was it right now? It had become such a part of me that without it I felt strangely incomplete. I missed it even though it would be useless on the icecap and was better replaced by the sit-ski as a way of getting around.

The feet-warming job done, I stuck my boots back on and allowed my self the little pleasure of laying back. Just for a second.

"More fuel Karen" said Pasi, throwing in the fuel bottle he'd filled outside, making me jump awake.

My body felt chilled to the bone.

"Oh… thanks… I'll get the water on" I replied, trying to sound with it. I pulled myself up by my knees with a shiver.

I pumped up the stove to pressurise it, glad of its plastic parts that would not stick to my flesh, let a little fuel drain into the burner and lit it with a match.

I held the match in my fingers for a moment, feeling its warmth.

My hands were tired and my fingers throbbed. The strain from days of skiing felt too much for their tiny muscles which were designed for tasks far lighter than hauling a body five hundred and fifty kilometres across the Greenland icecap. I once read there are at least twenty muscles and forty tendons in the hand and more again in the wrist. That's a lot of bits to go wrong. No wonder I felt in need of intravenous WD40. I had watched the others' legs as we skied along, seemingly effortless, while I felt racked with exhaustion. I was past feeling jealous about such things: I'd been paralysed for thirteen years.

The flame of the burning fuel began to die, the sign that the metal on which it stood would be well heated.

I turned on the fuel, the liquid turning to a gas as it hit the heated metal, the gas turning to a roaring torch as it hit the flame.

I felt the heat rise instantly in the tent, and scooped some snow into a pan and placed it over the flame.

I began sorting out the cooking gear but I longed to lie back, sink into the platform of down beneath me and let sleep anaesthetise the pain. In the daytime I craved the cocoon of my sleeping bag.

Zipped in I was safe from worry.

Zipped in I could repair my body and mind.

Zipped in I could almost forget there would be a tomorrow and another reckoning with the reality of my dream.

But at the end of each long day of skiing there were chores to be done. Tents had to be set up and reinforced against storms, gear sorted and cleaned of snow and most importantly of all, ice melted to wet our insatiable thirst and feed our shrivelled sinews.

I checked my fish tank thermometer. My feet were coming back to life. I checked the stove and added some more snow, and watched for leaks, not wanting to lose any precious fuel or drip it across the eruption of down bags and clothing that filled the tent.

The idea that we would switch tents as the days progressed had come to nothing and I wondered if it was creating a division between the two camps. I knew the guys didn't want to share with Anna due to the fact that she was often in a mood with them but didn't like that we seemed to be getting more segregated.

The structure of tent life was always the same; we melted ice all evening and we slept all night. The melting was mostly my job whilst Anna and Pasi did other tasks that I couldn't easily do. Pasi would be outside, shovelling snow baffles against the tent to keep out the wind. He would stake our skis into the ice and tie the tent guy ropes around them providing extra security in case the ever-threatening wind should pick up. He'd secure everything down for the night, every piece of equipment too valuable for our survival to risk being blown away. Anna would empty the pulk of essentials for the evening and choose bags of dehydrated food for dinner: spaghetti bolognese, curry or couscous and a couple of other meals masquerading as something more tasty than they were. They all tasted the same after a while but a welcome change to the day-long, week-long, month-long staple of peanuts. Each pulk still seemed to weigh close to a hundred kilos. Pasi's was so heavy and solid that it seemed like a stack of dead bodies must be hidden beneath its blue fabric but as a Finnish ex-commando, nothing seemed to phase him.

I hoped he was okay outside as the wind was really battering the tent and we'd been skiing in a white out all day.

"I am coming in" said Pasi, unzipping the door, the heat lost instantly, spindrift covering my feet. He slipped in quickly, crouching down to enter, his beard coated in ice, googles and big mitts on. He sat down in the porch beside me and zipped the door closed, then sat for a moment. I knew even he was tired.

"I am hungry" he said in his monotone voice.

"How is the weather?" I asked, a daft question when it was only quarter of a millimetre of fabric away.

"I am glad we have double poles for the tent" he said as he pulled off his googles, then turned and began taking off his boots.

The stove was a roaring tinnitus in our ears but each minute of its irritable bellow brought the temperature up further. After only fifteen minutes of burning fuel, the thermometer said the tent was warmer, now hovering around minus ten. The water began to bubble, the ice now transformed to our most precious commodity.

I made the usual round of drinks – hot chocolate for me, coffee for Anna and Pasi. Exhausted, we all laid back. It would have been so easy to fall asleep there and then in the sub-zero heat of minus ten but knowing the stove needed to be tended kept us awake.

"Pasi – your coffee!" shouted Anna, his cup falling over between the sleeping mats, spilling across the tent floor, seeping slowly from the mouth-hole in the lid of the plastic cup. The cup was righted and I mopped up the spill with toilet roll, almost too tired to care, knowing it would soon freeze and be brushed out of the door. But I also knew that we should stay vigilant and pay attention to the little things. It was little things that could lead to big things going wrong.

I pulled myself up and shovelled more ice into the pan. The next boil would fill our water bottles up ready for the morning and then we'd put them in our sleeping bags to stop them freezing solid overnight.

Pasi pressed buttons on the GPS, his blond wires of stubble dripping melt from his chin onto the silver matting that lined the tent floor for extra insulation. His jacket had sponsor labels sewn loudly across the red fabric, pristine white flakes still resting in its creases from his digging activities outside.

"Eighteen kilometres today," he informed us in his deep monotone, "and four hundred metres of climb."

"Is that all?" Anna sounded disappointed, the day having been the hardest so far, battling into a headwind, seeing almost nothing but the person in front. "I can't believe we've skied for nine hours and only done eighteen kilometres." Her headscarf sat tight across her forehead and hid the creases of her frown. "We'd do that in an hour in an adventure race." I understood her line of thinking and could relate to her frustration at how slowly we moved.

"Yes but you do not pull a one hundred kilo pulk when you are adventure racing," Pasi reasoned. "Err, Karen, the stove."

The snow was melting beneath the stove's base and the pan was precariously lopsided again. I reached out to grab it and Anna shoved some more ice underneath.

"If only Jacek had done what we asked and brought something to put the stove on, then we wouldn't have this problem."

"Anna, please don't keep going on about that" Pasi scolded.

"We can hear you!" In unison, Jacek, Harvey and Andy called from the other tent. "We're bored of hearing about the stove."

The lack of stove base was such a small thing, just a pin-prick of a worry with the icecap ahead of us. But a hundred pin-pricks would damage our chances of success and Anna was worried about that, perhaps frustrated too with her efforts to organise the scattered, haphazard bunch of near-strangers that our team essentially was.

I wondered how life was in the other tent. Tidy, messy, fun, smelly? Definitely it would be smelly. A Pole, a Brit and a nearly-Norwegian. Could they chat and banter easily? How was Jacek feeling, at sixty, with a bunch of people he'd never met before? And Andy who had never even been on skis, more accustomed to life in vertical places than horizontal? He spent his spare time swinging from overhanging rock walls like a monkey. When the helicopter had dumped us on the icecap, he'd put on his skis and asked "So how do you do it?" as he clumsily tried to shuffle, then fell flat on his face.

I barely knew Jacek or Andy and it had been at least ten years since I'd spent any time with Harvey. If things continued this way, I wouldn't know any of them much better after a month on the icecap. We skied all day in single file, one out front breaking fresh tracks, a trail of us behind with our heads down, moving with the speed of a funeral procession. We were each lost in our thoughts, focused only on placing our skis in the two parallel tracks ahead and on wondering what we would think about for the next month.

Why were any of us there? I'd wanted the adventure, the wilderness, an experience of the Arctic, along with the compelling goal the journey offered. But what about the others? Anna hated the cold and didn't like skiing. Jacek sold cars for a living in Warsaw and I wondered what had brought him here. Andy was more at home on rock and didn't want to be away from his kids for six weeks. Pasi and Harvey – well, they both loved being out in the snow and ice but there were already differences of opinion brewing between them about how things should be done. We were a random team, an unlikely mix and we'd never even met before the flight to Greenland.

Sharing with a married couple meant I was at intimate quarters with the squabbles that only happen between those who are close, a sign of the love and understanding that allows people to be how they really feel when they're tired and grumpy. But it reminded me somehow of the problems I'd left at home, of the challenges Suresh and I had. To escape, I listened to the laments of Robbie Williams on my mp3. His music wasn't my usual taste but a lullaby about his Gran somehow soothed me into a blissful land of bicker-free softness, a land where I could forget my own troubles, those I'd wanted to leave at home, those I'd spilled at the loch-side just a few weeks before. It had been the anniversary of our wedding and Suresh had been away. I'd driven the dirt track to the loch where we'd been wed – a beautiful spot beside a crescent of beach and giant Caledonian pine trees that had whispered in the breeze – and sat sobbing tears as the rain lashed against the window. I was afraid I'd made a mistake. I was afraid I'd committed to someone I couldn't make happy, or vice versa.

Cooking done, I switched off the roaring stove, only to realise that the roaring was coming from the wind as well, a low growl. I had a sudden panic about being so exposed, that this flimsy tent offered only the illusion of safety, and wanted to put the stove back on to mask the noise.

Instead I got into my sleeping bag with all my clothes and zipped myself in, like a kid hiding under their sheets.

I was just dropping off to sleep when the tent shuddered and sent down a shower of white ice again. The wind had continued to build through the evening. I brushed the flakes off me and seeing the thermometer gauge, noted my left foot had gone up two degrees to fourteen. At least it was on the rise. No-one else was sleeping yet.

"I'm coming round to use the Sat Phone" Andy called through the flapping of nylon. Pasi, the satellite phone beside him, scribbled in his note book recording the GPS data from the day.

Minutes later, Andy peeled back the crusty flaps at the front of the tent and launched clumsily into our space, knocking the shovel into the pan, which fell and poured its slushy contents back into the ice.

A small tenement block of fleece, he plonked his bum down and dangled his feet into the leg-pit that Pasi had dug at the front of our tent. "You should be careful where you get your snow from. Watch out for the yellow stuff" he said to me.

"The toilet's at the other end" I pointed out.

"We were in Patagonia once, on a climbing trip," Andy blundered on into a story, "really tired and thirsty after an epic climb. We hadn't slept for three nights because of a storm we got caught in but that's another story. Anyway, we staggered back to find the tent, but the wind was so strong that we had to crawl and when we got to where the tent should be, there was just a guy rope and no tent, so we searched around." He paused, wiping his nose on the back of his glove. "Well, we found some of our gear and we all felt so terrible but we got the stove going. Someone got this big lump of snow and put it in the pan – 'a nice cuppa tea' we thought – and waited for the snow to melt, and we were all really thirsty, really dying for the cup of tea, really cold and just wanting a drink. We watched it melt, gradually, slowly, then just when it was nearly melted, we saw it was a bit brown, then suddenly there was this giant turd in the middle of the pan. I mean, what are the chances of that, just picking the wrong bit of snow where someone had left a frozen turd?!"

We fell about laughing but I made a note to keep my hygiene radar switched on.

"Where's the sat phone then?"

Pasi rummaged between the bags, stacked in an orderly line like soldiers guarding the outer edge of the tent. He passed it to Andy who fumbled to take it with his fleecy hands. He shoved it in his chest pocket.

"It stinks in here, I'm off."

Icy flakes whipped through the door as he left, swirling into the porch like a mini-tornado. He zipped us back up into our nylon bubble. I lay back again and relaxed into the billows of down – jackets, sleeping bags, booties, mitts – soft heaps of comfort to absorb the weariness. I shut my eyes, watery from windburn and listened. It was noisy for such an empty place. Every small sound seemed amplified and the tent vibrated noisily like the taught skin of a drum. I imagined being outside and seeing our tent glow red in the dusky white wilderness, a sanctuary, like a fire-lit cottage in the midst of the dark wet Scottish countryside of home.

Andy's voice cut through my thoughts.

"Uh, guys" he sounded hesitant. "Come and have a look at this. Quick."

We glanced at each other and Pasi raised his eyebrows towards his shaven forehead. "Ooh, what could this be?" he said with a part-excited, part-intrigued expression. Quickly, he zipped up his jacket tight to his chin, pulled his hat on deep and dropped his feet into the pit to tie his boots. He unzipped the tent, turned back to grab his giant gloves and disappeared into the dusk.

A cold rush of air invaded the warmth.

Anna and I looked at each other uneasily, our minds racing.

"I can only think of two things."

"Me too"

In our minds were polar bears and storms, the most dangerous of all a Piteraq, the very thing that had brought disaster to previous expeditions. A Piteraq was the Inuit word for the fearsome storms that sweep down from the icecap, ferocious catabatic winds that race to the lower pressure on the coast and gain speeds of over a hundred miles an hour.

"Anna, quick, come out here" Pasi called, the sound of the others running around outside signalling something serious. Anna zipped up her down jacket, did her hat, boots and gloves and disappeared too.

I strained to see outside as she left, but saw only the flash of her feet in the darkness.

I was alone inside with the tent vibrating louder than ever now. I pulled my hands from warm pockets and fumbled for a head-torch, searching for its rubber switch, struggling to be dextrous with my tired fingers.

"What is it?" I called out but my words were stolen by the wind.

The sound had gone from a growl to a full roar.

I wanted to go outside, join the others and do whatever needed to be done. I wanted to face whatever was out there together but if I shuffled my bum through the pit and out of the front door, I'd only get plastered in snow, hypothermic and probably be more trouble than help. I couldn't hear what the others were saying but they sounded busy. I could hear scraping, shovelling and metal banging. Something serious was going on and I felt frustrated not to be out there facing it too.

"What's going on?!" I shouted again, but my voice was lost in the frantic flapping of fabric.

I felt useless, sitting doing nothing.

I unzipped myself from my sleeping bag and shuffled to the edge of the inner tent and began tidying the stove away. I detached the fuel bottle, nestled it upright into the snow so none could leak, folded the serrated legs of the stove and placed it in its small waterproof bag. I stacked the small pan into the medium pan into the large pan, cleaning each out with snow first before stuffing the lighter and matches into their waterproof case and inside the pans to make sure they kept dry. I was aware I was meticulously distracting myself. I put the lid on and tightened the pans together with a grubby strap, its rainbow-stripes grey with stains and stashed them in our limp cardboard box, which thanks to the bin bag beneath, was somehow surviving the days of abuse and acting as our kitchen cupboard.

What if it was a polar bear?

I'd heard stories of polar bears eating people alive, of stalking their prey for days, both seals and humans. The only way to stop them was with a high-powered rifle. The problem was we didn't have one. I thought of the rape alarm I had packed, the idea of it suddenly outrageously inadequate but I would find it in a moment anyhow, just in case it was a bear out there. I'd read they didn't like loud noises and after our decision not to bring a gun, it had been the next most unusual thing I'd brought to the icecap after the fish tank thermometer, yet again trusting my life to a five pound plastic gadget.

"Grab the shovel!" I heard someone call. "Over here. Quick."

"Make blocks of ice!"

In the corner of the porch, I placed another bin bag on top of the cardboard box, to protect the food and stove from drips. An emergency was underway and the best I could do was tidy the kitchen.

I searched out the rape alarm. At least it seemed a little more relevant.

I stopped, and listened. I could only hear muffled voices beyond the flapping of the tent.

What was out there? The sheets of crusty fabric suddenly felt like a flimsy excuse for protection. One swoop of a hungry polar bear's claw and it would be shredded, and any bear lost out there in barren expanses was sure to sniff our high smells. A bear wouldn't want our dehydrated rations – even we didn't really. The bear would want us. It would rip us apart.

If it wasn't a bear, it could only be a Piteraq and the wind would build and build to the power of a volcanic blast, flattening anything in its fetch. The tent poles would splinter, our shelter would be shredded maybe worse than by a claw, and we'd be naked to its vicious blasts. We would be left to perish in the inhospitable whiteness unless we could keep our tent from collapsing, then we might stand a chance of surviving a storm.

Bear or storm. Either one could kill us.

With a rising chill of fear I realised the seriousness of our situation. I began searching the tent for our EPIRB, another plastic gadget that would send an SOS to satellites. We always saw it as our magic bullet, bringing rescue at the press of a button but being out there was like being on the moon. No-one could pluck us from the storm. No spear or gun could save us from a polar bear. With all our gear and gadgetry, we were utterly alone.

The door of the tent was whipped open and Anna's head popped inside, her face almost completely hidden behind thick goggles and a face mask.

"Karen find the EPIRB and the satellite phone, and the spare battery" she said, then turned to head out again.

"What is it?" I said.

"It's a Piteraq – I think" she confirmed, the wind muffling the shouts and digging behind her.

I was relieved. A storm seemed better than a polar bear.

"You can see a haze of snow above the ice, maybe five minutes max before it hits us. We're building an ice wall."

She ducked back out and the zip was slammed down.

I was thankful for the news flash.

I listened to the shovels punching outside, to the frantic scrapes and squeaks of their construction work. This was it, the famous Piteraq. It seemed so wrong to have joked about it. Here was a force of nature that demanded the upmost respect. It could kill us.

I searched out the EPIRB and sat looking at it beside me in the tent. I didn't believe it could save us. The cold pulled drips from my nose as I rummaged for a tissue. The price tag on the packet said 'Johnstone's Chemist', a nostalgic flash of home, a reminder of the day I'd packed then gone for a picnic beside a loch and laid in the warm spring sun chatting, eating cherry tomatoes and tasting their sweetness.

Home comforts seemed a long way away.

Sensing urgency, I reached for the zipper again and strained to make out the hunched figures working furiously, the dark shapes of tools chopping out blocks of ice. I could just make out the pulks tied to the tents, the skis and poles all driven into the ground as anchors, piles of snow already banked up against them. The rope tying our two tents together was taut and vibrating, the wind getting stronger all the time. I shivered and wondered if my six pairs of trousers and down sleeping bag were enough to keep my legs from freezing. I willed them to finish the wall, so we could all climb inside and baton down for the storm.

I didn't want to sit there by myself.

Zipped back inside again I pulled out my diary and wrote a little, aware of how odd it was to be in the midst of an emergency, yet unable to do much to help. I was writing instead of working with the others to protect us from the lash of the wind but at least it was a distraction.

My mind and will were outside with them and I listened intently as my pen scrolled gibberish. Their voices sounded less knitted with panic and I sensed the wall must nearly be finished. I imagined the last block of ice slotting into place and everyone moving to spike their axes into the ground, to fix our tent even more firmly down.

'I'll huff and I'll puff and I'll blow your house down'.

Not if we could help it.

I listened carefully to the commotion outside, aware that the storm must be about to hit. I heard the guy ropes being cranked tight one last time before Anna ripped the tent zip open and launched herself in. Pasi wasn't far behind.

By then the tent was bending in with the force of the wind and the fabric flapped so strongly I was sure it would rip or the poles would break, or the whole thing just take to the sky like a giant human filled kite.

We all hunched inside and pushed back against the fabric that the wind pressed in on us, hoping that the poles would take the strain. Thanks to Pasi's foresight and information on how other teams had failed, the tent had double poles, which I assumed meant twice as strong, although looking at them bend I doubted it. It was still a comfort and instead of the fabric caving around us as I'd seen tents do in far lesser winds, it seemed to hold firm, the tent shuddering loudly, sometimes deafeningly so but it held its shape. I wondered at the strength of the stitching, imagined it splitting open like an over-ripe banana and exposing us all to the savage night. I watched the seams like a hawk, sure that one would twang open at any moment as the storm attempted to sweep us away.

During the storm, the ice wall we built to protect the tents was filled in with drifting snow. Most equipment except the tops of the tents was buried. ANDY KIRKPATRICK

9. REST

The muffled sounds of morning woke me, the stove bellowing once again and behind it, the wind too. Dim light filtered through the feathers of my sleeping bag and I moved to dig myself from under the layers of down with numb hands as they were every morning now.

First I thought about the pain, the soreness, the stiffness – then all that faded as I grasped that these familiar morning feelings meant I was alive!

"Did we make it?" I whispered, aware that this morning no-one was moving as usual and that we had slept in.

"Morning" said Anna.

"It looks that way" said Pasi, his hand coming out of his sleeping bag to touch the tent, as if to check it was still there, but also for a pat of thanks. I felt as if we'd had a big night out. Hungover from the storm, we were all awake but no one moved.

I lay for a while, mustering energy for the effort of sitting up, hoping that when I moved, my hands would recover from being numb lumps on the ends of my arms.

"Thank God for double poles" said Anna unzipping herself and sitting upright, still dressed in all her clothes, ready to face the weather if the tent was destroyed. "Are you boys still alive over there?"

Andy's voice called back "No!"

I reached an arm forward and Anna pulled me up. In hospital post-accident, it had taken me a month to learn to sit up, such a simple movement but so hard without the use of abdominals. Now so tired, I had regressed to a similar situation and was grateful for her help. I winced with the pain of moving my shoulders and she did the same as she peeled the plasters from her heel and exposed the raw skin beneath her blisters. We were a perfect advert for why not to ski across an icecap, our bodies barely holding together.

My hands were totally numb as if I'd slept on them, numb like my body below my break. I thought of the syrinx and tried not to panic that the feeling might never return.

I shook them hard and tried to make fists.

Slowly they began to tingle, dizzy as the blood seeped into them. I felt relief. I wiggled each one, then rubbed and stretched my palms to shake the life back into them.

Too slowly, my hands came back to me.

At last, maybe fifteen minutes later, I could hold a mug of hot chocolate, and I wished it wasn't plastic so that I could feel the warmth soothe my fingers.

Pasi unzipped the tent, and the loose fabric flapped crazily. Ridges of snow buried almost everything except for a few ski tips and poles that stuck out from the piles. The air was a haze with spindrift. We might have survived the worst of the storm but the tail of it was still blowing. It didn't look nice out there.

Bodies and voices started emerging, the pressure of bladders too great not to venture outside. Not for the first time I was almost grateful for a catheter and for the ease with which I could wee into a bottle and save having to shiver outside. Some of the guys had perfected the art too and they each had a bottle for peeing into, the wider-necked the better as far as size and safety were concerned. Anna had brought a 'she-wee.' A kind of pubic funnel to collect wee, though she confessed it wasn't easy and even with practice in her parents garden, it wasn't a foolproof method. She avoided the risk of spillage and went outside.

"Where is he?" I heard Anna say shortly afterwards.

There was a pause, then Harvey replied. "I don't know, I haven't seen him."

My heart missed a beat. "Who's missing?!" I called, panicked that we'd lost someone in the confusion of the storm. A bustle went on outside, something reminiscent of the night before.

"What's going on?" I asked again.

"We're missing someone" said Anna.

"How? Who?" I went over the night in my mind, wondered about scenarios, whether someone had gone outside to the toilet then got lost in the storm. Could they have survived the night or might we find a body frozen in the snow?

"What's happening?" I called again as I heard them digging. Why were they digging? Shouldn't we be starting a search, scouring the area beyond the tents? I shuffled towards the porch and reached to pull back the fabric door as a call went up.

"Here he is!" Harvey shouted, and I peered out to see a small red hat and a fishing rod. It was the gnome.

Buried – but found again – in the storm.

We'd had six days of hard graft and our bodies needed a break. Like toothache, the wind kept gnawing but having survived its worst felt good. Surviving it felt like a cure for the underlying fear I'd had about being caught in a storm. We decided a rest day was in order, and slept the morning away, no longer worried about the tent ripping from its footprint and appreciative of some time to recover.

Lunch was still a non-event but made better by a stream of hot drinks. We had no books or cards for entertainment but even if we had, we were too exhausted or distracted to bother. Pasi finished his magazine article and Anna dressed her blisters again and applied some luminous, mercury-based, banned substance she'd found somewhere in Eastern Europe. I preferred just to lie and relax or man the stove and rehydrate with endless cups of hot drink. The occasional visit from one of the others brought smells and entertainment to our day, and attempts to call home on the satellite phone made us feel less remote than we were.

Anna spoke to her mum, Pasi to the magazine editor, Harvey to his girlfriend, Andy to his kids. There was no answer the times I tried to call Suresh but I spoke to my Mum and Dad for a few crackly seconds so at least they knew we were okay. There were text messages from friends and family to reply to, and messages of encouragement from the school kids we'd hooked up with.

Before leaving for Greenland I'd spent the day with various groups of kids, primary and secondary and told them about our planned journey. We'd called our adventure 'Hands and Feet Across Greenland'. We weren't sure it made sense to others but it did to us and by then even more so given that my hands and Anna's feet were taking the brunt of our efforts. The hands and feet had grown arms and legs when Careers Scotland had got involved, along with year groups from four schools. Talking to the kids I'd told them all about the fears I had. Polar bears, storms, being fit and strong enough, eating dried food every day, how the team would get on, pressure sores and health challenges like not getting a frostbitten bum whilst going to the toilet. We asked them what things they would like to do and asked them to set themselves a personal challenge whilst we were attempting ours. They had to think about what would be hard and why and keep a log book to record their progress on one side of the page and if interested track ours on the other.

Knowing they were watching and texting helped me keep going on the dullest of days, and their projects inspired me too. There were plans to help with meals on wheels, raise money for charity, do the mountain bike black-run at the local forest and maybe hardest of all, one of the boys was aiming to be nicer to his little sister. It was frustrating that we couldn't update our blog as the laptop wasn't connecting to cyberspace like it should but a daily phone call to Anna's Mum became the alternative means and she fastidiously typed the reports from her daughter and posted them on our blog.

The rest day gave us time to catch up with messages and relax our weary muscles. The day after the storm passed quickly like a day with a cold, snuggled by a fire, doing nothing much but letting our batteries recharge. I began to be glad of the wind instead of worried, thankful for the excuse to stop and enjoy idle chat with Anna and Pasi. I wondered how different it would be if Suresh were here. Jacek wouldn't have joined us, and our tent splits would have been completely different, more likely a couple and either Andy or Harvey to each tent. As they say, 'two's company, three's a crowd' but Anna and Pasi were good companions for tent sharing really and I appreciated Pasi's dry sense of humour.

"What's it like to share a tent with two women?" Anna asked Pasi later that day as we busied ourselves melting water and preparing dinner.

He replied with a straight face "It would be okay if one of them wasn't my wife."

I was grateful for the simplicity of being single whilst there, just the simplicity of being with friends – tied to them but not bound. Laying there I thought about Andy, for once not being the joker, asking as we skied along if I got on with my husband. It was a blunt question. As usual I made positive noises.

"How come you never talk about him?" I didn't have a reply. He asked where he was, why he wasn't in Greenland with me and I made his excuses – bad back, work – but I could tell he wasn't convinced. I knew that there had been an answer to the question that lay deep down inside me, and being here in Greenland was a way of not facing up to that question; that all the physical effort and pain was just my way of masking a much deeper pain.

*We feared for the life of our seventh team mate and had to
dig him out of storm drift. ANDY KIRKPATRICK*

We were just a bit disappointed that the shadow we skied towards for a long time was only a solitary post. The relentless white horizon meant that we could see the slightest feature from a long way off. ANDY KIRKPATRICK

10. WEST

The next day was calm. We began our usual routine then got into file and followed our bearing West once again. Everyone seemed lighter and happier somehow, perhaps for surviving the temper of the Greenlandic Gods. There had been an underlying stress about meeting a Piteraq and now we felt a weight had lifted. Of course there could be worse in store but for the time being we didn't think of that.

Two legs in we shunted into the back of each other like a motorway pile-up and our parade came to a halt.

"I think I can see something" Andy said whilst squinting at the horizon.

We all scanned in the direction he pointed and one by one, the stronger eyes first, we saw a thin dark shape. Jacek peered through the binoculars but couldn't make out what it was. With a fresh energy, we made towards it, a few degrees of diversion worth it whatever it might be.

For a long time, it remained a small shadow in the distance, but gradually it gained form, thinner than it had first looked.

"What if it's a bear?" I said, knowing everyone was thinking the same thing.

"Not this far out" said Harvey, which was true but we had been told the story of a team being tracked by a bear and how a helicopter had been called to kill the bear.

The shape shifted and changed, coming and going like a piece of dirt in your eye, until it formed up into a stick-like shape. Like a person. Another human being?

We skied on with new purpose, daring to consider the possibility it might be someone, but it would be a chance in a million to meet anyone up here. Whatever it was, it didn't seem to be moving and as we drew closer, we saw with some disappointment that it wasn't.

It was just a steel pole sticking out of the ice. Inexplicably, randomly, in the midst of nowhere. Why would it be there? Maybe it marked a stash of supplies left by a previous expedition. We were tempted to dig down and search for whatever might be there in the hope we might find something other than peanuts or raisin-filled dehydrated meals. But perhaps someone would be relying on it, a strategically placed hoard of essential things, dropped by air and marked for safe finding. It was the most exciting thing we'd found on the ice, the only thing that wasn't flat and white, other than coffee, for nearly two weeks.

We skied on and left the pole un-tampered with, hoping someone else would find it more useful than us. We laughed about it and I felt the monotony and the burden of the early days on the ice dissolving.

I noticed the ice below my skis change as the day went on. What were small blue crystals in the morning became larger with all colours of the rainbow refracting through them in the late afternoon. Instead of the monochrome place I'd once seen it now seemed magical and colourful with the time of the day readable from the ice.

Someone once told me that the Inuit have fifty different words for snow, each one for a different texture or type. After weeks on the ice I could understand how that could be. Removed from the speed of modern life there was time to notice that an ice crystal wasn't just an ice crystal, that food and drink tasted better when you had to work so hard for it, that nature had patterns it was hard to notice normally.

There was a time when I'd assigned my need for adventure to being paralysed, then to being in the wrong job. I had thought that if my daily work was something I found more fun and meaningful, then maybe that need for adventure would recede. When I left the corporate routine I found so empty, I chose a new career where I could interact with people instead of a keyboard and have the flexibility and freedom of being my own boss. I liked it. Yet every morning as the computer sparked to life with its musical jingle, marking the beginning of a new day, new emails, new work, old things to finish, I found the blue ripples of my screensaver reminded me of somewhere else. I thought of cold waves breaking over my kayak, of low cloud hiding frozen mountains and I felt thirsty again to be ruled by nature's rhythm. I yearned for another adventure instead of the familiar scene of pixelated ripples and the gentle electronic hum.

But I was here again now in another adventure, like none I'd ever had before. This one was emptier than before, a road-less, boat-less, people-less vacuum.

We skied on, called by the horizon ahead though it was behind and all around us too. Space. The possibilities seemed limitless. There was only a compass guiding our route, no obstacles to limit our way except for our own minds. One could go mad there. One could find sanity there. We were skiing across the ice, into the emptiness around us and into the emptiness within. There was peace from worries and from decisions I was too confused or scared to take. We had an aim and therefore a direction, always northwest but I became sure there was another reason behind it all, an aim I couldn't even see.

The 'Greenland Girls' as they attempted to kite across the ice in the spirit of Nansen. ANDY KIRKPATRICK

11. 314 DEGREES

Our direction was 314 degrees northwest. That was the bearing we painstakingly followed. It would only change once, at DYE 2, the radar station about two-thirds of the way across the icecap where we would turn more sharply north. What was actually at the radar station was a mystery but we knew it had been abandoned at the end of the cold war and guessed it must be some drifted over Portakabins.

It was the job of the person breaking trail to keep their eyes on the compass and to shift slightly one way or the other to keep the needle lined up in the right direction. The leader also had a large kayak compass tied on the back of their pulk, so that the second in line could keep watch too and call to head right or left a bit if the needle went off line. Two pairs of eyes were better than one to keep us right – it would be easy to spend all day going in circles or re-tracing our steps, especially when the sun and wind weren't there to guide us too. I wondered at the skill of ancient cultures with only the stars or the sun as tools for navigation. As I skied across the ice I noticed some of the mental fatigue had gone, seemingly blown away by the storm. Sure, my body still rebelled each morning at having to move, moody at the hammering it was taking but the mental aches and pains had gone. It seemed the same for all of us and it felt at last as if we'd bonded as a team.

The wind blew the surface snow into wave-like forms called sastrugi, so the icecap varied from a frozen sea of ripples to angry, solidified waves that made us trip and stumble. With my skis fixed in a parallel position the first week had seen me fall over maybe five to ten times a day as I struggled to keep balance over the hard lumps of sastrugi. When I fell there was a thud and usually my arm would twist and get trapped beneath me. After only three days my ski pole had snapped in half when I'd toppled awkwardly over it and after that I worried about breaking the spare or even worse twisting a tendon in my shoulder and being unable to pole along. There was no room for injury in the light of our limited supplies and the difficulty of a rescue. As a result I'd concentrated harder and the days of skiing had become as mentally exhausting as they were physically, the security of the tent even more welcome at the end of each day. But now, so far into the journey, I felt like a kayaker who had mastered their craft and could balance and not fall from even the highest waves of ice.

Beyond my own aches and pains, which where more signs of over use but not of injury, other problems where emerging in the team. Harvey had hurt his back, most probably from the strain of hauling a heavy pulk. He also had a cut on his finger that was going slightly septic. It was symbolic of how hungry we all were that when he pulled the plaster off to clean his finger one evening, and a fishy stench came with it, all he and Andy said was "Mmmmm. Fish and Chips!"

At least Jacek was injury free, though suffering from general exertion and perhaps the effects of having almost thirty years over the rest of us. Already he looked too thin, his face more sunken behind his cheekbones. In many ways polar travel is a death march – too many miles with too few calories. We were all eating ourselves up.

Harvey and Andy said that as soon as the tent went up in an evening, Jacek was flat out. Apparently he'd offered to help with things the first few nights but had nearly burnt the tent down trying to light the stove so since then stayed clear of cooking duties and snoozed the evenings away, his rest punctuated by hot food and drink. Neither Harvey nor Andy minded, and either accustomed to being independent or control freaks, said they preferred to do it themselves anyway.

I was amazed that my body kept recovering and doing it all over again each day. The hardest thing for me was the peripheral stuff of being paralysed, the bodily functions that don't function anymore, my inability to thermo-regulate, bladder and bowels that needed managing like a baby. There were some silver linings of being paralysed that helped on the ice: I could pull my catheter out and pee as quickly as a man, but without exposing any flesh and I didn't feel the discomfort of cold wet toes squashed into tight boots or the pain of blisters on my feet. I was paranoid though about my catheter tubes disconnecting. If they did I'd end up with all my layers of trousers wet, increasing the risk of hypothermia or a frostbitten bum. On the ice there'd be no way to wash or dry my clothes and I'd stink for a month. Much worse, something could go wrong at the other end and it would be almost unmanageable without running warm water and a supply of clean dry clothes. I dreaded what might happen but knew too that living at such close quarters there would be no hiding anything, and everyone having to deal with problems that at home were very private seemed almost worse than the potential issues themselves.

Before leaving home I'd thought about all the things that could go wrong. They were all fears that had the potential to stop me from setting off on the journey. I tried to think of one small thing I could do for each problem. Every little strategy I could think of helped counter my fear and made me feel just a bit better about going onto the ice. I secured the connections between my catheter tubes with cloth tape, washed my bladder out daily to clear away sediment that collected to prevent the catheter getting blocked and changed the catheter bag regularly so that it didn't burst or leak. One small challenge I hadn't anticipated was that my catheter bag started to freeze at night, despite being quite close to the warmth of my body and within the cocoon of my sleeping bag. In the morning, it was like a 'slush puppy', a crushed ice drink that had the colour of orange juice. *Drink more water* I told myself, or else my catheter would block, and I didn't want to have to fiddle with tubes and syringes out there on the ice, even though I've become a skilled plumber of sorts. They were unique problems compared to the average icecap team but they were details that mattered, that would make the difference between success or failure, life or death.

The other problem I'd deliberated about was how to manage having periods on the ice. Sat in a sit-ski all day with my hips squeezed into it would make changing a tampon impossible. I sought advice from my friend, a family planning doctor, and decided to take the contraceptive pill continuously as it should stop any bleeding. It seemed a good strategy except that I reacted oddly to it and bled unendingly. It was a real struggle to manage and I didn't have the supplies to cope. It reached the point where I had only two tampons left. Luckily we were a team with 'modern' men, and my problem became everyone's problem, generating a whole bunch of bizarre ideas, mostly bad ones.

Over two weeks into the journey we were well established in our routines. As we slid along through softer snow, the late May sun a little stronger, our spirits were lighter than weeks before. Sometimes it became easy enough underfoot to break out from our single line and ski next to each other, alleviating the quiet monotony with stories and jokes. We stayed rigid in our system of fifty minutes skiing, ten minutes break, when we'd sit picking our favourite bits from our bag of snacks, amazed at the size of our growing mountain of excess peanuts.

It was too difficult to manoeuvre my sit-ski into a strategic position to pee and it wasn't like there was an obvious tree or patch of grass to target anyway. So, I just peed wherever I was, aiming the stream from my catheter onto the same small spot on the snow and challenging myself to get the hole it melted deeper and deeper. Then I'd pour my leftover peanuts into the hole, always surprised when despite the tiny diameter, it took nearly a whole bag.

"Look. I think I can see something." Andy broke our silence as he stared through the binoculars at the horizon.

"Probably another pole, or a dead bird" I said.

"Really, have a look," he persisted. "I think there's something moving."

Like the boy who cried wolf no one wanted to believe he could see anything this time, whilst also being scared he could and that it would be the bear that stalked our darkest nightmares.

"I'm telling you I can see something" he repeated, standing up.

We handed the binoculars around one by one, each fiddling with the focus dial trying to see something in the whiteness that filled the view.

"No, it's probably just a shadow from a steep bit of sastrugi or something" said Harvey.

"I reckon it's another dead sparrow" said Anna

"I can't see anything" I peered through the binoculars trying hard to make anything out.

"You're hallucinating, drink some more water" said Jacek.

Pasi remained silent and peered for longer than the rest of us, his time spent standing guard on the Russian-Finnish boarder giving him the skill to look harder than most. He slowly lowered the binoculars down whilst keeping his eyes trained straight ahead.

"Maybe it is a person. Maybe it is a polar bear" he concluded.

Now we all stared harder, squinting for better focus and shielding the sun from our eyes. We removed our sunglasses, put them on again, passed the binoculars around and around, debated and over-ran our ten minute break by a long way.

There was a black dot on the horizon and it was too big to be a pole or a dead bird.

"It is a person" said Pasi, the binoculars held to his eyes, "maybe more than one."

Regardless of what or who it was, we gave up on our speculating and began skiing purposefully towards it. It seemed to be on our course anyway, the 314 NW bearing pointing straight towards it. If we got closer and it began to look more like a bear, we could always divert course. Not that that would help.

We moved with a speed I hadn't realised we could, our eyes trained on the black silhouette ahead. Gradually, the dark shape appeared to split and multiply but then it would be elusive again, shimmering intermittently so that sometimes I paused to rub my eyes, not believing that we'd ever seen it.

But it was still there and now it looked like two shapes not one. Was it a couple of polar bears? Were we foolish to be skiing straight for them? Their form looked a bit too tall and thin for bears but I thought of the pictures I'd seen in books of bears with hunched backs walking high on their paws. Maybe they really were bears. A hungry bear would be a thin bear, especially if it was lost up on the ice a long way from food.

We pushed on regardless.

The closer we skied, the more the shapes looked like humans than bears.

"It's definitely people" Harvey was convinced, and soon we all were as four distinct figures crystallised in the distance.

We skied with a fresh found energy, astounded that in such a wilderness, there were other people. I had assumed we'd see nothing and nobody all month.

We waved vigorously and they flung their arms into the air too. They were only a few hundred metres away now, their orange sleds and pale blue jackets a dramatic sight. Their outfits and colours matched like a team, with rims of fur around their hoods. In contrast we looked scruffy and un-coordinated. We lifted our masks, keen to show we weren't from outer space, and there were cries of hello and cheerful smiles.

They were four women.

Four gorgeous women.

Four gorgeous Greenlandic woman.

Our four men responded with such friendly vitality that I wondered at their transformation, no longer tired, sore or surly in any way.

"Hello" I shouted as both teams drew together, everyone spontaneously giving each other hugs, as if we'd not seen another human for many years, as if we believed we were the last people alive on the planet.

Even before we'd had chance to finish our hellos, Andy, characteristically blunt and thoughtful, blurted "You haven't got any tampons have you?" Everyone laughed, especially when one of the women said "'Yes, too many! Here is a bag full!"

They were the first Greenlandic women ever to cross the inland ice, all four of Inuit descent and so strikingly attractive that the men seemed quite unhinged. We asked why they wanted to do the journey and their answer was refreshingly simple.

"Because we have never been to the other side."

It was only mid-afternoon and we still had two legs before our skiing was officially over but there was no question of going on. The girls agreed to stop too and an excited super-camp grew around us: three tents instead of two with skis and pulks scattered thoughtlessly in contrast to our usual careful organisation.

They had just one tent between four, a dome into which they squeezed with a corner allocated to each of them for gear and clothes. They told us what bad weather they'd had and how thankful they'd been for the warmth of the dog fur on their jackets that one of their mothers had carefully sewn on. Another's mum had made them special sealskin booties to keep away frostbitten toes. They had been stranded in a storm a week or so earlier, perhaps the same storm that had pinned us down too. To pass the time, they'd each had a vanity mirror in their corner and whiled away the time plucking eyebrows and beautifying themselves. I giggled at the picture that entered my mind and the disparity from the shenanigans in our tents. I envied that they seemed so bonded and jolly, the involvement of their families, the history and culture that connected them to the ice.

Later in the evening, all ten of us squeezed into one tent, something we'd thought too difficult with the six of us but given the occasion it just had to be done. Like a magician pulling a rabbit from his sleeve, Pasi produced a bumper can of fruit salad, a small bottle of vodka and prepared a celebratory cocktail.

"I can't believe you carried that massive tin this far with you!" I commented, though it never ceased to surprise me what Pasi had stashed in his pulk.

"It was for a special occasion" Pasi grinned "like this one." He handed out the cocktails in our big plastic mugs. Behind his hard exterior, Pasi had a kind, thoughtful inner.

"Mmmm. Nice. I've never had a frozen cocktail before" one of the Greenlandic girls enthused, and whilst it was a treat, it didn't have the edge over a good cup of tea or hot chocolate.

Our new friends were strangers but we felt close as family as we cuddled up tightly to fill the small space. The tent steamed up quickly and for the first time in weeks I felt a glowing warmth from friendship and adventure as much as from heat. This warmth grew stronger as stories unfolded and I mentioned that I'd only ever met one person from Greenland before and that she now lived in Denmark. Uiloq Oystein. I'd met her ten years previously, in a not dissimilar situation, cycling in the mountains of Kyrgyzstan. I recalled she was also a keen kayaker.

"Uiloq!" the girls exclaimed and she turned out to be the very same one, a good friend of theirs. They knew her phone number and called her on the sat phone there and then. Rumour has it that nobody on the planet is more than six-times removed from anyone else but in that moment I would have believed it was only two. Minutes later, our crackled voices exchanged surprise. Laughter pealed across the ice and we wondered at life's coincidences.

Amongst the stories there were other, less encouraging tales. A Spanish team further west on the ice had raised an EPIRB alarm days ago but only their abandoned pulks had been found. The terrain at the western edge was riddled with crevasses and broken ice, ridges and canyons that by now would be surging with melt-water and impossible to cross.

"It is pointless to go on" said the oldest of the girls, "it will be impossible for you to get over the ice to the land."

We knew the western edge of the ice would be a crux, but we'd been given the coordinates of an assured safe route along an ice road that had been constructed a few years ago for a car commercial – a gem of information that had been of great comfort.

"The ice road is no longer there" we were told by another girl.

We worried as the girls told us how difficult it had been for them to pass through the area and that they had almost given up before even reaching the ice cap. We would be almost a month later than them and the crevasses more dangerous, the valleys more deeply carved. There was a strong chance that snow bridges would have collapsed and that the lakes and rapids of melt-water would prevent our passage. Skiing through it would be like a game of Kerplunk – one wrong move and we'd tumble down into the ice to drown or freeze to death.

The girls didn't think we'd make it and suggested we'd need a helicopter to lift us over the last twenty kilometres.

It was terrible news. The part we'd thought would be easy, following a smooth road of ice, now looked insurmountable. Neither our budget nor our pride would allow that so we shrugged our shoulders but knew we'd carry the burden of uncertainty until the very end.

12. THE BOOT

It was a wild party by icecap standards but neither drunken nor late. Nevertheless as everyone said their goodnights and left the tent, the warmth of being together remained. A storm has been wailing all night and when we woke in the morning, it was still buffeting the tents and a fog of blowing snow surrounded us, blurring the ground. It would be a headwind for us, a tailwind for the girls.

Without much deliberation we decided to conserve our energy and take another rest day. It was a week since the last one enforced by the Piteraq. For the girls though it would be perfect, the weather not too wild but the wind on their backs and strong enough to give them a good push along.

With true adventurer's spirits they decided to use their tent flysheet as a kite and we watched them struggle as they clung to the guy ropes and extra bits of cord to gain some power from the great billows of orange nylon that flapped around them. The thin sheet tugged helplessly and looked like it would rip into pieces at any moment and be whisked off into the cloud. It seemed daring, even foolhardy to risk using their only form of shelter for an extra bit of propulsion but they were set on the idea and with each failed attempt they seemed to get more enthused.

"This is what Nansen did" someone shouted above the wind and I wondered how he'd managed to get a heavy cotton canvas tent airborne and keep it up there long enough to ski along behind it.

Each of them sat aboard a pulk and gripped onto a guy rope that led to a corner of their tent. But the tent wasn't square and it's zips kept opening and the lines twisting until each reasonably co-ordinated attempt disintegrated into a tangled mess and the girls were wrenched from their pulks by either the lines or their laughter. Their high spirits lightened my own and as the others filmed them, I peered out of our tent, laughing too. It felt like we were messing around in the local park instead of in the middle of a desolate icecap.

They persevered for ages and it wasn't until late morning that the girls eventually abandoned their efforts and packed the tent away. They were still cheerful. We said our goodbyes, sad to part ways and waved them into the distance as they began their single-file journey again. We watched for a long time until their four blue jackets became colourless and their figures merged into one black dot moving toward the horizon again.

Besides telling us how difficult the western edge of the icecap was, the Greenlandic girls had also talked a lot about pizza and chocolate brownies, after being invited for food by a couple that lived at DYE 2, the mysterious radar station we'd been heading towards for weeks. At first we thought they were pulling our leg and that perhaps it was a way to motivate these tired strangers. But they promised it was true and that at the radar station we would meet Mark and Lou and better still – they would make us pizzas! DYE 2 was still almost a week of skiing ahead but the news of other people and delicious food ahead had almost erased the bad news about the edge of the ice.

With our monotonous diet we were already fantasising about food and my mouth watered when I thought about a giant plate of chicken Caesar or a vanilla slice. Food turned into a group fantasy and the thought of dripping mozzarella and crispy pizza base or of biting into the soft chewy chocolate of a brownie was almost too much to bear when all we had were snack bags that were so well travelled and squashed that it was hard to distinguish a peanut from a raisin anymore. We thought about pizza every day, often every hour and the idea of possibly eating some spurred us on to ski faster.

The morning after the girls had left us we packed our kit away and skied on. Our days were still long but the nights felt longer than ever. We were at our highest point, on the plateau of the icecap around 7600 feet and at night it was noticeably colder. 'Minus 35 celsius' my fish tank thermometer reported one early morning when I'd left it out in the deep freeze. It was no wonder I slept in more clothes than I skied in, with layers of merino wool underwear – incredibly not that smelly after two weeks of continual use – buried beneath layers of fleece, synthetic insulation and down. Every day I was more and more thankful for my specially designed short sleeping bag, with it's thick down filling and cosy pile lining to keep my bum warm. With two pairs of thick socks and felt booties inside it, the combination seemed to be keeping me toasty. Now we were higher and it was colder, the others checked my feet again but it seemed that technology had won out over the cold. In fact I'd been warmer in Greenland than pigging at home in Scotland.

"Just checking your feet are okay," one of them would say, sliding their hand inside.

They always were, the heat pads in my socks radiating nice warmth. So the worries of frostbite diminished but they still kept checking my feet, more an excuse to get their own hands warm in the snug that my feet had become.

With two and a half weeks of skiing behind us, the icecap was flatter and the going easier than it had been. We were nearing its centre and some days managed to ski over our daily target of twenty kilometres. The ice had looked flat the whole way and the effort required to ski forward was our only gauge of gradient. Sometimes it would feel especially hard yet look slightly downhill or be pancake flat but feel like skiing through glue. Rarely was it easier than expected, except occasionally in the late afternoon when the snow warmed up and we could glide along. Thankfully, I'd stopped falling over so much, so I was less worried about injury and had extra energy for skiing forwards instead of feeling exhausted from all the scrambling back up from the ground. I had finally begun to feel stronger through the effort, my body adapting. Being on the flat I no longer needed a bungee cord to keep me in the pulk tracks, and was free to ski where I wanted, the kind of freedom I could only experience in a kayak or ski. Total independence. I could take my turn at the front.

Anna was still reading the book about matadors in Mexico, often trailing at the back as she turned its pages or talking on the satellite phone to her mum, telling tales of survival and near-disaster. With so much talk of what might go wrong it seemed we were tempting fate; it was only a matter of time before something did.

"Aarrrrgh" there was a cry of despair from the back of the line, and we bumped into the back of each other as we each came to a stop.

"What is wrong?" Pasi called from the front.

Anna had stumbled over her boot, which had come away from the binding on her ski. The toe piece of the boot, with a metal bar that connects it to the ski, had broken away. It was irreparable – impossible to clip into the binding, which meant she couldn't ski.

It was a disaster, and we all stood around a little in shock. We had a spare set of skis but no spare boots. A broken boot was unheard of.

Without a ski she would have to walk, the snow perhaps up to her knees at times. Progress would be reduced to a slow trudge. Once we got to the crevassed terrain nearer the edge of the ice it would be downright dangerous – not that we would ever get that far. Perhaps on skis we could make the edge of the icecap in ten days, but without skis it would take another month.

The thought of rescue was in everyone's mind, as well as the fact that in the middle of the ice we were as far as we could be from help.

Everyone stood looking at her boot.

We racked our brains for ideas, but duct tape was all we could come up with. Pasi wound the roll around Anna's boot so many times that the front bulged with the black shiny tape and it seemed impossible that it could come lose. We skied on and thought positively. After all, duct tape was wonder stuff; it had held my canoe paddle together when it snapped in half not to mention keeping my car wing mirror in place for three years, so surely it would hold the toe of the boot in place for another few weeks.

It did hold but badly and by the end of the day the tape was in tatters. It was a problem. We had to find a better solution if we were to carry on as a team, and so that evening our tent was transformed into a workshop and the night was spent experimenting.

With the kind of ingenuity I'd only ever seen in an Indian bike repair shop, Pasi and Harvey devised a fix with wires, screws and more obligatory duct tape, using one of the skins of a ski – a thick carpet like material used to grip the ice – to make a makeshift binding.

The next morning, Anna gingerly pushed her foot into the binding and began skiing. It held well and we made good progress, but skiing with a free heel meant a lot of flex and torque through the toes and by early afternoon she had to resort to walking again.

I could sense that the boys thought that reading her book had somehow contributed to her failing over and breaking the boot, and it was unfortunate for Anna, who was still racked with pain from her blisters, that her boot issue was now slowing us down. It was yet another doubt that hung over us. It seemed unfair to have reached the highpoint of the icecap and really started motoring, for the broken boot to have happened.

Something better had to be found, so none of us were reluctant when we agreed to an early finish for the day.

Back in the tent we took on traditional roles, the guys fixing Anna's boot while she and I made tea. They pondered over the intricacies of the broken boot, fiddling with screws and bits of wire, while we mused over how to make dinner tastier, longing for a rack of spices instead of bags of palm fat.

The only person missing from the domesticity was Jacek, who slept, as he did every evening, exhausted after skiing and unsure of how best to help the team that buzzed around him. I wondered how many sixty year olds I knew that would consider skiing across Greenland with a bunch of strangers from another country. Perhaps Jacek and I had something in common in our unwillingness to lie back and accept limitations or conform to expectations of what we can or cannot do in certain circumstances. I wanted to be able to do anything I ever might have before paralysis or at least get as close as I could. There were days when Jacek and I trailed at the back together. We said little but there was an unspoken understanding between us about why we were there and a knowledge that we'd never give in.

"If you can do it, so can I" Jacek had said to me earlier that day and his words spurred me on through a patch of exhaustion.

By the time food was ready to be dished out, Anna's boot was clamped tightly to the ski with the best repair possible, given the limited tools to hand. We tucked into foil bags of curry and sympathised that Anna would have to put her foot into a cold boot in the morning. Clamped to the ski, it would be impossible to keep it warm overnight – normally boots went into our sleeping bag with us to stop them from freezing. In the morning we'd have to warm it up with a bottle full of hot water to save her foot from frostbite.

In a way the boot incident, like the storm, was something that let us get closer as a team.

The broken boot did nothing for Anna's enjoyment of the icecap and she trudged at the back, still sore with blisters, her pain added to by one cold boot that took all day to thaw out and warm up.

Although Anna and I had done much of the organising to get to Greenland, on the ice, Pasi, Harvey or Andy usually led the way and broke trail out front. Anna was used to taking the lead and seemed quietly frustrated with this macho trend. I'd had years of using arms instead of legs so was used to being slow next to able-bodied friends and bringing up the rear. At a break one day, Anna came skiing through from the back and, without stopping, said she

*Easier going terrain, I'm skiing along and feeling the yawning
space and a great sense of freedom. ANDY KIRKPATRICK*

would lead the next leg. As we sat and ate our usual snacks from our snack bags, we watched her trudge into the distance. We knew she was in more pain than anyone, and had every right to be more exhausted and in need of a rest but instead she carried on. She had something to prove, that she was not to be underestimated or pitied. I guess no one had bothered to tell her that after Pasi we all thought she was the second hardest person in the team. She had nothing to prove to us but then maybe it wasn't for our benefit.

Unfortunately as we sat eating and watching her move off we saw her begin to veer way from our bearing, heading South. She was already too far away to hear our shouts, and so Pasi sped off after her to pull her back on course. We skied after him, all a little angry at the waste of energy, even if really it made no real difference.

When we all re-grouped, the atmosphere was tense and Anna was only speaking to Pasi. None of us knew how to break it until Andy finally stood before Anna, grabbed her shoulders and with a friendly shake and a jokey shout said "You drive me crazy…" It was enough to get conversation moving again.

"The thing is, no-one ever agrees with anything I suggest" Anna responded, looking as if she was holding back tears.

There was a short silence, then Andy replied. "I think you're wrong there."

Finally we were all able to smile again but we knew we were sticking plasters on a deeper wound. Anna wanted to call a halt to skiing and have a group pow-wow, taking a few days if necessary to talk everything over. But rather than face the risk of analysing our problems together for fear it might terminally ruin the fragile team that we were, we all insisted there wasn't time; we needed our spare rations in case of bad weather rather than for days of discussion or squabbling without making progress over the ice. It seemed the only problem was between Anna and the rest of the team and so in a way, without any discussion, we chose to just let her get on with it.

We just wanted the path of least resistance, to let the past go and concentrate on getting to the other side. Perhaps we should have stopped and talked. It might have made things better but instead we skied on, avoiding confrontation.

13. DYE 2

The endless, featureless white that yawned around us gave the illusion that we were going nowhere, but the GPS assured us that there were now more kilometres of ice behind us than ahead. It would only be forty-six kilometres more to DYE 2, the abandoned cold-war radar station and the landmark that had been our goal for three weeks now. From how far away would we see it? How big would it be? How many days before we spotted it on the horizon?

It was a long-awaited view when we finally saw it. A tiny dot at first. Just a blip on the flat horizon but a blip that must be huge to be seen from so far away.

It grew larger through the day and whiter in the hours we skied towards it until it's giant dome seemed to dominate our view. From where we were it looked like a large black box, the size of a small block of flats, with a radar dome perched on top, both an eyesore and a wonder that such a thing could be built there. From first sighting, it took us two full days to reach the dome.

Knowing that DYE 2 was within a few hours reach we sped up over the last ten kilometres, to our surprise crossing a large area of groomed ice a hundred metres wide that stretched out of sight in either direction.

"Blimey – it's a runway!" said Andy, looking left and right as if to check no planes where coming in to land, the ground obviously prepared by a snow plough.

"Look," said Harvey lifting up his ski pole and pointing "there's something coming."

We looked where Harvey was pointing and saw a figure skiing vigorously towards us with no pulk or gear. An arm went up in a wave and we waved back, sure that it must be the infamous Mark or Lou who lived beside DYE 2.

"Hey! Good to see you, I'm Lou!" she called, sounding as happy to see us as we were her.

She stopped close by me with a look of surprise on her face, presumably never having seen anyone in a sit-ski out there before.

"Are you the pizza lady?" asked Andy.

"Would you guys like something to eat?" she asked.

She only had to ask once.

We followed her towards their place, a Weatherhaven hut about a kilometre from the giant dome. It looked as if it had been designed to survive a nuclear blast, anchored down with cables and big steel pylons. All I could think about was pizza and brownies. The man of the house appeared and introduced himself as Mark, Lou's husband. The two of them looked like out of place ski bums or post apocalypse survivors with their dark tans and well worn in clothes.

Everyone went inside the hut, Pasi piggy-backing me in to a waiting chair, the warmth instantaneous.

"Woah! You guys have been out on the ice for a while" Mark observed and it wasn't until later he confessed it was our smell that gave it away! We were immune to our own odour, thankfully unaware until then of how bad we stank. To save them from suffocation, we retreated outside and took our smelliest things off, before re-entering and starting again.

"Cup of tea or hot chocolate anyone?" and we all made mmming and oohing noises at the mention of a hot drink.

It was bliss to sit in the warmth cradling a mug of hot chocolate.

"Would you like some food?" Lou asked and we all grinned inanely at the thought. My mouth watered at the prospect of pizza or chocolate brownies.

"I've got a pot of spinach and tofu stew on the go."

My mouth stopped watering.

It was hard to disguise our disappointment. Spinach and tofu just wasn't a patch on the mozzarella and crispy pizza base that we'd drooled after for the last week. We quickly recovered though, grateful for the hospitality and happy for any fresh food that came without a foil bag or raisins. After devouring the first plate, we went back for seconds too, and when the chocolate hob-nobs appeared, all self-control disappeared. Harvey and Andy strategically positioned themselves at the biscuit table and demolished at least two packets, guilt-free, as we listened to stories of the Hercules planes that landed each week with fresh supplies of goodies.

Mark and Lou lived on the ice for the summer season. Their job was to piste a runway for US planes to practice landing on ice. It sounded straightforward enough to prepare the snow with the big piste-bashing machines, to maintain the runway and mark it clearly with flags and to send weather forecasts to the pilots that would be flying in – but there was nothing simple about living and working on the ice, the conditions constantly against them. Another part of their job meant playing host to any researchers that might visit to gather data or core the ice and of course to take in passing skiers like us.

We chatted about DYE 2. Mark and Lou called it "Dye-Mart" as it was their source of extra supplies such as tools, nails and toilet roll. Apparently you could find most things you might need in there, like a fully-equipped ship, except it had been abandoned instead of sunk.

"It was abandoned in 24 hours, back in '98" said Mark, filling us in on the historical background of the place. "It was deemed as unsafe, structurally unsound but there's rumour that was just made up by the authorities. They reckoned the cold-war was over and it wasn't needed anymore. Instead of decommissioning it like they should have, a label of structurally unsound gave reason for immediate abandonment. Much cheaper and easier for them than a responsible decommission." He went on, our attention captured. "It's an eyesore. It should never have been left like that." He told us how the place had been a time capsule for many years, like a cold war Mary Celeste, until the ice road had been built and people had driven 4x4's over the ice to strip the place.

"I was told there was a fish tank in there with fish in it – only frozen solid… well until someone smashed it."

"Mark loves it over there, but it gives me the creeps" said Lou.

"If you go over there you need to be careful, it's quite dangerous."

It was hard to appreciate the size of DYE 2 until you finally stood beneath it, or beside it, as it's weight had caused it to sink into a large wind blown hole a few hundred metres across. It was constructed like an oil rig, a large multi-floored box standing on six giant steel legs, the idea being that they could be jacked up as the ice settled. The base had held over a hundred soldiers and technicians, there to watch out for an attack from the Soviet Union, the giant radar part of the DYE line that crossed the Arctic. It was an enormous, spooky fossil of war. We looked around for a way in and saw a flight of stairs leading up from the bottom of the pit. The base was hard ice that had been formed by snow melting on the station and dripping down.

"Let's go down!" Harvey suggested. I felt uneasy as I watched him begin down towards an icy ledge below which the gradient became steeper. Once the others had established the best route down, they came back for me. The sit-ski had no brakes and on anything other than flat ice I had little ability to control it. Getting down into the pit took a strong mix of trust, teamwork and adrenaline but eventually we all stood on the frozen lake beside the rusting skeleton of a half-submerged digger.

It was cold in the shadow of the rig. The metal crackled as it cooled in the evening air and sent shivers down my spine. It was eerie, like we'd entered the set of an apocalypse thriller. The prevailing wind had banked snow against one side of the structure so you could scramble from the pit up ridges of old snow to the metal staircase that led up to the platform. Andy and Harvey climbed up there first and were hovering at the bowels of the platform shouting about an ice tunnel that led into a pitch-black corridor.

"We're going in" they shouted. We watched them disappear then heard their clunks and bangs echoing above us. Whilst they explored inside, we teetered gracelessly about the sheet of blue ice, inspecting the lumps of metal that protruded from its depths.

The place had an air of mystery.

When Andy and Harvey re-appeared they were like excited boys who'd unexpectedly found a secret world, like in The Lion, The Witch and The Wardrobe. They effused with stories of what they had seen, of abandoned drinks at the bar, plates of food still on the table, a whole roast chicken, cans of coke and beer that had exploded in the cold, shelves full of HP sauce and toilet rolls, a world that was literally frozen in time.

"Are you coming in?" asked Andy "I think you should."

I was tempted to play a disability card, the idea of getting up the stairs and inside a little worrying.

"I will carry you" said Pasi.

On Pasi's back with Andy and Harvey pushing we staggered up the stairs while Anna went on ahead. The first obstacle was squeezing through a metal door marked 'Danger – do not enter' and beyond it I could see the inside looked like an over-frozen freezer compartment.

"I've found you something to sit on" said Anna returning, her voice calling out of the darkness.

I squeezed through the door with some help and found Anna had discovered what looked like a meal trolley. It seemed a bit undignified but I transferred onto it and was taken on a tour of the first floor.

It was pitch black apart form the odd chink of light through frozen windows, the floor littered with rubbish, the whole place having the feel of a recently raised ship. The others seemed to find the place exciting but I was keen to get out of there, the moan of the wind and groaning metal sending shivers down my spine.

I was pushed into what had been the kitchen, with big metal freezers that were probably warmer inside than out. Food and tins littered the floor, and Andy picked up a hunk of chicken and pretended to take a bite.

Anna stayed with me as everyone else went up the stairs to the next level, the floors spiralling up to the radar on the top.

I was glad of Anna's company as we heard the others stomping around upstairs, making haunted house noises.

"Thanks for staying with me" I said. Anna gave me a smile back but I could tell something was wrong. "Are you okay?" I asked. Anna had put her heart and soul into this trip and so far it had been nothing but ill feelings and pain for her. It seemed that she was unable to see the beauty and wildness of the place and was caught up with melting stove bases and jobs that others hadn't done. "You okay?" I asked again. She turned and smiled but didn't reply.

By the time we skied back from DYE 2 – the escape down the stairs taken a little easier when I pointed out I had very osteoporotic bones, weakened by years of not weight bearing – Lou was standing outside waiting for us.

"We thought you might like some dinner?" she asked, the smell of real food drifting out to us long before the invitation.

After dinner they offered us a 'Camp Raven' style shower; a tiny wooden shed in which they put a bucket of warm water. The prospect of removing any clothes and exposing bare skin to the bitter cold was far from appealing, and we agreed that it was "all for one, or none for all." If one showered, we'd notice how bad the rest of us smelt.

None of us bothered.

I was intrigued by Mark and Lou, how a couple could survive without anyone else up there in the middle of Greenland.

"It's usually a job done by couples like us" they explained "and it's make or break for most. It normally leads to marriage or divorce."

Our days stranded by bad weather in the tent gave us some idea of the strains of being cooped up in a tiny space, cold and remote up on the ice. It would certainly be a good test of a relationship, a six-month laboratory to really test what you had. Maybe all couples should be sent there as a pre-marriage test, though it would take an unusual pair to enjoy the job.

I tried to imagine Suresh and I doing it.

I couldn't see it.

We'd go mad after the first few weeks, maybe much sooner. Like anyone who meets a solid couple like Mark and Lou, it made me question my own relationship. I still hadn't spoken to Suresh since I'd left home, and there'd been no messages of support like the rest. I was surprised not to have heard something – anything, even a simple X in a text to show that he loved me. I often wondered if I had only married him because I believed I was unlovable and destined to be single forever, that I was just bowled over that he had proposed. Someone had once said that I would always be single as I'd break any man I went out with, that I could never slow down and no man would put up with it. Now I was there in the middle of Greenland. I wondered if they'd been right.

I knew coming was a mistake for our relationship, that staying at home,

We saw the giant dome of the DYE 2 radar for days before we reached
it. We had no idea it would be such a giant and eerie fossil of the
Cold War. ANDY KIRKPATRICK

*The Camp Raven shower cubicle at around minus thirty degrees
Celsius wasn't too tempting! ANDY KIRKPATRICK*

having babies, settling down, would make him happy. He didn't want me to
come because he loved me and because I'd turned my back on those things,
I'd turned my back on him. It had been a choice and I'd made it. Even so,
everyday I held some hope that it wasn't all or nothing, I kept expecting a
simple satellite phone message – 'Missing U' or 'Hope U R OK'.

But there was nothing, just a void. Loneliness. The stretch of emptiness
between us scared me more than Greenland – maybe that's why I was there
– facing the icecap rather than what was at home.

"I think you should have the last brownie" said Andy, coming over to me,
bringing me back from my silent pity party. "It's all downhill from here but
I think you might need it."

I took the brownie from him – still warm and soft, chewy in the centre –
and looked around at our small team, all smiling like veterans even though
the war was only half over. They were good friends and in their company, I
couldn't possibly feel lonely.

14. DOG CAMP

W e sipped hot drinks and ate fresh blueberry muffins, still warm and
moist from the oven. We were reluctant to leave Mark and Lou's
hospitality and the cosiness of their hut, so we drew out conversation until
we'd had so many cups of tea and trips to the toilet that it seemed we would
stay all day. There was a pause in our chatter and we knew we had to go but
somehow another half an hour flew by before we pulled on our jackets and
boots and opened the heavy metal door to the blinding day.

We gathered outside their hut in the blue-sky cold of late morning,
knocking frozen chunks of snow from our skis and jiggling our feet and
shoulders to keep warm. I cupped my hands and breathed re-assuring warmth
into them, willing sensation back into my fingers again. They were cold from
the morning ritual of fiddling with buckles and securing my feet and legs into
the sit-ski, an awkward job and hard to do with gloves on. In that pleasant,
prolonged way of saying goodbye when you don't know where you'll next meet,
we talked longer outside the hut whilst taking group photos and enthusing
that we'd definitely meet again.

"You be careful near the coast" said Mark.

"We've made it this far – what can go wrong now?" I replied. "Erm actually
quite a lot!" I replied to myself, everyone laughing.

"We will" said Pasi.

We finally jolted our stiff muscles into action, calling goodbye and skiing
into our line formation, this time on a new bearing slightly more northerly
than the bearing we'd followed for the three weeks to DYE 2.

The daytime sun was warmer than it had been, and the ice was different
from before; more crystalline, more forgiving to our skis as they forged a path
through the bumps and ridges. The first twenty minutes was painful, a shock

to our recovering bodies and we broke the discomfort with pauses to look back at Mark and Lou's hut. We reached the carefully prepared runway of snow, smoothed with their piste-bashing machine and marked with parallel lines of flags. Through habit we paused at its edge and looked around to make sure there was nothing coming before we crossed, as if we could have missed the roar of a Hercules coming in to land. Apparently they only practiced their landings on Tuesdays, barely scraping the ice on their way through and slowing only enough to off-load a new sack of supplies including muffin mix and chocolate biscuits.

I was already feeling hungry.

The undulations and irregularities of the runway zone made the skiing more challenging, the sit-ski wobbling over the bumps and ridges and almost capsizing me. It was reminiscent of the first week, exhausting on my arms and shoulders as they strained to hold me upright and hard work for the others who skied close and lunged to catch me if I nearly fell. Only now I felt strong, like a kayaker shooting rapids, able to hold my self up against the ice. Taking my fleece off the night before in the warm hut I'd noticed I'd grown a huge pair of shoulders and an equally impressive set of lats, which Andy had described as looking like two loafs of bread stuck to my back.

The skiing was very slightly downhill from there on, even though it didn't look it, but the altimeter and our speed indicated it was and so as I left the runway I gave a mighty push and felt some glide.

It felt as if I was flying at last, the snow smooth and less sticky in the warmer sun. I slid almost effortlessly along, at times so easy that my arms lay loose at my side and my shoulders able to enjoy a ride like they'd never imagined they could. Everything shimmered, inside and out. I tingled in the way that happens in inspiring or special moments. I forgot about the effort, the relentless heaviness of skiing uphill, the sore muscles and aches that had radiated deep from my bones, the draining weight of worry and fear. In spite of everything we'd gone through, I would have endured it all a thousand times over to feel what I felt that afternoon and in the days of downhill that followed. The space that yawned around us had reached in and touched a space within me. Despite the uncertainty that lay ahead, I felt at peace.

I pushed on beside the rest of the team and thought about our next waypoint. Camp Raven and DYE 2 were already just dark shapes barely visible behind us. Our next waypoint didn't sound so attractive – it was called Dog

Camp, though I never discovered quite why. There was no building there and neither dogs nor tents, but it was where the road of ice should start. The road had apparently been built so that cars could be driven up onto the ice, for an advert that was made. It seemed incredible that such an idea had materialised considering the technicalities of the job and the budget that would have been involved. Then again, DYE 2 had been constructed up there just in case of a war so nothing was beyond belief and hopefully, it would help lead us safely through the serrated western margin of icecap.

Someone had kindly given us the coordinates from their icecap crossing, not only for Dog Camp but also for the 'first bend in road', 'second bend in road' and others that would guide us along the road and through the dangerous terrain ahead. The end of our journey and the end of the ice road would be at Point 660, the place where a dirt road butted up to the icecap and led to the town of Kangerlussuaq. Once we got to Dog Camp it would be an easy route to safety, though I worried that it would be too slippery for my sit-ski. That is if the Greenland girls were wrong and the ice road was actually still there. If not we were in big trouble as it had been the promise of the mythical ice road that had made the whole venture seem possible. There was no way I could cross dangerous broken ice fields. The ski had no ability to edge and grip the ice, so might slide off and plummet me into a crevasse or one of the big ice rivers I'd heard of, rivers that rushed along deep canyons before dropping into bottomless holes.

The next days went by uneventfully and in contrast to what had passed, it felt holiday-like to be skiing along with only a thin silk thermal and a sunhat. The reflection of the light on the ice was so blinding that we used duct tape to block out light on the gaps around our sunglasses and lathered sunblock on our noses. We made nose-flaps from duct tape for extra protection but the intensity of the sun was impossible to avoid. Freckles erupted where freckles had never been before as if we were being morphed through some sort of ageing software.

The relentless days of exertion and calorie-deficiency were also taking their toll, tiredness etched into our thinner features.

We religiously stuck to our system of fifty minutes of skiing but in the clear weather we weren't glued to each other's heels with the fear of getting lost and warmer sun meant the trail wasn't so hard to break. We skied slightly apart, our differing paces scattering us over hundreds of metres but we always stopped together for breaks. During our ten minutes of rest, conversation flowed more easily, the tension of the earlier weeks gone. Maybe we had become used to the routine of adventure that tied us together and to the quirks of each other's personalities.

We paused for a break one day and it was Pasi who noticed we were one down.

"Jacek is slow" he said, with an expression of concern on his face as he looked back into the distance and squinted. I managed after a few minutes to turn my skis until I could see him, hunched and sitting on his pulk.

"Tired" I almost whispered, knowing the feeling.

"But he's stopped early" Pasi looked frustrated, and I felt disappointed for Jacek that he hadn't made it to the break.

If the leader skied for fifty minutes and then stopped, the person at the back might be skiing for an hour before they caught up. Jacek had been going for fifty minutes and called himself a break. I shivered and realised I'd get cold waiting for him to catch up. Jacek had been very kind, and carried my down jacket on the top of his pulk. Every time we stopped, he'd wrap it around my shoulders to keep me warm and cosy. Besides stopping hypothermia it made me feel looked after and I appreciated that a lot when everything from waking to sleeping felt such hard work.

I looked at Jacek sitting alone in the distance and wished I could look after him too. There was little allowance for weakness in our group, though I wasn't sure quite why. Maybe it was the place, the time pressure, the physical and mental demands of the journey. Or perhaps it was if one person showed signs of weakness, then it was a mirror to us all of our own struggles and a reminder of the fine threads by which it all held together. My broken ski pole, Harvey's bad back, Anna's blisters and damaged boot, Jacek's tiredness – they were all sore reminders that failure was possible and after all that we'd given, we didn't want that now.

"We need to take some weight out of his pulk" suggested Andy. "I've asked him to give me some but he's too proud to let me take it."

"He has no choice – he is too slow" said Pasi with authority.

I looked back at him sat alone against the empty landscape, nothing but a problem all of a sudden.

I knew the cracks in our team had been hidden successfully for a while but now they were surfacing again. There was a cauldron of disagreement, a months worth of niggles thrown into the pot, and I wondered whether it would stay calm or boil over. I breathed silent relief when Jacek began skiing again after only a short while but by the time he caught up the official ten minutes had become half an hour.

That night it was put to him that he had to lose some of the weight from his pulk. As Andy said he was a proud man but he was no fool. He had pulled his weight so far but thankfully he agreed.

"Land!" someone shouted, and like an apparition, there it was, stopping us in our tracks – just the thinnest band of something on the horizon marked by a bank of cloud that lay above it.

After twenty-six days on the ice, I could understand the life of a mariner and the excitement of seeing something other than sea.

"We have to celebrate" Anna called out. "Here, I've got some Percy Pigs."

"Okay" I agreed, with no idea what they were.

"Here you go, Marks and Spencer's best sweets."

We chewed whilst staring ahead at the dark strip before us.

"How far d'you reckon?" I asked between chews.

Harvey stood beside me. "About fifty kilometres."

"Fifty four" Pasi reported, whilst pressing buttons on the GPS. "To Point 660."

"We did that distance yesterday. If we go well again, we could be there in one more day." I thought out loud.

"The ice seems okay just here, but look over there," Pasi pointed ahead. There seemed to be a hollow, bluish in the bottom. "I think it is a lake."

We skied on again. The lake was beside us quicker than I'd expected and it was odd to see a landscape that wasn't entirely flat and a colour other than white. We followed a wide rounded ridge, the lake on our left and another hollow to our right. It was dramatic to be looking down, hard to get a sense of scale and strange to have a view more complex than a flat white horizon.

We dropped down in height, the lake behind us and the snow became heavier, wetter and almost slushy in texture. Smaller ponds of blue appeared all around us, and we wove a route through, picking lines between patches of white as if we were drawing a dot-to-dot.

"Only four K to Dog Camp" Harvey read his GPS.

Only four kilometres to the ice road or maybe it would be a slush road.

This morning four kilometres would have seemed so easy but now, weaving a convoluted safe route between the growing ponds of melting ice, it seemed a lot further.

The pools started to merge and there was only a narrow passage of white slush between them. I teetered carefully across, gingerly poking my poles in the water either side of me, cautious not to fall as I nudged forward. As the pools got deeper, I stopped worrying about getting wet and hypothermic but about drowning instead. The possibility of tumbling into the water whilst bound in my sit-ski filled me with terror, though I was hopeful that the others would pull me out in time to save me.

There was a commotion ahead and I looked up to see Pasi, sprinting but hardly moving, like a clip from a comedy cartoon. The slush was like quicksand and he fought to keep his skis from sinking, racing for the safety of the white bank ahead of him. He whooped loudly when he made it.

I studied the crossing and saw there was no way I'd make it, not without some speed to carry me through. I'd either sink or fall but either way get wet. I wished I'd brought a dry suit. I'd considered it, conscious of my inability to warm up if I got wet but decided it was too much carriage.

Within minutes, Pasi was pedalling his legs again, crossing back to the rest of us. He had a plan, and he swiftly put it into action, tying rope from his waist to the front of my ski and explaining that he would sprint again whilst I got towed and balanced behind. The others would stand on firmer patches of snow to help stop me from toppling. We got on with it quickly as there'd be more of it and worse to come.

As Pasi lunged forward, I was wrenched into motion, stabbing the tips of my poles quickly either side of me, praying not to topple into a hole. One of my skis rode up onto a bump and I tipped dangerously to one side but I speared the slush just in time to recover before an almighty rush forward as Pasi gained ground. A few frantic seconds later, I saw Anna's stretched arms reaching for me and she grabbed my sit-ski and yanked me over a lip to safety. My feeling of vulnerability was replaced by relief not to have fallen into the icy water. If we could navigate through this, maybe we weren't such a bad team after all.

The next few kilometres passed uneventfully, but the landscape changed dramatically. Between the pools and lakes were blocks of ice, wind and water-weathered formations that after a month of blank canvas were almost startling to see.

"Okay" Pasi spoke in an upbeat tone, "Dog Camp is only two hundred metres ahead."

We all looked up expectantly. I hadn't imagined a huddle of fur-coated Inuit or a spiral of smoke rising from a fire with dogs laid around. In fact, I wasn't sure what I'd imagined Dog Camp would look like but I hadn't thought there'd be nothing. There wasn't even a crooked old hut or any abandoned junk; just a slight hollow that might provide shelter from a blasting wind.

We all scattered in search of the ice road, pulks abandoned haphazardly around Dog Camp. I'd dreamt of getting there the night before, felt the relief of finding the ice road, our much-needed route to safety. In my dream it was a glistening ribbon that whisked us off the ice like a conveyor belt, the six of us ambling happily along it, taking photographs of the spectacular ice formations that were carved around us. It had been a beautiful and easy way to leave the icecap.

I watched the others, circling around, clambering to high points for a better view, eager for a sight of something road-like. I willed the moment when one of them would shout out 'Over here!', but as the minutes passed by, it struck me that the search might be prize-less. If a whole lake could appear in a matter of days, then a whole road could certainly disappear within a year. How could anything man-made withstand the forces of a place like this, the power of such a giant mass of ice?

Each of them returned to base with stories of the horrors ahead, gnarly treacherous ice formations and no sign of a road to take us through.

"What's it like?" I asked, knowing the answer, the stress of what was to come already growing on everyone's faces.

"Well the Greenland girls weren't kidding" said Harvey.

"It looks very hard" said Pasi.

"I think we need to start wearing climbing harnesses and rope up" said Andy. "It looks like the most terrifying bit of ice I've ever seen."

Jacek sat down on his pulk and said nothing.

"Oh – but what an adventure!" shouted Andy.

'Land' suddenly seemed a long, long way.

15. KEEP PUSHING

There was no ice road. All that lay between us and safety were thirty-five kilometres of perilous terrain. From our viewpoint just beyond Dog Camp, it looked impossible to cross. The fringe of the ice was a crazy mosaic dissected by crevasses and flows of melt-water. Rivers had carved deep canyons that looked un-crossable and if we got caught the wrong side of one we'd be forced off the ice in the wrong place. Ordinarily that might not be an issue and the rocky vegetated ground beyond would be easier to travel across than the shattered ice but only if you could walk. In a sit-ski I'd be stranded. We needed to reach Point 660.

In the middle of the icecap it would have been hard to get help. Too far for a helicopter to reach without re-fuelling and logistically complex, but so close to the edge now it would be relatively simple. We'd have to hope of course that our insurers would be amenable and probably we'd need two helicopters to get us all in.

But a rescue would be defeat.

Everything we'd done and come through would be for nothing.

As I considered the steps involved with rescue, it dawned on me, uncomfortably, that I was the reason we might not get off the ice under our own steam. Everyone else could sprint through slush, jump across streams, climb up the house-sized blocks of ice. If we called a rescue, it was purely because I couldn't walk through the mess that lay ahead. Someone would have to come with me, to help at the other end, to find my wheelchair that should by then be waiting at Kangerlussuaq airport. We only needed one helicopter, the rest could continue without me. Two of us would be finished whilst the others struggled on, but it would feel like we were the ones left behind.

I lay in my sleeping bag working out how it would play out, waiting in the hostel. We'd have all the luxury I'd dreamed off for a month; a toilet, water from a tap, heating, a bed you didn't have to inflate – but it would all be empty knowing the adventure was still happening without me. There would be the disappointment of not quite making it, of not finishing together what we'd started and worse there would be the guilt that I'd spoilt it for the person who had to leave it all behind and come with me. The more I thought about a rescue, the less appealing it was. I looked at Pasi and Anna, both quieter than usual and wondered what they were thinking, acutely aware that if we carried on this would be our greatest test.

I tried to focus on the 'how to' rather than the 'how not'.

The meltwater we'd already encountered had just been dribbles compared to what lay ahead. It was clear I wouldn't be able to pole through the lumps and pits that we could see let alone over the ever-bigger torrents that pummelled through the crumpled ice. I imagined the others having to push and tug me along, the twist and torque on everyone's backs and the high chance of injury. The guilt of a rescue or the guilt of causing an injury; what would be worse? I was in a rut and thinking the worst, unsure of what to do for the best.

I expected a debate, a discussion of the pros and cons but we hadn't got to where we were by chance. Even if there were cracks in our team that gaped wider than those in the ice ahead, we were still a good team. There wasn't really a dilemma to discuss: rescue just wasn't an option unless there was an injury, unless it meant life or death.

"That looks like a good line" Pasi pointed down a precipice and through the humps immediately ahead, each one growing in size until they were more like small hills.

And so we began again.

We each developed a strange technique as we slid haphazardly down shiny blue slopes. The others edged their skis or fell over just in time to prevent a dunk in the pool of water at the bottom of each pit. Instead of propelling myself with the ski poles, I prodded them at the ice in front as a way to slow myself down. I juddered dangerously down the slopes, conscious that one bad move could stake a pole into my face or rip a shoulder from its socket. It was a bad technique but other than that the only way I'd learnt to slow down a sit-ski involved making fists and digging my knuckles into the ground but that didn't work on solid ice.

The pulks caused problems for the others. Going downhill, the heavy weight accelerated like a toboggan into the backs of their heels and contorted the towing wires so badly I was sure they'd break. Uphill, the effort of dragging the pulks looked immense and they often capsized on the contours of the climb, their fabric tops grating across the ice. The dead-weight of a capsized pulk was almost impossible to pull, the friction against the ice too much. The others all put skins on the base of their skis to gain more grip for dragging the heavy loads upward, but even then it was tough. Eventually the skis got changed for crampons and I wished I could be rid of my skis too and somehow gain some control over the slip sliding away and the fear of disappearing through a hole into the ice, but skis were my only means of moving.

The terrain became so difficult that we had to work in shuttles. That's the 'royal we', given that I couldn't shuttle myself let alone anything else. The first up a slope would un-hook their pulk, teeter back down on their crampons being careful not to trip headlong into a cold pool and help drag the capsized pulks to the top. I effectively became another fragile load, as trying to propel myself up and down the steep icy edges was a futile and dangerous activity. I waited my turn for some helpful, able hands to grab hold and yank me upwards and onwards. Then I gripped my poles so tightly that my hands went numb on each hair-raising descent all the while wary of the consequences of one wrong move.

Again I felt vulnerable and acutely dependent.

You chose this Karen. Why do you get yourself into these situations?

But I knew the answer without thinking. I only had to look around me. We were in an incredible place.

Incredibly dangerous.

Incredibly scary.

Incredibly tough.

But also just incredible – the clear blue pools of water, the twisted ice architecture, the deep canyons formed smooth like giant water slides.

All morning we pushed on, pulling and pushing, grunting and groaning, giving the ice everything we had.

"That's one kilometre." Pasi fiddled with the GPS and reported its statistics.

"One kilometre!" I expressed my surprise. The effort and stress had made it feel like twenty.

Another kilometre later, utterly exhausted and disillusioned with our slow progress, we stopped. Pasi decided to scout ahead for the best route. Harvey went to do the same, guided by another set of GPS coordinates someone had given him as a suggested route off the ice. They headed in different directions.

We rested, and pulled out the food bags in need of energy. I opened a fresh bag, keen to find new chunks of chocolate hidden amongst the peanuts but the first thing I found was a folded piece of paper. I smiled, remembering the scene in my kitchen back in Scotland; two good friends had helped me weigh and measure equal quantities of peanuts, raisins and chocolate into each of the plastic snack bags before we shipped them out to Greenland. My friend Joseph had scribbled notes on bits of paper and folded them into some of the bags.

"They'll cheer you up" he'd grinned, scribbling some more.

For all his notes, we hadn't found one until now. As I read his words, my smile broadened. In his neat, artistic scroll he'd written; "Keep pushing. Not long now."

I laughed. It was just the message we needed to hear, another coincidence to encourage us on our journey. 'Keep going!'

It was the boost we needed.

From our viewpoint we could see Harvey and Pasi forging ahead but in widely different directions. They couldn't see each other and each was waving for us to follow them. They were the two with the most experience but at times their opinions competed. They needed to work together, yet the closer we got to the edge of the ice the more the differences they'd tolerated in each other became strained. Whichever way we went, we needed to go together. We followed, but in the middle, none of us wanting to chose one over the other, remaining hopeful that a central line would bring us all together again.

The closer we came to the end of the journey, the more the strain took its toll. Each of us was tired, our patience frayed, less willing to compromise and bolder in expressing opinions and sticking to them. We disagreed over most things now; from the best route off the ice, to the small doings of daily living. That morning as we left camp, Andy had stood on the tea bags he'd left scattered, smearing the leaves across the ice. Anna had shouted at him to pick them up but like a naughty kid, he rebelled and left them. We wanted to leave as little trace as possible on the ice and smeared tea bags didn't fit with our ethos. I felt ashamed later that I hadn't backed Anna up and cleaned the tea bags up even if Andy wouldn't and I was sure he'd wish he hadn't left them too.

This day was harder again, and now I began to feel seriously in danger of either breaking a bone or drowning, as pulled by Andy we moved along the tops of ice ridges, big steep drops on either side. A slip by either of us would see us both plunge down. Andy – always the easy going one – was dragging me wherever he decided, ignoring the group and taking routes of his own, with single-minded focus and no room for negotiation. I saw a stubbornness I'd never noticed before, a total unwillingness to give up. It would normally be a good trait but being tied to him like that didn't feel so good.

"Slow up a bit!" I shouted to him from behind. "It's a fine line between being stubborn and being dead!" Several times I'd feared for our lives as he yanked us through streams and over crevasses.

"Just trust me. We can't waste any time getting through this. It's melting more every minute." Our team joker, our peacemaker, was suddenly showing another side, a bloody mindedness that explained how he'd climbed the things he had. Most of the time I'd seen him as a friendly teddy bear character but now he was made of steel.

"Just go steady when we cross this water" I pleaded as we splashed into an area of melting ice, and wished for the dry suit I hadn't brought.

He was silent.

Silent meant 'be quiet and don't interfere'.

I couldn't have known then how well I would come to know that.

With one leg to go Andy sat on his pulk next to me, everyone done in. "Don't worry," he said "this is the best bit."

"What do you mean?" I replied, just wanting it to be over.

"The worst times are always the ones you remember most fondly – the times when you're really tested, the times you want to give in, the times you think you'll break."

"Mmmmm" I replied, sounding doubtful about his logic, but I knew what he meant.

"People like us don't want easy lives because we're not easy people."

Maybe he was right, but a bit of 'easy living' seemed like a nice option then and there.

"This is a category two experience" he continued.

I raised my eyebrows and nodded for him to continue.

"Category one is an experience you enjoy but have no memory of. Category two is one that's miserable at the time but you remember vividly and fondly.

Category three is one that's miserable at the time and that you would give anything to forget."

We were immersed in a category two experience – it was tough but already I knew I'd look back at the journey and want to do it all over again.

As we skied onwards, I thought about Andy's theory. Was it possible to categorise experiences so simply? What about life at home, life with Suresh? It had been really hard for the last few years. If I applied the category theory, I'd grade it as a three – not because he was a bad person, far from it, but because we only seemed to bring out the worst in each other. Some people seemed to think I was brave going to Greenland but they didn't realise the cowardice in it, that facing the hazards of the icecap seemed easier than facing things at home.

When the ice ends, you'll have to.

Lost in my thoughts, I bumped into the back of Anna, our progress stopped by another obstacle – yet another icy torrent that carved through the blocks of ice before us. I pushed the thought of home to the back of my mind, where it had been buried for the last month and did what I did best – put on a brave face to hide the coward within me.

Am I a coward?

No you're just scared.

Scared of confronting your real life in the real world.

As I looked out at the horizon, knowing the land was growing near, I felt a fear. Fear of the end, the end of our journey, the end of the escape. I knew that the one thing that anyone travelling looks forward to the most was the thing that scared me most.

Going home.

16. POINT 660

Our team and our kit literally fell apart on those last few days. It was as if the harshness of the ice had ripped the hearts and stitching from us all. The closer the land came the greater its pull, yet it seemed to never get any closer, always beyond another line of ice cliffs or just over another stream. As we staggered along two of the pulk harness systems broke so dragging them by hand whilst walking sideways was the only option, making the team look as if they were part of a frantic retreat, rather than at the end of a fabulous journey. The reality was Greenland had taken all we had and now it wanted more than we could give.

The others wore crampons with their skis long abandoned in such rough terrain, but I depended on my skis for every inch of movement. Stones became exposed in the ice and they scraped chunks from my skis as I pushed over them.

But I was beyond caring.

The end was all that mattered.

I dreamt of food, warmth and safety.

We crept closer.

I thought I could smell the land.

It wasn't about kilometres any more but metre by painful metre.

Gone was any glide.

The skiing was over for me.

Now it was just shoving, pushing, stumbling.

It's not getting any closer.

My head was strung out, muscles and sinews tight enough to twang.

Your shoulder will rip any moment...

My hands were on Anna and Andy's thighs to balance myself from a fall.

Their thighs are like rock.
My shoulders feel like that too.
This has to end soon.
I've had enough.
And there it was.
The end.

The other side of Greenland, a deep moat the last obstacle, the trench spanned by a simple plank of wood.

Everyone stood there panting, sweat dripping from their faces, clothes streaked with glacial mud, laces trailing, pulks battered and upended.

"Point 660" said Pasi looking at his GPS. It was the first time I had ever seen him tired.

I held onto Andy's neck as he carried me over the plank, then up the dirt road on the other side, my feet yet to touch down on this soil I'd given everything to reach.

Pasi carried my ski, and put it down on the gravel where we'd be picked up. He and Harvey guided me down into it again.

It felt like landing on the moon.

I bent over and ran my fingers through the grit and sand.

I imagined this would be the high point of the trip. The end. But it wasn't.

Running my fingers through the dirts I fought back tears – both of relief and sadness. The sand and grit were the same as the grit and sand on the helipad in Ammassalik. I sat back up and without thinking tried to move, instantly realising I was stuck. I wouldn't be able to move until I got my wheelchair back.

Suddenly I didn't want it to be over.

We waited patiently in the sun for the all-terrain vehicle to arrive to take us to Kangerlussuaq. Everyone was quiet until someone suggested we cook some of the food we had left, but everyone was happy to wait now until pizza in town, and maybe a beer to celebrate.

Whilst we waited, the weirdest thing happened. A small crowd of tourists, mainly American, crested the hill of gravel that led to the dirt road, our own ride coming down the hill behind them, my heart jumping a beat when I saw my wheelchair balanced next to the driver.

The tourists teetered towards where we sat, unsteady on their feet, until a small crowd surrounded us.

"Wow, have you guys been on a day-trip or something?" One of them asked whilst inspecting our dishevelled state through thick glasses.

"Oh no, we've crossed the icecap."

"Wow, and did you break your leg up there or something?" said another one, an older lady wearing a thick home-made balaclava.

I restrained myself from facetiously answering 'Oh yeah, and we just happened to find this special sit-ski in the middle of the icecap' and instead said "No I can't walk."

"How long did that take?" Another asked, looking mildly impressed, picking up his SLR camera to get a picture to show his grandchildren.

"Twenty-nine days" we answered in unison.

"Wow – how far have you skied?" asked yet another balanced on ski poles.

"Five hundred and fifty kilometres" said Anna proudly.

"How far is that in miles?" they all asked.

"Twenty thousand miles" said Andy.

It felt like it.

Climbing a ridge on Zinal Rothorn in Switzerland, age 21. This was seven months before I became paralysed. ALUN POWELL

The Team. Back row from left: Jacek Olesinski, Pasi Ikonen, Anna McCormack & Harvey Goodwin. From row: Andy Kirkpatrick & me. MARK & LOU.

Pasi helping me into the tent after a particularly cold, cloudy day skiing.
ANNA McCORMACK

Sitting there looking out at absolutely nothing I wondered if I had what it would take to make it to the other side. The words of all those who'd said it was impossible seemed all too prophetic. ANDY KIRKPATRICK

The secret to staying warm in Greenland was never letting myself get cold in the first place - that meant a lot of clothes at times! ANDY KIRKPATRICK

This is one of my favourite photos from Greenland - the sit-ski beside our tent as a mild storm blew through. It reminds me of both the beauty and the wild desolation of the icecap. PASI IKONEN

Harvey helps me back up from a fall. In the first week I fell over a lot as I got used to balancing the sit-ski over lumps of ice. PASI IKONEN

Harvey suited up and about to venture out into the storm to dig the tent out. This had to be done every two hours to stop the tent getting buried.
ANDY KIRKPATRICK

*Bad weather harried us for much of the first half of the trip, with winds that
threatened to break the poles on our tents, or bury us whole!*
ANDY KIRKPATRICK

Nothing could have prepared me for the sight of El Cap. It's simply massive, and looking up at it from the valley floor it seemed intimidating and impossible to climb. ANDY KIRKPATRICK

The complex logistics of big wall climbing. The haul bags were super heavy with ten days worth of food, water and equpiment. The guy who took this photo has a telescopic camera lens and hangs out on a bridge in the valley reporting on El Cap climbing activity. TOM EVANS

Although four thousand pull-ups may sound like a lot, a clever system of pulleys meant that I was only hauling half my body weight. Nevertheless my arms were trashed each evening. NATASHA SEBIRE

Swinging out in space below El Cap. The fact that it's so overhanging was good as otherwise it would have been much harder to haul myself up against the friction of the rock face. NATASHA SEBIRE

Being so high up for day after day felt seriously exposed. I liked getting to the portaledge, looking upwards and imagining that I was just lying safe on the ground. NATASHA SEBIRE

This shot was taken after my scary rope tangle. I must have just stopped crying, but you can tell I wasn't too happy. I think Andy's face says it all (he gave me a Snickers bar in an attempt to cheer me up). NATASHA SEBIRE

You might imagine that one of the scariest parts of big walling would be sleeping on a portaledge. In fact by the time I'd reached the end of the day I was so tired I'd have slept sitting in my harness. NATASHA SEBIRE

Me hanging from the top of the wall, my upper body on the lip while my legs hung below until Tash and Gemma could pull me up. I guess this picture sums up what it feels like to climb El Cap. ANDY KIRKPATRICK

Preparing to set off back down from the top of El Cap - a far tougher and more hazardous journey than getting to the top. Luckily Tash and Gemma were there to help us. NATASHA SEBIRE

After a nine hour piggy-back we reached the car park at the bottom of the wall. It was a huge relief to have made it back in one piece. Little did I know that somewhere on the way down or collapsing here in the car park, I'd actually broken my leg! NATASHA SEBIRE

Ten years old and wide-eyed at El Capitan. Little did I know... MIKE DARKE

Exhausted but re-united with my wheelchair after a week without it. Freedom at last! NATASHA SEBIRE

17. FACING UP

The first morning home I moved through my house with its soft carpets to the front door, my body still unused to my wheelchair, my mind still back there in Greenland. I bent over and picked up the letters that lay at my door, marvelling at the complexity of a postal system, the idea of tiny pieces of sticky paper that allowed other pieces of paper to travel further in a day than we had in a month of crossing Greenland. I looked at the white paper and thought of snow.

The whole world had become a marvel.

This life was paradise.

I opened the old wooden front door and peered outside at the view, feeling the warmth of the June sun on my skin. I noticed how luminous the green moss growing on the tree at the bottom of the garden was, the sweet smell of flowers, the loud singsong of birds – so many birds. The layers and depth and brightness all seemed more intense than I'd ever experienced before.

Inside the house it was the luxury I noticed. Water available in an instant, heat from the radiators at the press of a button, the softness of the sheets and the way the pillow held my tired head. When I went to fill the kettle and I was enthralled by the tendons in my hand as I turned the tap and sat there for a while, wondering at the design of the human body and watching the rush of running water and the droplets that spurted onto the tiles and onto my face. I had spent days melting water, each drop as precious as fine wine.

I noticed the detail of every moment as if seeing it for the first time.

I found myself really enjoying each act or movement, each small or simple thing. I wondered why everything seemed so different from before I'd gone away. It was as if all my senses were heightened after so many days in the nothingness of the icecap, with its lack of colour and form and stuff to muddle my senses.

There was so much texture to life at home that I'd never noticed before but there was also a void – the space where Greenland had been, the feeling of longing to return to a place I'd grown to love. There was also the void that I had travelled to Greenland to escape.

The space between Suresh and I seemed larger than ever. We hadn't spoken at all whilst I'd been away. At first I'd worried and wondered why not, thought about what was right between us and what was wrong and what should be done to fix our wounded relationship. I'd skied alone with my thoughts day after day, trying to come up with a plan to make it right but after a while the hypnotic routine of skiing meant I'd lost all track of what was or what might be. I'd let go of thought and been absorbed into the silence of the icecap. But now back at home, our conversations stilted and strained, the silence between us was screaming at me to do something.

Perhaps my heart had hardened with the ice but I felt unwilling to accept things as they were between us anymore. I'd tried. We'd tried. So hard we were exhausted and now with the ice between us, it felt harder and emptier than ever. I could see for the first time that I was with Suresh for the wrong reasons. I'd been hurt before and had some crazy belief that because of the wheelchair I'd be single forever and I didn't want that. I lacked confidence and he'd proposed. In my vulnerability I'd accepted and had thought it was real but beneath it all there was just this fragile thing in me that needed to feel loved. He'd come along at just that moment and swept me away, a knight in shining armour. The shine hadn't lasted for long though because he couldn't fix me or make me happy, and I could never make him happy either. I couldn't be the wife he wanted.

I would have to be the one to smash us to pieces in order to save who we were.

Breaking up was the hardest thing I'd ever done. It's easy to be strong in the face of nature but harder in the face of a lover. But where once I would have wept, slept, then fought hard to try again, I found a certainty that surprised me. I was sure beyond a question that breaking up was the right thing for us both and for once I had to learn to let go of something I'd worked hard for. A failed marriage – to become divorced – would be a failure that would stay with me forever but I knew it was right. I didn't know why – it was all beyond words. But I knew that somewhere in those frozen expanses, in the vast nothingness of the icecap and without any conscious thought, things had changed.

I moved out.

And so I found myself on another adventure, only now a solo one, a familiar one, in a new flat by myself, in a new city having moved to Inverness. A few months before my life had been in a pulk the size of a large kids sledge; now it was in a small mountain of cardboard boxes. As ever it was the simplicity of the wilderness that steadied my nerve back in the 'real' world. As with all adventures it was an odd mixture of the excitement of the possible and the fear of the unknown but I trusted it would lead somewhere worthwhile.

Sat in my new kitchen, unwrapping plates and cups, the share of our life together, I wondered if without Greenland it would have been different. If I'd stayed then maybe I might by now be settled or pregnant. No. The answer was simple; Greenland was inside me, the vast thrilling emptiness, the anger, the peace, the beauty and the terror. It was inside me all along. Going there or staying home would have made no difference – there was a wildness inside me that would always be there and I could never wish to tame it.

The one thing I knew without doubt was that Greenland would be a blessing for both of us – one day. Despite all my weakness, in Greenland I had found the strength not just to cross the ice but to face the hurt and failure of the unbearable at home and so – hopefully – save us both.

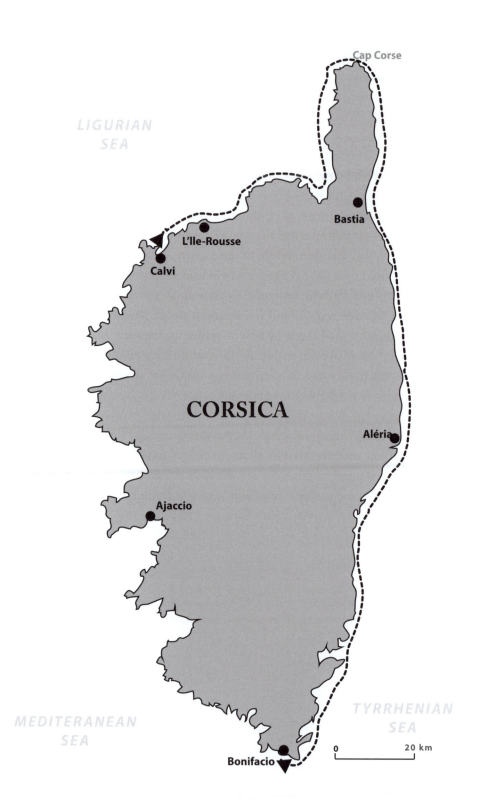

LIGURIAN
SEA

Cap Corse

Bastia

L'Ile-Rousse

Calvi

CORSICA

Aléria

Ajaccio

MEDITERANEAN
SEA

TYRRHENIAN
SEA

Bonifacio

0   20 km

CORSICA

Kayaking beneath huge cliffs on one of the calmer days at sea. Four paddlers, three great companions with me. KAREN DARKE COLLECTION.

18. DOWN BY THE SEA

Eight months passed. It was February. Snow had piled high on the bonnet of the van and four of us climbed in, excited to leave behind the Scottish winter. The next stop would be the Mediterranean. We were all single, all a little bruised in different ways, all in search of something that we hoped we'd find on the sea. The plan was to kayak, around the island of Corsica. We had a roof full of kayaks, a van packed with food, and we were rich in time with a whole six weeks to spend away.

It had been a while since I'd been on a long kayak trip. The last big one had been in 2004, an epic journey of 1200 miles from Vancouver, Canada to Juneau, Alaska. Whilst it had been relatively incident free, I still thought of myself as a bit of a liability in a kayak, at least vulnerable if the conditions got tough. I'd been told early on by an 'expert' that I'd never be able to kayak as I had no control of my stomach or hips, and so I'd just be sat in the boat with very little ability to control it. When kayaking in a big sea your body is reaching constantly, shifting and leaning, keeping your balance as the sea moves around you. As I'm unable to control my stomach muscles it means that when I lift my arms up to hold a paddle my body slumps backwards and forwards and gives me less ability to manoeuvre the kayak. Even sat in my wheelchair it takes the upmost concentration to lift both arms up above my shoulders, one hand always having to hold onto something for balance. To overcome this in a kayak I'd made a sort of girdle that I wore around my waist and hip area, like a 'splint' that when wrapped beneath my buoyancy aid allowed me to stay upright. The most improvised splint I'd ever made was from an old plastic fish box and a bread board I'd found amongst debris on a beach. The splint support was only a marginal victory though. Sometimes we might have to cover fifty miles or more in a day in the kayak, and that ideally requires the core muscles of the body to twist and do much of the work. I was reliant on arm power alone. This meant I was generally slower than others and if a headwind kicked up, then my lack of ability to put real power behind the paddle could be dangerous.

Besides the girdle, I also used blocks of foam to keep my legs out to the sides of the kayak, helping with stability. It all worked well as long as it didn't get too windy and I stayed upright but as to what would happen if I rolled the kayak? Well, I'd practised but that could never be like the real thing. I had a 'rolling-float' on the deck of the kayak, with a very large handle and a cord that when pulled would open a small cylinder of gas. The idea was that if I rolled, I'd grab the rolling float, pull the cord – woosh! It would inflate and I'd pull myself up enough to get my head clear of the water to breathe. It did work but the only time I'd capsized in anger, I'd panicked, forgotten to use it and just tried to push myself out of the kayak instead. There were many reasons why that 'expert' had been right about my abilities in a kayak but it was often being told I couldn't do something that encouraged me to try harder and learn how to. Despite my best efforts and the fact that I loved to kayak, I still felt vulnerable when the wind got up or the sea got rough.

On the long drive south, following the infinite grey ribbon of the autoroute, we were buoyant. Barry had the wheel, smiling broadly as was his way and with his Wirral accent he always sounded cheery. He'd taught himself to kayak mostly by going out solo in the rough waters near his home but had progressed fast. He'd kayaked all the way around Britain in an epic two-month journey just the year before. Jon was squashed between Barry and me, the dashboard and the gear stick, his mischievous chuckle also making us smile. Jon worked as a kayak instructor and was as skilled on the sea as he was on rivers or in surf. His kind, gentle nature always made me feel safe. Carol was in the back, amongst the boxes and bags of food we'd brought with us for the month. Also a kayak instructor – I was in safe hands – she was as excited yet nervous about the trip ahead as I was, and her playful caring way and soft Irish lilt made her the perfect female companion for the trip.

To avoid the danger of us spending too much time brooding over the difficult love lives we'd left behind, we made a deal. We were allowed one song each – mine was a Coldplay number – and one short story and moment of melancholy to go with it. After that we'd put the past behind us and have the adventure ahead.

Late in the night with the engine humming and the scenery still flashing by, an old memory popped up. In 2000 I'd cycled the length of Japan and while there I'd been interviewed several times by Rioko, a TV producer, who had persistently asked me as I cycled through the islands "What are you searching for?"

I'd said I wasn't sure, that I just liked cycling, being outside and exploring new places.

"It's like you're searching for a missing jigsaw piece," she'd continued, but I hadn't known how to answer and hadn't really known what she meant.

Since then there'd been so many journeys and so many miles. But that night, buzzing down the motorway towards Corsica, I could sense what it was because it was in the van and in the adventure; freedom, laughter, friends, strangers, connectedness, excitement. The missing piece was hard to describe because it wasn't anything exact. It was nothing that could be given, nothing anyone else had as such but a combination of many subtle things, of feelings and people and events. It was being, not doing. It was happiness. Although it sounds trite, it was love but in the bigger sense, not just the love of one person.

Many hours later and a lot of miles and memories behind us, we arrived in Nice. We grabbed a few hours of much needed sleep in the van before making the early ferry crossing over to the island of Corsica. The winter Mediterranean was bigger than I expected, a large swell rocking the ferry and waves that scared me at the thought of kayaking in them. I wondered how well both my body and new kayak would cope with the seas as I looked out of the ship's thick windows, knowing yet again I was asking a lot. I also knew I was dependent on my friends and that me being part of the team would make a difficult trip much harder. I've always hated asking for help from anyone but sometimes there is no way around it. Once underway we'd be working our way around the three hundred or so miles of rocky coastline, our kayaks packed with all the food we'd need for the trip, along with camping and safety gear. Just as in Greenland I knew that success or failure was all down to being a team. I just hoped I wouldn't let my friends down.

~

I slid my legs into the narrow cockpit of the kayak as the surf crashed down just short of the bow, my eyes on the job at hand, my mind trying to ignore the fact that in a moment I'd be paddling out into those waves.

Next I slid my bum in like a cork into a bottle, then attached my spray deck and zipped up my buoyancy aid.

"Ready Karen?" Jon asked as I picked up my paddle, wishing I could have a little practice first before heading into the sea but knowing this was it, all the kayaks lined up and loaded to go. It was the first time I'd ever sat in this kayak – it had arrived brand new and wrapped in plastic just the night we left for Corsica.

"Guess so" I said, lifting up my new carbon fibre paddle, and with a big heave the three of them pushed me out into the waves, slowly at first, then fast as the sea took me with it.

The waves crashed down towards me but I knew I had to stay focused, keep my mind strong and punch through. The water crashed over me but the boat kept spearing through. Another wave rolled in and I paddled hard again, punched through it once more. I heard the the others shouting encouragement from behind, and I powered on towards the calmer water beyond.

We had begun in the northern town of Calvi, our plan to paddle clockwise. When locals asked us later where we'd come from they raised their voices in surprise and when they discovered we'd paddled Cap Corse, "Oh la la!" was often their response. Cap Corse was a thumb-like promontory of land that jutted out at the northeast end of the island. It was a dangerous place where the wind and tides could whip up the sea, with rip tides that could whisk you far off-shore. But lady luck had been with us the day we'd kayaked around the Cap and the sea had been near calm.

I was glad of that. I didn't want danger. There was a level of risk purely from the nature of kayaking but I was thankful for the lack of underlying stress. No polar bears. No Piteraqs. No frostbite worries. No relationship worries. There was just a wide open sea, a warm sun and good uncomplicated friendship.

Just before we'd left Calvi I'd put my wheelchair on a train across the island, to Bastia in the east. From that moment I knew I'd be forced to depend on piggy-backs or bum-shuffling to get around and I totted up how long I'd spent without my wheelchair in the last twelve months. For something I was so dependent on for mobility, it was a long time. With Greenland and Corsica it would be two months at least and although I sometimes felt grounded without it and craved the independence it offered, it would be useless in the kind of places I wanted to be. A wheelchair wasn't designed for mountains, icecaps or sea or for the rock and sand that we'd live on that month.

As I paddled out into the ocean away from the breakers, Barry, Jon and Carol moved up around me, a pod of kayaks. I felt my heart miss a beat, knowing we had started. I was back, in synch with nature's rhythms again. We would time our days with the tides, sleep on the beaches and watch the rocky mountains burn red as the sun rose or set.

We'd barely begun before we became stormbound. The weather was angry and the sea too rough to continue and hardly away from town, we were forced to camp on the edge of a car park. It wasn't wilderness and it was hard going without my chair. It was the beginning of a feeling I carried with me, of holding the others back. It would be easier for them without me, without the piggy-backs and the extra kayak to lug up the beach and without the weaker paddler. The feeling lurked in me and it wasn't unfamiliar. I recognised this sense of being the slowest and weakest and most vulnerable. Sometimes I felt like a burden. I fought hard against it, never wanting to succumb to the potential limitations of not being able to walk but I knew that I depended on the willingness, support and friendship of those with me to do the things I did.

Someone once told me I was the 'lowest common denominator'. What they meant was that what I could do (or couldn't) dictated what we could do together. They didn't mean for it to be hurtful but it stabbed at me to hear how they felt. I know that others have to compromise what they might otherwise do when doing things with me but don't we all when it comes to being with others?

There are situations in life that are difficult but we have to make the most of the circumstances we have. I try to do that. There's opportunity every day to dwell on the difficulties and the impact of those on others. I try not to do that too much. We're all different. We all have our weaknesses and we all have our strengths. My weaknesses are obvious and in the wilderness, for all that I love it, they become more apparent. I'm just grateful to have friends that will go there with me and that don't remind me of them.

I was lucky to have that in Corsica.

Two weeks later as we kayaked into Bastia, the sea was so big that we were hidden from each other between the crests of the waves and I couldn't wait to find my chair. I wanted terra firma. I was looking forward to being away from the perils of a windy day on the water, stress free and freewheeling the streets of the town. I would have stayed in Bastia for a day at least, to feel the knot of tension in me unravel but there was no time to appreciate the little luxuries we'd been without – a shower, a toilet, a café – as after a stretch and a short walk and a bag full of chocolate croissants, the others were ready to go.

It was dark as we left the ramp in the small harbour but it was calm. Paddling in the moonlight had a hypnotic effect and inside I felt relaxed again. As we passed the main harbour entrance, we waited, stealth-like against the giant boulders of the outer wall as pilot boats led a huge ferry out. It's engine droned on by and with the decks lit up it looked like a tall block of flats at night. It turned slightly south, roughly in the same direction we were headed, towards Bonifacio, a week of paddling away along a very long stretch of beach. There would be surf and I'd be scared and probably get wet and just for a moment, I longed for my hip and abdominal muscles to work so I could steer and balance my kayak.

We paddled into the night with the moonlight reflecting off the gentle roll of sea. With the others paddling alongside, I looked towards the twinkling shore, then out to the black space of sea and felt content.

As we approached the beach to camp, the rumble of surf terrified me and ate into any sense of calm I'd felt earlier. Jon landed first, promising to flash a head-torch at us if it was good enough to come in and land. When the flash came, Barry offered to escort Carol in first and grinning at me – he liked the surf – told me "Keep warm, don't go anywhere and I'll be back to paddle in with you." I watched them disappear towards the blackness of the shore, admiring Barry's easy and confident way. Self-taught and a master on the waves, his humour and nature always made things feel easier and more fun than they otherwise would. A while later he returned.

"Right, Carol's had a good swim but don't worry, you'll be fine."

I felt my confidence plummet even lower.

"Just come alongside, grab hold of the back of my kayak and cling on."

Minutes later we were whizzing towards the beach on a roller of foam, Barry powering on his paddle, me weebling and wobbling. I didn't even bother trying to control my own boat but at least it meant no swim and as we crashed onto the beach the only flood was one of relief.

The long beach lasted a week with a surf landing to spice up the end of every day. In reality the waves were probably no bigger than my three nephews could make in a bath but I still fretted over it and preferred to eat a 'floating lunch' to avoid an extra landing. We found a rhythm – mine painfully slow for the others some days, my shoulders bearing all the work – but the views helped ease the monotony; the high mountains of Corsica on our right framed with blue sky and turquoise sea, open water stretching towards Italy on our left. Greenland and all the change and turbulence of life at home felt a million miles away, life simplified – sleep, eat, paddle, eat, paddle, eat, sleep – back into the cycle of nature.

The memory of home was only sparked when I occasionally turned my phone on and it beeped to announce new texts. There was one from Andy – *Hope you're having fun. I've moved out of home, renting a house in Sheffield, near the kids' school. Would be good to meet up when you're back.* It had been months since we'd met, and we'd barely stayed in touch. It had seemed best that way – there was something about him that stirred feelings in me that were better left buried. He'd had stuff to work out. Now though, I wondered what was best.

At last the beach ran out. We'd reached the bottom of Corsica. We turned a corner in the low cliffs, at last heading west but almost instantly the wind hit. The sea got sloppy, waves chopping into our kayaks as they bounced off the cliffs. I was knocked off balance by each wave, wobbling dangerously until I was certain I'd soon capsize. The sea was so confused that every small movement I made with my head or shoulders was critical. Every tiny muscle I had worked overtime, responding to the feedback from the rolls of the kayak.

"What's the worst that could happen?" I'd asked myself, but it didn't work in the positive way I'd hoped. Instead I imagined being smashed against the cliffs, or drowning in the turquoise water.

I'd called out to the others, "What do you think?" and then without any words, we'd turned back. I was relieved. As we landed on the beach back around the sheltered corner, I breathed out at last. Barry and Jon were good to go on, probably excited by the tougher conditions and the chance to use their skill but I'd felt a limit, one I hadn't always been good at recognising. There was a time to push on and a time to back off. If we continued I'd no doubt swim and it would be difficult, with heavy-laden boats and cliffs that went on for miles. There weren't even any beaches to land on for shelter or rest. We still had well over a hundred miles to go but I couldn't go up against the sea. The sea always wins.

We were stranded for days, camped on a sandy corner of the sheltered beach watching the wind howl through the narrows between Corsica and Sardinia. We waited and waited, playing card games to pass the time whilst sand found its way into everything we owned and everything we ate. The locals told us it wasn't even that windy for the time of year. On the fourth day, the whitecaps were bigger than ever and I did what I'd never done before.

I decided to stop.

Stopping probably sounds like nothing to most people, just the sensible and obvious thing to do. But my pattern wasn't to do the sensible or obvious. I always pushed. I didn't like to give up on things. But if becoming paralysed by falling off the cliff had taught me anything, it was that sometimes I should back off, that sometimes it was the right thing to do.

Carol said she was happy to stop with me so whilst we packed up for the land, Barry and Jon repacked for the sea. With the help of a kind couple we'd met on the beach, I borrowed a wheelchair from the local hospital. It was a heavy metal tank but it was better than nothing and I could keep it until we boarded the bus. We would catch a bus north and with luck my own wheelchair would be waiting at the train station at the other end. If we got really lucky, the bus driver might take us straight there, to save me sitting for ages on a pavement at the bus station whilst Carol ran across town to find it.

Luck. It always seemed there was a lot involved. But it wasn't really luck. It was usually about the generosity of people, about kindness from strangers, about being willing to trust that if you try, then somehow it will all be okay. It's like magic; if we try, trust and give when we can, then the world will hold us in return.

The bus journey took us high across the mountains, through quiet window-shuttered villages where the only sign of life was a single plume of smoke, an open boulangerie or a rusting Citroen passing by. The bus twisted and turned through hairpin roads, giving us glimpses of the sea, more distant than it had been for weeks. I longed to be out there but was also glad not to be wobbling amongst the waves. It was a new experience to have avoided teetering on the edge of danger and not to have pushed myself to the relief and exhaustion of a journey's end.

With the hum of the bus engine, I finally relaxed into the fact we'd stopped.

I had decided to stop.

There was a time when the gung-ho part of me that didn't want to know limits would have pushed on but over the years my adventures had changed me. They'd given me a respect for nature and for myself that meant I need not continually push on like it was all a form of self-harm.

I stared from the bus window at the passing views. I looked up at the high peaks and did my trick of imagining a giant hand brushing across, imagined the sound my running shoes would make, tap tap tapping across their heights.

I felt a sudden and rare pang of sadness when I considered that high places would be forever beyond me, well any high place beyond the tarmac.

But there are many other places yet to visit I thought, trying to be positive and not dwell on what couldn't be.

But where next? I wondered.

It had been some year. Both a year of change and a year of pain. But without pain we don't change and without change our experiences become limited. For the short-term at least, it's more comfortable to stay with the status quo and not rock the boat – avoid the discomfort of facing our fears or a new set of circumstances. I knew from experience that the longer I resisted change, the more I risked becoming unhappy and losing a part of myself along the way.

As the bus wound down from the mountains towards the town and the sea, it struck me that there are different kinds of fear. There is good fear, the kind that should be listened to, the kind that preserves us and helps us survive.

And there is bad fear. That includes a fear of the unknown, or a fear of the past repeating itself.

Stopping paddling was 'good fear' I decided. I'd been scared to go on and it didn't matter that I'd stopped. There'd been a good reason – immediate danger – and in fact, stopping could have saved my life. My fear about going to Greenland had been 'bad fear'. It was fear of the unknown. My fear about a life without Suresh was 'bad fear' too. I'd been scared of what the change would mean. They were both fears that could have stopped me, held me back, kept me stuck, dragged me down and if I'd listened to that fear, I'd no doubt be unhappy.

All those years ago, on the cliff, I'd not listened to my fear. I'd pushed on when I should have stopped.

It felt good to listen and respond to fear in the right way.

The bus descended back down to the sea and I felt peaceful.

I was happy to have stopped.

EL CAPITAN

19. SO IT BEGAN

'Back mid-March. Could meet up then.'
I pressed send, at last replying to Andy's text, then sank back into my sleeping bag to the now familiar sound of waves crashing on the beach. We were still in Corsica, camping and kayaking and making the most of the time we had left before the long drive back to Britain.

Finally we met up in York one April afternoon. Andy was doing a talk there, storytelling about his climbing exploits.

"You should come along and see some pics of El Cap" he suggested.

While my fall from the Scottish sea cliff had utterly changed my life fourteen years before, the journey across Greenland was about to bring another huge change. I couldn't have known it at the time but two conversations would change the course of my life again.

The first was a flippant suggestion.

"Greenland is boring" Andy had said, sat beside me on his pulk chewing peanuts, both of us looking out at the vast icecap before us. "We should have gone to climb El Cap instead."

I'd looked at him and laughed out loud, the sheer daftness of his suggestion. Me climb El Cap! I'd thought about the iconic rock face before – one kilometre high, near flawless and either vertical or overhanging, nestled in the famous Yosemite valley, California. It was something way beyond me as a climber when I could walk, so the idea of spending a week climbing it now was totally crazy.

"Isn't this hard enough?" I'd asked, wondering if he was just pulling my leg.

"Maybe we should do it after this?" he had replied, turning and looking straight into my eyes with a seriousness that was most often hidden.

It's perhaps a good job that we can't foresee which of our throw away ideas will turn into reality. Otherwise we might not think them up in the first place.

The second was a moment of honesty between friends.

"So are you looking forward to getting home?" Andy had asked me at the end of crossing the ice.

"Not really" I'd replied, which took him by surprise and my words had surprised me also. But it was true. "There's difficult stuff to sort out when I get home."

"If you don't mind me asking, is it your husband?" He asked, and I nodded. "You know what – you can love someone all you want, and be loved back, but it's no good if they want you to change into someone you're not. The stuff they don't like about you is the stuff that makes you who you are and without it they wouldn't love you anyway."

I was a bit taken aback that Andy had pieced my problems together so well.

"I've been married for sixteen years and not one has been easy because of climbing. My wife says she loves everything about me but the part of me that wants to climb. The problem is that that's who I am. I don't seem to be able to live without climbing."

"So how do you manage it if it's like that?" I asked. I thought of Suresh and me, of our differences, the pressure I felt to settle down and have kids and be 'normal'.

"Dunno. I'm still trying to figure that out. Maybe you either have a marriage where you don't compromise and one person is unhappy or you both compromise and neither one is happy or you split up and find someone who can accept you as you are."

"Are you happy?" I asked, feeling it was my turn to put him under the spotlight, wondering if Andy was running away from something like me.

"No" he said, "but I have two kids."

Two conversations weeks apart. I could never have known how much these would lead to my life being changed beyond recognition. We couldn't possibly have conceived what lay in store for us. Looking back it's as if the icecap held something mysterious that affected both our destinies.

20. ROPING UP

I was ten years old when I first saw it.

El Capitan stood like a giant, a massive shining wall of rock that made everything else look miniature. We stopped at a roadside viewpoint, the kind of stop my brother and I always hated getting out of the car for, with Mum and Dad enthusing about another view and another photo. But that day was different. There was this awesome big rock to look at and it pulled us from the back of the car like nothing had before. My mouth had hung open as Dad pointed out the climbers that clung to the rock face, small dots in the colourful wall of granite. How could anyone cling to a vertical wall like that?

I thought they must have super-human powers.

I'd stood on the Eiffel Tower as a kid and thought I was on top of the world but El Cap was four times higher my Dad said. It was no wonder it cast a magical spell over me.

That had been twenty-five years ago. I'd always wanted to go back and always assumed I would but never found enough impetus to make a trip there a priority. My childhood visit to El Cap was folded in fond memories of a year living in America – my parents had done an exchange, swapping houses and jobs for a year – and I'd never cared much for altering the good memories with a view through adult eyes.

But unexpectedly there was impetus now. It was ten months after returning from Greenland and Andy and I met up.

"So, what about climbing El Cap?" he'd suggested and because it was the second time he'd mentioned it and because of the expression on his face – he was serious – and because my life had gone topsy turvy – so why not – the idea lost all its flippancy.

El Capitan is aptly named. It's a natural wonder of the world, a giant granite wall set deep in the Yosemite Valley in California. The valley was carved by glaciers, with some of the highest and steepest rock walls in the world. El Cap diminishes them all though. It stands tall above the rest, a stunning drape of rock, 'the Captain'. In my memory it was an enchanted place, a kind of fairytale castle except not a castle at all. It was appealing to return there and to be one of those dots on the wall with superhuman powers. Yet it was a stupendously stupid idea.

"There's no way I could do it" I retorted.

"Maybe. But let's have a go at climbing a tree" he grinned "just to see how it feels."

I felt nervous.

I felt intrigued.

What if I could?

How would it be to feel the fur of a rope in my palm again? The sensation of a cold metal belay device in my hand? The rattle of a harness racked with gear? To have a rope coiled around my neck?

I felt excited enough to agree to try. We met up near Edinburgh, a rough halfway between my home in Inverness and his in Sheffield.

"There's a park near the Forth Road Bridge. Just on the north side" I suggested. I'd kayaked from there a few summers before, memorable because friends from Aberdeen had driven down with two sea kayaks tied to the roof of a fancy sports car. The kayaks were way longer than the car and the angle of the roof meant they sat like rockets waiting to be launched. It had looked as dangerous as it did ridiculous but somehow it had all gone smoothly, apart from a fraught rescue when my friend capsized in the chop of the Firth of Forth.

The daffodils were out, Spring just starting to struggle through – they weren't out in Inverness yet – and we stood in a cold breeze looking across the grassland towards the Firth.

"We need to find a good tree" Andy said as he strode purposefully away towards the wooded edge of the park. I would come to know his resolute stride better than I realised.

I followed slowly with the effort of wheeling through mossy grass, happy when he stopped having found a suitable tree with a big thick protruding branch and plenty of space beneath it. As I looked up at the twisted gnarl of the tree and at the rope hung over it, the idea of climbing again seemed more insane than ever. It was fourteen years since the last time I'd climbed.

And fallen.

Andy emptied his rucksack and I bent down to look. Familiar yet forgotten sounds and sensations triggered memories that I couldn't place. It made me think of someone looking back at their life, at the objects in a trunk of old belongings left to go dusty in a loft. Andy threw a thick rope over the branch and tied one end off to the base of the tree, the rope dangling free for thirty feet.

I struggled to remember what to do with the ropes and climbing gear, some of which I'd never even used before. Andy clamped the teeth of a shiny piece of gear onto the rope, and showed me how it moved up the rope smoothly but gripped when you pulled down.

"So this is jumaring" he explained. "One of these is attached to your waist, and one is for your hands. Move one up, then hang on it while you move the other and you can shunt yourself up the rope."

He made it sound simple. As I listened, I thought how I'd never even jumared when I could walk.

The explanation over, it was time to slip into the harness. 'Slip' doesn't describe it well – that's what I did when I could simply step into it and slide it easily up my legs and over my hips before clasping it tight around my waist. Now it was more of a wrestle. I picked one foot up at a time and gently fed each through the respective harness leg loop. Getting it as far as just above my knees was easy enough but for the rest I had to lift myself up whilst Andy yanked the webbing into position, careful not to twist it into a tangle beneath my bum. Mindful of the risk of pressure sores, I asked him to insert some bits of foam between my skin and the rough strapping. The whole procedure of getting the harness on took more than twenty minutes. In the past it took less than two.

There was another twenty minutes fiddling with slings to set up the hauling system, but at last we were ready to climb. If you could call it climbing. I just had thirty feet to pull myself up the rope.

I pushed the blue jumar clamp up the rope, the rope sliding through smoothly and it locked down when I pulled. I tried to do a pull-up and lifted out of my chair, the rope sliding through another gold coloured jumar on my harness as my body lifted. I relaxed my arms and found I was suspended a few inches off my seat by the gold jumar. I slipped the blue jumar up and repeated the operation, lifting a few inches at a time. I quickly realised it would be no speedy affair.

It took at least half an hour to get myself suspended part-way up the tree. It was hard. Bicep-burningly hard and it felt uncomfortable. The tape of the climbing harness cut into my legs and although I couldn't feel it, it was pinching down on my flow of blood.

"People have died hanging in harnesses you know" Andy informed me, doing nothing to reassure. "They hang too long and toxins build up in their leg and when they stand up again the toxins hit their heart and that's it."

"Well at least I can't stand up."

"If we climb El Cap, we should make sure you don't hang too long though" he said, looking up with a concerned expression.

People walking their dogs through the parkland glanced across, surely wondering what was going on, an empty wheelchair, a woman twisted up in ropes hanging from the tree. It looked like some form of torture.

That's kind of how it felt.

I reached my high point when the rope ran out around the giant branch. I looked beyond the park, across the Firth of Forth, at the ships that sailed beneath the railway bridge and its curtains of red iron. I noticed the current on the water and the whitecaps that blew up with the easterly wind. It was special, to have a perspective I didn't normally get. It was nice to be up there and to have a view.

In that moment and with that view, I felt a flicker of enthusiasm for climbing El Cap. It would be good to escape the world of 'short-arse' and a novelty to be up high. I didn't quite grasp just how high that would be.

It was a few months after the shenanigans up the tree when I was invited to an event in California, *No Barriers*. It was a practical sort of conference, bringing together technology, disability and outdoor adventure – the ethos to help encourage and enable people with disabilities to access the outdoors. The organisers had invited me to give a talk about crossing Greenland.

One of the *No Barriers* team is the pioneer of paraplegic rock-climbing. Mark Wellman was a park ranger before a stumble in the mountains paralysed him. A few years later, he climbed El Cap, the first paraplegic to do it. I'd read his book about it a long time before, called *Climbing Back*. Someone had given it me to read during the long months of hospital but it hadn't been what I'd wanted just then. It had all been too close and too painful.

It was lucky for me that Mark was running a workshop on 'wheelchair climbing' so I signed up to join him, eager to learn what I could.

We gathered at a road-cut. The view was great but the constant stream of four-wheel-drives growling by reminded me we weren't in the wilds but in the gas-guzzling US of A. A bunch of guys with vein shot arms waited their turn. Some were in wheelchairs, others the walking wounded. The atmosphere was thick with testosterone as guys with rippling muscles and sculpted bodies took turns to pull effortlessly up the dangling rope. I squinted up at them, high up and closer to the beautiful blue sky and hoped I'd get up there as easily as them. The sun baked down on us and the hours seemed slow but at last the queue shrank and my turn came around.

It took ages to get into the heavy-duty harness, more like a giant nappy, trousers with a big padded bum. It was quite a contrast to the usual thong-like harness that regular climbers use. Mark had designed them especially for the job, with straps and velcro galore to help secure them to the legs, and an integral belt to tie the rope into. They would distribute the pressure, so I wouldn't die hanging or risk getting sores where the harness straps would otherwise dig in.

Tied into the rope, I pulled in the stretch until the tension came on and I was ready to leave the ground. On my first big effort I felt the blood surge to my head and biceps.

"Grrrrrr" I even made a growl of effort to match, but I didn't even budge an inch. The second effort I tried even harder.

"Grrrrrrrrr." The noise I made even surprised me, the kind of grunting that I usually heard from the beefy eastern Europeans in the gym.

My bum lifted off the ground. I swung sideways and my backside skimmed over the boulders. Again and again I exploded with effort but my muscles just couldn't pull me more than a few centimetres at a time. The technique needed what I didn't possess, pure power, my muscles more accustomed to steady endurance. Sweat poured from my forehead and grit ran into my eyes but I was determined to keep going, to get to the high point up in the shade of the overhangs. Five minutes later, the chest harness cut into my underarms, which by then quivered like jelly. Depressingly, I was still suspended only a few metres from the ground. I felt disheartened. I looked down to the group below, eager for some hints on how I could improve my technique.

"If you're going to climb El Cap, you're gonna have to eat less chocolate or go to the gym." Mark passed his verdict, and the queue was getting longer.

My time was up.

On the way home, I stared out through the plane window. The Rocky Mountains poked out above a thin layer of cloud. In the years closely following my accident, a view like that would have drawn my thoughts to memories of climbing tainted with sadness at what couldn't be anymore. Now the sight of the rocky peaks drew my mind to climbing again, except this time to the possibility instead of the impossibility.

The possibility existed and yet it felt impossible for me. I'd been so slow. I'd been too weak. But someone else had done it, so why couldn't I? I didn't like to fail. I especially didn't like to fail where others hadn't.

Back home, I phoned Andy.

"I'm just not sure if I can do it" I confessed. "I was a complete weed. Even if I live at the gym I don't think I'll get strong enough. And he said I should eat less chocolate, but I don't eat that much anyway…do I?"

21. IS IT WORTH IT?

Andy was having none of it. Stubborn and positive, he insisted we should try again.

"We just need to put a pulley in the system" he suggested, "there's no point in beasting yourself if you don't have to."

Mark Wellman had hauled himself up El Cap doing 'neat' pull-ups, kind of like drinking whisky without the water. With the rope running through pulleys I'd need less effort to pull my weight. I'd make less progress with each pull but my muscles wouldn't get so pumped from over-exertion.

"If you're super strong you might manage twenty straight pull-ups but how will you feel on the four thousandth pull-up? By adding two pulleys you'll reduce the effort and the distance, meaning you'll need to do double the pull-ups but you'll go faster in the end." Andy convinced me.

I agreed that overall it probably wouldn't be slower, and a lot easier than grunting my way up the wall with my full body weight.

We met again at a climbing wall in Aberdeen and Andy produced his pulleys and the new harness. "So you reckon a parapenting harness is safe for climbing?" I asked Andy as he unfolded what looked like a padded seat rather than a normal harness. It had been kindly donated by a parapenting instructor in the Lake District. "Check out the colour" he laughed at the bright pink fabric. "Just try and ignore the high mortality rate in paragliding. With a climbing harness on top for extra safety it'll be fine."

Rigged up I started up the rope again, only this time with much less effort. It wasn't easy to get into a rhythm but soon I was inching up the wall slowly but methodically.

"If you see El Cap as a kilometre high wall you'll never get up it. But if you just climb it an inch at a time then you can do it" Andy called up to me, trying over hard to be motivating.

In less than twenty minutes I was at the top of the wall. I could finally grasp the possibility that I could do it. The next step would be climbing outdoors on real rock.

Kilnsey Crag is an overhanging wall of limestone in the Yorkshire Dales. It's too hard for a climber of the standard I'd once been, but was super steep so perfect training for jumaring. I wanted to keep things low-key, keen not to stray into the sensitive subject of climbing with my Mum and Dad. That plan didn't work out. Yorkshire Television got wind of our intention to climb and wanted to film it for a series called 'Is It Worth It?'. Andy called on his friend Ian Parnell to lead the climb so that he could second whilst climbing alongside me. He would encourage me to haul myself up the rope that Ian would dangle from the hood of the overhang. I had the feeling again, of finding myself in the thick of something that was all someone else's idea. I was being swept along.

The idea of climbing again was never mine. It was all Andy's and as a consequence, climbing Kilnsey Crag and being filmed had just kind of happened. On one side there was Andy, imagining himself in my shoes, eager to help where he'd hope someone would help him if circumstances were reversed. On the other side was Charlotte, the TV producer, looking for a good angle. I was just the pawn in the middle, happy for the novelty and for a chance to try something I thought I'd never do again but also revisiting things I wasn't sure I wanted to.

The morning of the climb arrived. Charlotte and her small crew arrived at my parent's house. My Mum and Dad looked apprehensive as the crew began interviewing them, digging into their feelings about me going climbing again. They spoke positive words and smiled for the camera but I could see beneath it all that it wasn't easy. I thought of the torment they'd been through and felt bad that it was all being stirred up again by the prospect of me going back to the rock.

I felt guilty.

I justified it with talk of how safe it would be and of the extra ropes we'd use, and how experienced Andy and Ian were.

I watched my Mum and Dad's faces as we ate breakfast, my guilt intense though I tried not to let on. There was little point as we were going anyway. Our spoons clinked on cereal bowls and the blackened toast turned the kitchen

My first attempt at climbing since being paralysed. Despite a lot of effort I was barely clear of the ground. "Eat less chocolate and go to the gym" was the recommended antidote! KAREN DARKE COLLECTION

smoky, and there was a jolly pretence about us all. Underneath it though, I saw their fear but couldn't face it, because I felt it too. Who was I to do this to them but then who would I be if I didn't?

They waved goodbye as we reversed from the driveway, and my Dad shouted after us "Be careful!", just as he had a hundred times before. I was a teenager again, excited to be off on another climbing adventure, saying "yeah, yeah" to his concern, feeling the déjà vu. We drove from the busy West Yorkshire valleys to the space of the Dales, and as we went I understood that their dilemma was the same as my own. How can we let ourselves be free to take risks, to explore and discover but to love ourselves enough not to cross a line into stupidity and to pay the ultimate price for it. Could I do that yet?

The gentle roll of the Dales and scattering of grazing sheep calmed my nerves. For right or wrong, stubborn or stupid, my unending need to explore took us to the base of Kilnsey Crag.

It dripped like I remembered it always did, water falling like a fine curtain from the lip of land at its top. It's an impressive knobbly wall of limestone, patterned with moss. It looked overhanging enough to make me glance at Ian's arms. Could he climb it?

Within an hour of arriving, Ian cruised up the crag like it was covered in step ladders, and we heard "Safe!" echo down from the overhangs. Instead of the fancy harness pants I'd used at the California road-cut, I put on my parapente harness, big and padded like an armchair, super comfy and glowing pink. (A few years later, Major Phil Packer would be offered the same harness for his attempt on El Cap, and refuse it for being girly pink, far too un-cool for a military man!). A regular climbing harness went over the top for extra safety. I tied the rope into both, sifting my memory banks for climbing knots, realising how rusty I was and how nervous that made me feel, like a pilot that hadn't flown for fifteen years. I was trusting my life entirely to Andy and Ian but then wasn't that always the way with climbing? It demanded the ultimate trust.

Andy climbed up alongside me, pacing himself to match me, calling encouragement across the short stretch of limestone between us. His words spurred me on and distracted me from fear and when I paused, I looked out through the wet curtain at the soft green folds of the hills and thought how beautiful it was, how peaceful, how strange to be climbing on Kilnsey Crag. If I'd let myself, I might have shed a happy tear.

It was good to be high again.

It was good to have a view.

And it was good to be on an adventure with friends.

The pulleys made things easier, more an act of endurance than strength. It wasn't the same artery-exploding effort of my American experience and Charlotte and the cameraman gradually became midgets as we climbed upwards towards the Gods. They wanted drama of course, tears and jeers for the footage. I wondered if they'd picked the wrong person to film; apparently I was an emotionless sort of child, showed no huge highs and lows.

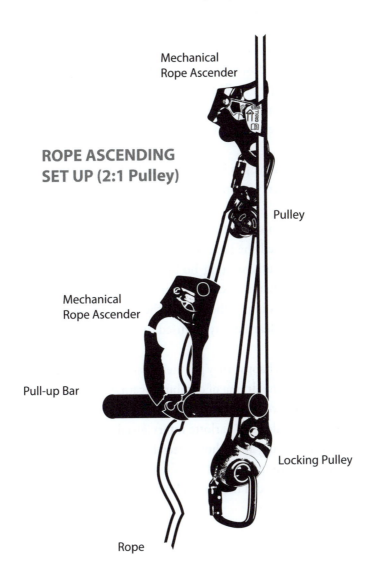

ROPE ASCENDING SET UP (2:1 Pulley)

Mechanical Rope Ascender

Pulley

Mechanical Rope Ascender

Pull-up Bar

Locking Pulley

Rope

At last I shunted up beside Ian, hanging in the shelter of the overhang and Andy scrambled up into the huddle too. I whooped a 'Woohoo!' because it was the end of the rope, a top of sorts and I felt I should. It was special to be there and I felt far from emotionless but I heard the effort in my 'woohoo' and knew I was performing for the camera, for the effort of getting there and for the guilt.

Ian abseiled down first and was back on the ground within minutes, whilst Andy fiddled with slings at the belay point and jogged my memory on how to descend safely. The metal of the belay device was cold on my fingers, the gadget like none I'd used before, a different generation of shiny anodised gear. I handled it with uncertainty. Arrows and labels explaining how to use it made little sense. Andy had to rig it up and I felt stupid for being there and not knowing how to get down. When the time came, I inspected the drop below and flicked the rope that I'd abseil down. Checking the rope below was a habit I hadn't lost, to make sure its length ran free. The rope snaked briefly beneath me, then stopped. There was a split second of silence as our brains registered the situation.

"Shit!" I met Andy's eyes as he swore and the horror hit us. The rope I was about to abseil down was only five metres long, just the tail of the knot that Ian had tied.

It was another near miss, another great adventure, the kind that would've once been told and embellished over drinks at a pub. Only now there wasn't the foolhardiness of youth or gung-ho bravado. I'd nearly died once and had more near misses than I cared to remember. I didn't want it again. The reality of what we were doing, of the risks, of the potential for disaster burned deeper into me and the fear I always refused to back down from gained the upper hand.

The camera crew was happy. They got their drama in just the right measure and I got a measure of the drama of climbing again.

We did some more 'woohooing' at the bottom, and shared a bottle of beer the crew had brought along. Charlotte interviewed me and asked me 'Is it worth it?' I said something about how special it was to be back on the rock, about how you can't live in fear. But I was living in fear. The incident at the top had scared me and so did the possibility of climbing El Cap.

Pulling up into the roof of Kilnsey Crag, Yorkshire. With a pulley system in the ropes the job of hauling up was much easier than 'neat pull-ups'. IAN PARNELL

22. DOUBLE POSITIVE

Ilike people who believe that anything is possible. They don't put extra obstacles in the way of challenge but somehow diminish the size of those that already exist. They see opportunity instead of disaster and their glass is half-full not half-empty. When the shit really hits the fan, they can still find humour – it's a life saver – and shadows of doubt either don't exist or don't get mentioned, just tossed to the side as worthless. They behave as if all is well. They believe that all will come good and somehow it does.

I was attracted to Andy for all of these reasons.

The greater the challenge, the more he seems to enjoy it. Maybe that's why Andy and I seem to work. There's nothing easy about living with someone who gets around in a wheelchair. The world isn't designed for people that can't walk (although in the years I've been paralysed I've seen the urban world get more and more accessible), so it's a pleasure to be with someone who seems to thrive when things get difficult. 'Challenge' should be my middle name, and it seems like we are both attracted to it. Maybe it comes from growing up in Yorkshire. No doubt it goes with climbing mountains.

To say that Andy believes things are possible is wrong as he doesn't have to believe. He just doesn't doubt. He gets on and does it. We were cycling together one day and came to a line of giant boulders blocking the road ahead. The gaps between the boulders were too narrow for my handbike to fit through. Andy began trying to shift a boulder that was at least twice his size, and I'm sure more than twice his weight.

"Don't be mad" I called over to him above the wind, "It's massive. Watch you don't hurt your back!" It seemed ridiculous to even try to move such a mass of solid rock.

He didn't answer, but next thing he was wielding a long metal rod he found in some rubble at the side of the road, and prised it under the boulder.

"What are you doing?" I called over, even though it was obvious.

He was silent, which roughly translates as "Don't ask stupid questions. I know it looks mad but just watch."

Sure enough, the boulder nudged sideways. With another five minutes of effort and levering, the gap widened right up. I rode my bike between the boulders.

"Better than a dead end" he concluded.

As we cycled along, I thought how his lack of doubt and sheer physical strength must to be the ingredients that have allowed him to climb hard and stay alive. It's definitely not been down to fitness or good planning!

It was being stubborn and unwilling to give in that led me into falling off the cliff and hence to life in a wheelchair. Despite all the obvious signs that I should have backed down and let someone else take the lead, I pushed on, positive and determined that I could do it. However, the same traits that got me into trouble mean that I now refuse to let being paralysed stop me. I won't give in to the fear that it could. That normally means I see opportunity in everything and say yes to just about anything.

After Kilnsey Crag, Andy suggested we go climbing together again – we needed more practice if we were to consider El Capitan. Uncharacteristically, I wavered at his suggestion and there were two good reasons why.

The first was that if there's something I remember from school maths it's that a positive and a negative together make a negative and a positive and a positive together make an even bigger positive. A double positive has to be good most of the time but Andy and I together can be a lot of positive. I recognised that our combined stubbornness and unwillingness to give in is a potential formula for misadventure. If we went climbing together again, both 'woohooing' about how good it would be or pushing on regardless, we could get ourselves into a lot of trouble.

The second reason I wavered was simple. I'd taken the wrong decision once and because of it put myself in a wheelchair. As a result, I didn't trust myself.

I didn't know if I could make the right decisions for myself on a rock-face. It went deeper than that too but that would be venturing into the realms of self-psycho-analysis and it's suffice to say that my judgement hadn't always served me well. On top of all that, Andy and I had become closer and in the early days of our relationship it felt like a lot of pressure to put ourselves under.

And so I wavered.

If we were serious about El Cap though, we did need to try something a bit harder. I didn't want to get there and find I just wasn't made of the 'right stuff'. Andy's way of seeing difficult things as easy and his effusing positivity worked to end my wavering. The BBC Scotland 'Adventure Show' also wanted to film me climbing something – which felt a bit weird given it was all so experimental and me so unsure – but the two things seemed as if they might work. The crew could act as back-up if something went wrong and having more people around might help ease my fear.

The Old Man of Stoer is a sea stack on the west coast of Scotland. It leans like the tower of Pisa, two hundred feet high, a precarious stack of rock broken away from the cliffs and separated from the mainland by a channel of water. It's an exposed, elemental sort of place. Waves that have travelled the Atlantic crash at its base, wind whistles through the gullies around it, seabird guano is dribbled down its black wet faces. It's a tower that the next storm will weather a little smaller, gradually weaker, until one day it will disappear with an almighty crash and be swallowed up by the waves.

The Old Man is a difficult place to access in the best of circumstances. Climbers reach its base by scrambling down the cliffs from the mainland then strip off to swim across. Our plan, the only feasible one we could think of, was to reach it by sea. The tides were strong and powerful around the Point of Stoer, but if we timed it right, we might be able to kayak around and reach the base of the sea stack.

It was a calm summer's morning as we drove northwest from our campsite, the film crew promising to be at the Old Man when we got there. The dramatic skyline of mountains invited us onwards, promising adventure. The journey got slower as the roads became smaller, with cattle grids and sheep ambling at the roadside. I felt a flicker of nerves as we drove down the hill, grass green and short like velvet, into the village of Stoer. We parked as close to the sea as we could.

It was nearly time for action.

As was usual we'd made life harder for ourselves by overdoing it the previous day, an easy paddle from the campsite in Ullapool turning into an epic. Once we'd got out there the water was so calm that it merged with the sky, the Summer Isles had glistened on the horizon as if hanging there like clouds and we couldn't help ourselves. Almost fifty kilometres later, weary and hungry because Andy had dropped the banana cake overboard, we'd limped back towards the campsite. With the tide against us each hour had seemed to pass more quickly and the cluster of lights in Ullapool had never seemed to get closer. We'd missed our meeting with the film crew and we'd missed dinner. We had finally landed on the beach not long before midnight just in time for a last order at the campsite curry house. The camera crew had suggested we ditch the attempt on the Old Man given we'd overstretched ourselves that day but we didn't want to let them down and insisted we'd be okay.

"It's only sixty metres" we joked. "How hard can it be?"

Ah, bravado. It would only get us into trouble in the long run.

By the village of Stoer, the sea was still glassy in the bay and it was hard to imagine the rougher water that might be smashing onto the cliffs around the point. There was the usual faff involved with any kayaking trip, not least the trauma of wriggling into a dry suit – at least it was easier than the wrestling match of a wetsuit – before we were ready to launch.

Andy was still quite new to kayaking and not so confident in his balance. Almost as soon as we were afloat, he said he felt unstable. Minutes later, I watched him land on a beach.

"What you doing?" I called over, but there was his characteristic silent response meaning 'don't ask, just watch me'. He crouched over his kayak and began loading the hatches with small boulders from the beach.

"I won't be able to right you if you go over with all those rocks in there!" I shouted, but he was undeterred. His brow furrowed deeper as he continued loading the rocks in.

When we began paddling again, I tensed as our kayaks lifted and fell with the roll of swell. I could feel the adrenaline in my arms and my fingers tingling. We kayaked across a wide bay, my mood matching the murkiness of the sea, deep green in the shade of the wet cliffs. It felt like we were beginning something that might end badly and that we were taking on more than we could or should. I concentrated hard knowing that one capsize would be the end of the whole thing. It would be a cold swim even in dry suits and another calm forecast could be weeks or months away. Something about our little adventure felt different from ever before. I felt cautious, nervous, vulnerable.

Was I pushing too hard again?

Was this really a good idea?

I wondered as the swell took us up and down what had changed.

I thought about the double positive thing we had going. Andy had enough confidence for two of us. I found myself asking *What if? Are we taking things too far?* They were questions I wasn't used to considering. I realised I was becoming the cautionary negative voice, watching out for us but I worried that if neither of us asked those difficult questions, we'd get ourselves into trouble.

A while longer and we emerged from the shadow of the cliffs. The bright red and orange of our kayaks looked cheerful as the sun glinted onto us briefly. It reminded me it was summer and that this wasn't necessarily so serious.

It was meant to be fun.

We kayaked cautiously towards the point. I was preoccupied with what lay in store around the corner. *Would there be a raging tidal race? Standing waves?* I'd only kayaked in a tidal race once and will never know how I stayed afloat. I'd been gripped by terror for the five minutes I was stuck in it and had sworn never to get into one again. There were some skills you could work on and get better at but balancing in white water isn't one of them when you're a weeble from the chest down.

As we approached the point I noticed how tired I felt, the muscles on my shoulder tops screaming after the effort of the previous day.

Paddling towards the Old Man, the solid cliffs on our left ran out and became more broken and their aspect changed to face northwest. I'd been concentrating hard to match the map to the coastline but it was hard to tell exactly where we were. Without noticing we'd paddled further than I thought, around the point and past the crux. There was no tidal race. We'd done it! My hands relaxed on the paddle with relief.

Andy seemed disappointed.

It hadn't been tough enough.

We'd timed it well. There was no rip tide, no standing waves. We paddled obstacle-free into the channel that led to the Old Man of Stoer. I stopped paddling as it came into view.

It seemed higher than sixty metres.
It towered above us.
It looked very black.
It felt very intimidating.
Andy grinned.

I felt myself waver again.

The ominous feeling I'd woken with intensified as we approached the base of the stack. I couldn't seem to shift it, despite the clearing sky, calm sea and the cheery voices of a few strategically positioned camera crew from the BBC *Adventure Show*.

At the base of the Old Man a shelf of rock sloped out towards the open sea. It was the only real place to land, but as the waves swept us onto it I felt my heart leap into my head. The rock was jagged and sharp and I cringed for the kayaks as we scraped to a stop, glad they were plastic not fibreglass.

We were in the shadow of the stack, its black rock threatening. The waves broke around us, leaving a tidemark of white foam. I felt my heart beat faster. This was it. I was going climbing again, not just in a tree or by a roadside. This was real.

A real adventure with real danger.

My plan was to bum-shuffle from the kayak to the start of the climb – my usual means of getting around without a wheelchair – but the rock would have grated my backside to shreds. One puncture or one small patch of broken skin in the wrong place could be the beginning of the end for someone in my position. I've met people with plate-size sores on their bums, grounded in hospital for a year or longer. At best a bad pressure sore would mean weeks or months in bed, at worst a serious infection that could lead to death.

I was grateful for Andy's strength as he piggy-backed me across the sharp stuff to a smoother mantel of rock where we could begin climbing. His friend Paul Tattersal had hiked in earlier in the day and led the route up the Old Man already. The rope he'd placed snaked down from above and I watched it swing in the breeze as Andy scrambled around to reach it.

The route I'd take wasn't really a route, more a line through the void beneath the dark overhanging face of the Old Man, where the rope now dangled. I felt helpless, a passenger along for the ride but not part of the team, my skill and confidence eroded after years away from climbing and the scar left from falling. I sat watching but without really watching, my mind taking it all in; the white froth of breaking waves, the gurgle as swell rushed into the hollows around us, seabirds circling around the stack as if it were prey, an inquisitive seal sneaking a look at the big black salty rock that poked out of the sea. Close up it looked more like a lopsided dribble tower – the kind you make on the beach as a kid – than a sturdy stack of weathered sandstone.

As I looked up I wondered if my arms had it in them.

It should have been obvious but I realised like a slap to the face that the last time I'd been in this situation had been fifteen years ago.

Another sea cliff.

Another sunny day, excited to climb.

A day that ended badly.

It was no wonder it felt ominous. All the ingredients of my accident were there; an overhanging cliff, the sea crashing beneath, climbing, a traverse and a swinging rope. It disturbed memories that I'd buried deep and didn't want to uncover.

I shuffled towards the end of the ledge, shuttling a gel seat and a neoprene spray skirt from the kayak beneath me, careful not to catch my bum on anything sharp. I pulled in the slack rope, not daring to look down over the edge and into the murky sea below. I began clipping myself into the system; two jumars, a pulley, a belay device, slings and extenders, two ropes. It was a colourful jumble of gadgets and as I fastened things together, I checked and checked again, doubting myself until I asked Andy to check everything was right too.

Finally there was no delaying it anymore.

"Take in tight!" I called up the tower to Paul who had me on belay.

"Got me tight?" I asked Andy more quietly, trying to hide the panic in my voice. He stood close by, using a second rope to lower me out sideways.

"Yep. Go on, I've got you" he reassured – this time I knew he did. I took the plunge and launched from the edge, closing my eyes as I felt the initial lurch. Tentatively opening them again, I took it all in.

Air.

Space.

Too much air and space.

As Andy lowered me steadily out, the rope was jerky. I felt myself tense and adrenaline surge through me.

My fingers felt dizzy.

Dizzy with fear. Dizzy with the realisation that I was climbing again. Sort of.

"Shit, I'm climbing again!" I said quietly to myself, but felt swamped by the experience. Everything seemed intensified. The slow lower out seemed to be a treacherous swing beneath the world's largest overhang, the gentle lap of the sea below seemed an abyss of swirling currents, the tower above looked even taller than El Capitan. There was a terrifying twang as the rope freed from a snare on a protruding edge above and I lurched downwards.

A small cry of terror left me.

I felt so vulnerable, my life trusted in a rope passing over sharp rocks, a single rope not even as thick as my finger.

How did I ever do this? I wondered, amazed at how once it hadn't bothered me to hang from a single rope over the edge of a cliff. It seemed like madness or suicide to swing like a monkey on something not much thicker than string that ran so close to rocks as sharp as knives.

"You're okay. Come on, start climbing!" Andy brought me back into the moment.

Come on girl, you can do it. Voices in my head talked me into action.

Climbing has a power to quiet all those voices in your head. Fortunately in that moment, it did.

By the time I began pulling on the jumars and inching up the rope, my head had quietened. The demand to concentrate took away the fear and doubt, until there was nothing except my hands on the rope, my focus so sharp that I noticed the pattern of its weave, its slightly furred texture – the rope far from new and I hoped it hadn't taken any falls, – the cold metal of the jumars, a piece of duct tape that curled and was stuck with dirt, the flash of yellow bike grips that covered the pull-up bar. All that existed was the moment and each next small thing I needed to do to stay safe and move upwards. I hypnotised myself with the rhythm; sliding one jumar up, pulling myself on it so the second jumar at my waist slid up too, then resting before repeating it all again. Each pull-up gave me about ten centimetres of progress but I didn't think or notice how slow I moved.

I was sucked into the detail of climbing.

Slide up, pull, slide up the other jumar.
Slide up, pull, slide up the other jumar.

Nothing distracted me. There was a job to do, a length of rope to cover as quickly as I could. Time disappeared. At one point I noticed the wind. It seemed to be getting stronger. I looked down at the sea, whiter than before and a tug of angst nagged at me.

You have to get out of here too.
Then the focus returned.
Slide up, pull, slide up the other jumar.

Perhaps three-quarters of the way up, the overhang subsided enough that I could finally touch the rock and my hips dragged against its rough crystals. They grated pink fabric from my harness and I was glad it wasn't my skin. The touch of cold rock triggered a flood of associations. Nothing specific, just feelings of being in mountains, big spaces and endless air, laughing with friends about reaching some crazy high place, connection to something bigger and brighter than 'normal' life could offer. It awakened in me memories of why I did it; fingers reading the rock like Braille, the ballet between body and stone, problem-solving like Sudoku could never be, survival like modern living and its comforts just isn't.

But swinging in space on the end of the rope, I could barely touch the rock and it wasn't quite the same. It was never about adrenaline or rope work, gathering fancy racks of gear or pushing the grade. It was as simple as the touch of the rock.

I reached up to a ledge, slimy and wet. Something rustled and I jumped, pulled back and jerked onto the jumars. The rope bounced and my heart beat double. My focus was broken and I felt my fear rise again. My fingers were trembling.

"It's a Fulmar's nest!" Paul's voice carried down on the wind.

I hung for a while to let my shakes calm down. I considered a face-to-face encounter with a protective mother Fulmar. It seemed bad to disturb them and I wondered if they'd be more startled by me than I was by them. If only they knew what a threat I wasn't, that their slightest yelp would be enough to break me. I looked for an alternative route but the vertical hang of the rope meant there was one route only, directly up. I was powerless to do anything except scrape on past them. I hoped the mother Fulmar wouldn't try to peck my eye or gouge a chunk from my bum with its beak.

My nerves were so on edge from climbing, that passing the Fulmars I felt like Frodo passing through the Gates of Mordor!

The Fulmars cried out as I wrestled by and I cried too, my silent tears dripping into their nest. I got past them with my eyes and backside intact.

The final haul was tough, the overhang gone and the pull-ups hard with the friction of the sandstone. The summit wasn't too soon coming. When the rope finally ran out at Paul's feet, he reached down and pulled me over the edge, and I let out a small yelp as my shoulder wrenched and my torso twisted.

I was face down, on top of the Old Man.

Exhausted and relieved.

"I am never, ever, going climbing again" I stated, with assertiveness in my voice that hadn't been there all day.

And I meant it.

Now more than ever I knew I couldn't climb El Cap. Unlike Greenland and all my other trips, this time I knew I couldn't do it. The problem wasn't my broken body but my broken mind.

I wanted to get back down on the ground and never leave it again.

23. SUPERABLED

The morning after the Old Man I was tired and dehydrated, puffy-eyed from lack of sleep. Muscles ached that I'd forgotten existed. It was a feeling I liked. It was satisfying, knowing that the soreness was a legacy of two great days out. It gave me the sense of having done something special, of pulling something off against the odds. Nothing else gave a feeling like it.

The day had been topped off by the kayak trip back from the Old Man. There'd been a strong northerly wind and I'd worried about the tides around the point back towards the village of Stoer.

"Give us the keys and one of us can drive your car round to the southerly beach" one of the camera crew offered. With a large swell and the occasional breaking wave to contend with, his offer was hard to refuse. A tailwind would be a lot easier.

By the time we'd left the Old Man, the wind had died back a little and the swell was rolling and hypnotic.

"I can't believe we did it" I confessed to Andy as I felt the stress of the day ebb away.

"El Cap here we come" he replied. It was only a few hours before that I'd declared I'd never climb again. I chose to ignore him.

I concentrated on staying upright.

I focused on my paddle cleanly slicing the water.

I looked at the horizon.

I boxed the thought of El Cap away.

The June sun glinted off our paddle blades. As the evening drew in and the horizon got more orange, a pod of dolphins magically appeared and swam alongside us. The drama of the day sank with the sun and as I looked towards the reddening horizon, Andy and his kayak a black silhouette against a backdrop of playing dolphins, I felt still inside. Satisfied.

It's okay. You did it. And everything is okay. A voice within me muttered.

We would soon land on the beach and it would almost be dark. The adventure would be over and the need to do anything would vanish for a while.

For a day or two, there would be a quiet space.

∾

Lying in the tent the next morning I looked out at the sea, tired and thoughtful. I dragged my thoughts back to the present, rubbing my shoulders to help them into action. I burned with the thirst of dehydration so climbed up into my chair to go in search of water, just as the film crew arrived. We hadn't even begun breakfast. They wanted to interview us for the feature about climbing The Old Man. It would be aired on the 'Adventure Show' in the next few weeks.

Andy went first and made lots of positive statements; "Amazing, great, glad we did it", all the noises that viewers of the Adventure Show probably wanted to hear. He said how if he were in the same position as me, he'd hope that someone would do the same for him. He meant help him have some crazy adventures again, the kind that are harder to have when you can't walk.

"There's just so many things you can't do and places you can't go when you're paralysed" he said to the camera.

I found his words hard to hear. They were a reminder of my limitations and emphasised how he was helping me. I needed help but I didn't want help. I wished I could climb like anyone else. He didn't mean it to sound that way but it made me wonder if I should only do things that I could do on my own. For adventures in the wilderness I had to rely on help, feel grateful, feel helpless at times and give up some of the independence that mattered to me so much to me.

Why do you not like being helped? my voice inside asked. I contemplated it for a while.

I like to be independent. I don't like to put people out. I don't like to be reminded of my shortcomings. I don't want to feel weak. I don't want to be reminded of my disability. I want to feel able. Capable. Strong.

Later, I looked out over the bay again at the calm, grey-sky scene and thought of an American guy I'd met. Mike was paralysed from the neck down in a diving accident. He could still move his arms though they were a little weaker than normal.

"I want to be superabled" he'd told me.

He'd always been sporty but now he was a triathlete – he'd completed in an impressive list of marathons and ironman races. He must have an iron will to drive him on. By striving to do more he said he combated his feeling of being disabled. Maybe I was cut from the same cloth, though I suspected I'd still be striving to climb high and run far regardless of being paralysed or not.

I try to stay strong. I learnt it from my Mum – putting on a brave face when things get hard. She's had it hard when it comes to her health but when you ask her how she is, she only ever says "Okay" or at worst, "Fine thanks."

On the Old Man, spinning above the sea, I'd tried to be strong but it had taken me to the edge. Andy had seen it in my eyes and my trembling hands. I'd felt the fear like a lump of lead and it had seeped out in my private tears. The sea, the rock, the rope and climbers; they'd all triggered my pulse to quicken and my head to thump. The adrenaline had kept me moving but inside I'd felt motionless, almost as paralysed as my paralysed body.

The climb had ripped the scab off a deep wound. It had exposed something messy that I hardly dared look at. It was about being vulnerable. It was about being human.

When it was my turn to talk to camera, I also talked about how great it had been. "It was crazy but good to be climbing again. I was scared, but it was worth it." I said stuff like that because it was easier that way, to put on the brave face and soldier onwards, the 'have a nice day and don't give too much away' style that so many of us have because we're too scared to admit how we really feel or too busy to notice or because we don't want to bother someone.

I had noticed how I felt but I wasn't ready to try and explain it to a camera.

It wasn't a surprise when the final cut of film showed the 'oohs' and 'aahs' of a great day outdoors and me at the top of the Old Man saying "Amazing, great, scary…" but no sign of my words, "I'm never, ever, going climbing again."

When the film crew had gone we packed up and drove home. We'd had the best of it. The fishing boats rocked in a roughening sea and the rain settled in over the mountains as we drove towards them, the windscreen wipers on their fastest setting but still not quick enough.

"So what do you think about El Cap now?" Andy ventured.

"Hmmm. Yesterday was good practice," I tried to be positive but who was I kidding. I could hear the waver in my voice. It was a crazy idea.

"Maybe we should forget it" he ventured further and I knew he could read me.

"Maybe" I agreed.

The Old Man of Stoer was an intimidating place to practice climbing again. CAILEAN MACLEOD.

24. IRON WILL

Andy left shortly after that for Patagonia. It was July so mid-winter down south. He and Ian planned to climb Cerro Torre. It was a rocky pinnacle not dissimilar to the Old Man of Stoer except ten times bigger and colder. It punches from waves of ice instead of sea, with a frozen mushroom-shaped deathly-looking summit instead of a gentle ramp with a team of climbers waiting to haul them up.

I watched him pack and wondered if I'd see him again.

Be careful, don't take any risks. I was surprised to hear my Dad's familiar voice of caution in my head but I resisted saying the words because I knew they hadn't worked on me. There was no question, going climbing was a risk but maybe a risk worth taking if it keeps you happy and sane.

I was content to be at home and ride my bike through summer lanes. As I rode, I thought about Andy and Ian and wondered how it was for them in Patagonia. I tried not to worry but couldn't help it – the person I loved was fighting the elements on a very precarious looking mountain in the southern hemisphere, a frozen rope the only thing keeping them tied to its unpredictable face. *Would they make it? Would they stay safe?* They were questions I pushed back down because there was nothing to be done; they were in the hands of each other and in those of Patagonian Gods.

Instead I thought about the logistics of climbing El Cap. I still held the idea at arm's length feeling very non-committal about actually saying I'd do it. There seemed so many hurdles to cross just to make it feasible. I couldn't get any insurance unless we climbed with a minimum of four. Where would we find climbing partners mad enough to join us? Was I strong enough? How would I get to the bottom of the face? Was Andy strong enough to piggy-back me up there as he'd suggested? How would I cope on a portaledge, a flimsy fabric and metal frame I'd have to sleep on every night – our only place to sleep when hanging from the cliff? How the heck would I go to the toilet suspended from a cliff and unable to squat and hover?!

I mulled over all the problems and grappled with everything that needed to be done. I needed some practice climbs with sleepovers to test the portaledge. I needed to track down a special rucksack used by the military for carrying injured people. I needed to do lots of cycling to get my arms strong. I needed to buy an inflatable toilet seat…the list was endless and often seemed too difficult to solve. Really I just lacked commitment to solve them. I deliberated more than I'd ever imagined I could about the sense in going climbing again. Especially to El Cap.

I buried the idea away again.

In the late summer, Andy returned from a wet time in Patagonia with stories of days spent in damp miserable snow-holes, lying around in drenched sleeping bags waiting for decent climbing conditions. I might once have felt envy but I was glad not to have been there, playing the waiting game that climbers do and watching the prize disappear with each wet day.

Besides, I was distracted by other things. I had a race the next day. It was a race I'd been training for all summer to stand a chance of finishing.

The Aberfeldy half ironman is renowned for being brutal. I'd jumped at the chance when my friend Jay suggested we do it together. Once a regular in a triathlon club, it was a race I'd always aspired to do but it seemed too gruelling for my ability. It begins with a 1.2 mile swim in Loch Tay, one of Scotland's coldest, followed by a 56 mile hilly cycle up and down some of the country's steepest mountain roads, and finally, as if I wouldn't be tired enough by then, a half marathon. I'd been training for months but after a trial swim in the loch a few weeks earlier, I doubted I was fit enough to finish. After an epic getting into the neoprene wetsuit, I'd floundered about in the water shivering and trying not to drown. I'd worn three caps to stop my head from freezing and they squashed my face so badly that Jay had nick-named me the aqua-hamster.

It was an early start on race morning. Andy was there to support but was bleary-eyed from flying around the world and driving north with his kids, Ella and Ewen. The three of them encouraged me on as I bummed down the ramp into the loch. Other competitors strode into the cold water and swarmed around like aliens in their black neoprene outfits.

There was an intoxicating buzz of anticipation.

The cold stole my breath as it seeped through to my chest and I felt a lurch of dread as I was immersed in the dark weedy water. Minutes later the start-horn blasted and there was a frantic flailing of arms as everyone began swimming towards the distant buoy. I quickly found my position at the back but I was lucky that a seasoned triathlete had offered to swim alongside me. She'd realised I was anxious the previous evening and offered to accompany me. There was also another woman, a channel swimmer and all-round crazy girl – her channel training was to swim non-stop for twenty-four hours in Scottish lochs with no wetsuit – and she rowed a boat beside us. I was in safe though slightly mad hands.

I was last out of the loch but it felt a big accomplishment just to have done it. I got changed into warm dry layers as quickly as my frozen hands would let me and even took time for hot chocolate and a bacon butty before climbing into the handbike. It was an amusing contrast to the serious athletes who were counting every second and would be biking in their swim gear. With fifty miles of pedalling still to go, the leaders in lycra were already sprinting back for the final run. I tried not to feel disheartened. We would be out all day.

Andy followed in the car and Ella and Ewen jumped out regularly and ran alongside the bike to feed us. After a few hours, most other competitors by then probably packed up and heading for home, the rain started to come down heavily. Giant puddles sprayed up with our wheels and down on our heads as if we were sitting in a power shower. It was as wet as a wet day in Scotland gets. The weather was so bad that Andy offered us a lift but there was no way we were stopping. It seems to be my pathology, to always finish what I set out to do.

I didn't want to stop. It felt wrong to admit that I was enjoying the grim weather and the challenge that came with it. I liked the focus it demanded. I liked a bit of suffering.

I wondered not for the first time, whether the exercise and my addiction to moving was a way of covering a deep unrest. A dis-ease within me. Did I want to be more than I was? Was trying to be strong and capable a front for something lacking? If it was, it ran deep because I'd always been like that as long as I could remember. Since way before my accident.

Eight hours into the event I pushed my race chair like I was drunk, the fun of the day mutated to pain. I thought of my first big race, the London

Marathon. After twenty-three miles I hadn't even recognised Simon, my own brother, as he jumped from the crowd and cheered me on. My arms had barely been able to punch the wheels anymore, my torso slumped over my knees as if I'd drunk a litre of whisky. Not that I'd know. I don't even like the stuff.

I'd finished that race and I'd finish this one.

I kept on punching the rims, my gloves sodden with rain and the skin on my fingers rubbed raw. The cold penetrated my bones and my arms felt stiffer with every push.

At last, after 8 hours 45 minutes, a small wet huddle of folk marked the otherwise deserted finish. It was over.

It was so wet that my brake was ineffectual and I bumped to a stop against a kerb. I was cold, exhausted, and missing Jay. Somehow I'd lost him on the run. I waited by the finish and minutes later, he staggered in. It turned out that I'd lost him when I'd missed a short loop of the run route. Technically it meant I hadn't gone the course. I was beyond caring for a few hundred metres, but was bothered that we'd lost each other. He'd been my inspiration to give it a go and it would have been fitting to finish together.

Andy and the kids had followed us in the car the whole way round. The hum of the engine behind us had been simultaneously annoying and comforting, right to the grey wet end. They were my heroes and I was theirs.

I slept like a baby.

On the drive home the next day, El Cap crept into conversation. Andy asked me if I was still on for it but with the weekend's event it was the furthest thing from my mind.

"To be honest I haven't thought about it" I responded truthfully, the idea buried because it was both what I wanted and what I feared.

But I knew deep down what I thought. Guilt for the hurt I'd caused my family the last fateful time I'd climbed stood in the way of me saying 'Yes' and my desire to climb it stopped me from saying 'No'. It seemed impossible to choose between them.

"If you can finish that race, you can climb El Cap" Andy stared straight ahead, as if concentrating intently on the empty road north. It seemed that the doubt he'd had after the Old Man of Stoer was replaced by a confident certainty.

He was right I realised. I could. I was fit enough.

But I was stuck, torn by the dilemma between what I could do and what

I should do.

A part of me knew we would go – why for goodness sake, when I'd nearly died once and knew it could only be traumatic – but I wriggled around the dilemma, doing what I could to avoid any decision. I was in denial and finding ways to deceive myself. I invented scenarios of arriving in Yosemite and just looking at El Cap, then leaving on a sight-seeing holiday to the California coast.

Another week passed by.

We'd both kept three empty weeks in our diaries for the potential climb. September was our month, if we went. Another week went by and a guy Andy knew – Aaron – asked him to climb El Cap. He offered to pay for his flight out there in return for his expertise. It was like a free ticket to Mecca for Andy and too tempting to pass by. He was definitely going. The question was, would I?

When I have a hard decision to make, I often toss a coin. Heads I do something, tails I don't. Then I watch as the coin lands, looking for the faintest flicker of relief or disappointment within me. It doesn't matter how the coin lands. It's how I feel when it does that shows me my real answer. It tells me the truth that I've held all along but which for some reason I haven't been able to hear or face.

I tossed a coin.

I found my answer.

I gave the airline my credit card details over the phone. With the booking made, I hung up and closed my eyes for a moment, acknowledging what I'd done.

You're going to Yosemite!

But really I knew there'd never been any doubt.

Feeling nervous about swimming in the cold loch at the Aberfeldy Half Ironman. ANDY KIRKPATRICK

25. GUILT

With the decision made and plans underway, new parcels arrived in the post each day, mostly gadgetry ordered from various climbing websites. The sewing machine was busy as I stitched a seat to hold a gel pad and fiddled with the parapente harness to make it as comfortable and safe for my skin as I could. I focused on small details that would make the difference between success and failure. Part of me saw the plan as others might and as my parents would if they knew about it – dangerous stupidity. Through all the preparation I sought to justify my decision and to make what lay ahead as safe as I could.

After all the preparation and justification, there was still one obstacle.

Guilt.

Guilt for what had happened in the past. Guilt for anything bad happening again.

What if I die?

Living on the other side of the world and talking at the distant end of a phone line, my brother Simon seemed the best family member to test the idea on. He was young. He was adventurous. He wouldn't be a protective parent. He'd understand. I dialled his number.

"Oh, Andy and I are thinking of going to California. We'll probably go up to Yosemite." I tried to nonchalantly slip it into conversation. "He's climbed it fourteen times you know."

"But he's not climbing it this time?" Simon asked, with a hint of suspicion in his voice that I was sure I wasn't imagining.

"Oh I doubt it" I tried to sound jolly so as not to give away the heavy burden I felt inside. How could I tell him? "But there is a vague possibility…"

There, you've introduced the idea.

"So he might?"

"Well, we're not really sure. We might try it together but probably not. It seems a bit mad. I'm sure we'll just go sightseeing, have a holiday, you know."

You're back pedalling already. Be straight. What are you afraid of?

I'm afraid of being selfish.

I'm afraid of hurting him again.

I'm afraid of hurting all of them.

He went quiet.

"Are you mad?" he asked me and rightly so it felt.

The phone call was quickly over.

The coin was tossed and my answer was revealed but I still tried to ignore it. I pointlessly tried to deceive myself that most likely we'd have a holiday on the California coast.

The next morning, a one line text arrived.

"Please don't climb. We've nearly lost you once. Sorry to sound like Mum and Dad."

Fear was back again. Simon's and my own.

I cried.

It's easy with hindsight to see how clever the mind is, how conflict in our head is just conflict deep inside us. Like a battling courtroom, the debate raged in me. One part of me was better at laying its case. My ego. The 'me' that had stood on the Matterhorn all cocky and thumbs up. It had more skill, better justification strategies, the ability to defend what was plainly mad and the strength of will to win at all costs. My ego wanted me to climb and it had been busy looking for approval from my brother. It was a cunning defence strategy that had failed.

My brother was a parent now too.

His response just escalated my guilt.

"We don't have to do it." Andy kept opening get-out doors for me. He was picking up on my guilt and making some of it his own and with it he wavered at the idea of us climbing El Cap.

"Our flights are booked. You're climbing with Aaron. Let's just see what happens when I get there." I surprised myself at how well I could sit on the fence.

Did I really believe we'd choose the beach holiday?

I told my Mum and Dad we were going on a fly-drive to California.

After all, that's probably what it would be.

A glimpse of El Capitan from the valley bottom. KAREN DARKE

26. THE WALL

I blinked, hardly able to believe what I could see as El Cap came into view through the trees; a blinding granite wall shooting out from the shadows of the forest, reaching up towards the clouds. I'd never seen anything like it. Except I had, when I was ten. I thought it would look smaller. I hoped it would look smaller, but instead it was taller and mightier than even my little person's eyes had seen it.

I couldn't imagine being up there.

I noticed Andy watching for my reaction, glimpsing at me from the steering wheel as we drove into the Yosemite Valley past moss-coated conifers and damp blocks of rock the size of houses. El Cap appeared in flashes through breaks in the trees.

"I wish I could take a picture of your face" he said, grinning. He looked excited enough to burst. This was the place he loved most in the world, this valley, that rock-face. He'd lost and found himself a dozen times up there. Maybe he hoped I'd find something there too.

"We'll go to the meadow" Andy said. "You get the best view from there."

The meadow stood below El Cap, separated from its wooded base by a road lined with cars and tourists, a big open field of grass where people came to stare – to feel humbled.

I wanted to be a tourist like all the others that sat in groups amongst the long grass, in awe of the great pulpit of rock, enjoying the views, the sense of greatness, the soothing rustle of grass in the breeze, feeling relaxed. Instead I looked up and felt anxious. I noticed the irritating sound of traffic, the grating laughs of people enjoying themselves and felt more tense than I could ever remember. I chastised myself for feeling that way. How could I shake the impending sense of doom? I'd be defeated before we began if I didn't change it and try to think positively.

"That's the Nose." Andy broke my thoughts and pointed to a prominent corner leading up the middle of the face. "To the left of it is Pacific Ocean Wall. It's called that because that big dark patch to its right is shaped like North America. The rock up there is diorite, very loose and dangerous but most of the rock's diamond hard."

It took me time to take it all in.

"Can you see the climbers on the Nose?"

I squinted and wished we had binoculars.

"Bright red. Two-thirds of the way up. You can see their haul bags hanging down too."

At last I saw them, just tiny red pin-dots way up high.

Andy continued describing the details of the wall and pointing out the routes he'd climbed. His voice was alive, electric.

If El Cap was a shrine, he was a devoted monk.

I could only think about what could go wrong. I thought about my parents and the guilt if anything was to happen. If I died I wouldn't be able to feel guilty. Or would I? I wasn't certain about afterlife but probably the guilt would go with me somewhere. If I did have another accident it might destroy my parents and it would probably destroy me too. I thought again about my brother's words; don't climb, we nearly lost you once.

You don't have to do it. You can just say no.

But I knew I wouldn't. It was as if climbing the sheet of rock before me was a bizarre part of my destiny.

I've trained as a hypnotherapist. I understand how we create our own reality in every moment with the thoughts that we think. What we think affects how we feel. It changes the chemistry in our body. It influences our mindset, our health and every interaction. Knowing this I tried hard to change my thoughts but there were three words I just couldn't get rid of.

We could die.

Andy's smiles and jokes couldn't hide the dangers but if I kept thinking about them and worrying about the 'what ifs' then things would go worse rather than better. I needed to change how I thought.

We could die but if we're really careful maybe we can be safe.

It helped a little but a little didn't feel enough. How could we be extra careful? We could use an extra safety rope and clip into more belay points than usual. I could tie myself to the rock like a trussed-up chicken so a big plate of wall would have to come down before I would fall off, which did happen from time to time but the chances were low. Even with extreme bondage to the wall there were other things that seemed overwhelming. It would be just Andy and me up there.

On the route, Andy would be leading, climbing up, putting the protection in and getting the rope up for me to follow, each length of rope a 'pitch'. He'd be busy climbing, pushing upwards all day and I would be down below, alone on a folding bed – a portaledge – freaking myself out with thoughts that could kill us and with climbing skills so rusty that they could kill us too. I wasn't safe enough or confident enough to be left alone. El Cap was too big for the two of us.

What if we find some more climbers?

More would be better. We might be on the wall for ten days. I would need company and distraction, extra eyes to stay extra safe.

It might even be fun with other people.

But who the heck would climb with two random strangers, one of them paralysed, on the world's biggest big wall?!

I doubted there was anyone. It didn't even seem worth entertaining the idea. What kind of fool would approach a stranger and ask them to put their life in your hands? The stakes would be high and the highs would be real. One small mistake is all it would take.

I looked up again and imagined how long it would take to fall down the wall, twice as high as the World Trade Towers were; to spin and flap and see your death coming up metre by metre.

It's a fool's game. I heard my Dad's words again.

Sorting gear at Camp 4, ready for the wall. ANDY KIRKPATRICK

27. CAMP 4

We pitched the tent at the down-market climber's campsite known as Camp 4, beside a big green metal bear box – designed to keep the bears off your food – but we had little more than ketchup and toothpaste to stash inside it. The camp looked dusty and shoddy, a kind of climbing shanty village. Camp 1 was presumably the most upmarket with a nice pristine shower block but Camp 4 just had an all-in-one cubicle and from the state of it, it was used for plenty besides showering. Most tents looked well settled in, like they'd been there a long time – months – even though there was a six day limit allowed for anyone to stay there. Climbers. They'd find a way around anything that might stand between them and a glorious hunk of rock.

The campsite was buried well into the forest, pine trunks reaching tall and blocking views of the giant rock walls that surrounded it.

I was glad to shut them out for a while.

I wandered around the trails of the camp – hard work with my wheels digging into the dirt and catching on stones – taking it all in. Dust. Muscles. Testosterone. Drying ropes. Empty haul bags used to carry all your food and water up a big wall sat leant against trees. The clink of metal climbing gear being sorted and selected for climbs that could take weeks to complete – hanging day and night on the wall. I felt like I was going back in time, revisiting a place I'd once lived.

A climber's mess.

A climber's paradise.

There were large boulders scattered between tents and the largest, the size of a small house, had a small crowd at its base. I watched for a while as climbers took turns to tackle the obvious crack-line up through it's front.

"Midnight Lightning" Andy appeared beside me. "There's always people trying to climb it."

Seeing their hands grapple with the rock I imagined the touch of Yorkshire gritstone, cold and abrasive on my fingertips and was filled with a memory of bouldering near Otley, getting almost to the top of a tricky crack line then running out of strength, panicking, shouting for help and being so grateful for the strong hand that appeared over the edge and pulling me to safety.

I didn't miss bouldering.

It was still late summer but the valley bottom was over a kilometre above sea level and I felt the chill as soon as evening arrived. I wrapped up in a thick jacket and sat listening to Andy chatting with Aaron. The two of them had been in the valley a few weeks but hadn't got up El Cap yet.

"I just couldn't do it" Aaron explained to me. "It freaked me out being up there."

Andy had agreed to climb El Cap with Aaron – who was a Swiss banker – in exchange for an air ticket, the usual fee to be guided over three thousand dollars.

"Yeah you should see how much Red Bull he drank and how much he smoked. Nervous or what?" Andy continued. "We were a couple of days into the climb and Aaron shouted up to me, 'Andy I wanna go down' and I said 'You'll have to pay double the guided rate' – meaning failure would cost Aaron six thousand dollars – about a thousand dollars a pitch. He was quite happy with that, said he'd do anything to get out of there."

Of course once down Andy didn't ask for the money.

"It's normal to be terrified and want to give in" said Andy, obviously disappointed for Aaron. "When you climb El Cap all it takes is not to give in."

I looked at Aaron. He was strong and fit and I wondered how I could possibly do it if he couldn't – after all as soon as I'd seen El Cap I wanted to give in.

As the evening grew dark the camp came alive with smoking barbecues, the hum of petrol stoves, mellow chatter and accents and languages from all over the world. The clink of climbing gear was a continuous white noise. Everything but the creak of rusty bear-box doors and the sharp smell of pine reminded me of the climbers campsite on the edge of Chamonix – Snell's field. The toilet had been worse at Snell's though but I'd spent a couple of great summers there, excited about the route we were about to tackle or exhausted from the one just done. It had been so long ago I'd forgotten those memories but now I missed it and for the first time I felt glad we were planning to climb. I didn't want to feel like an outsider, an impostor or a tourist. I wanted to feel at home here – a climber again.

But I didn't feel at home.

All I felt was afraid of the wall.

In contrast, Andy seemed very settled, in fact more so than I'd ever seen him at home. He spent hours chatting to other climbers. Some he knew. Some he didn't. Some were never-met Facebook friends. Some just seemed to know of him and for the first time I realised that his eleven day solo climb of a route called Reticent Wall had earned him a place in El Cap history. Listening to him banter and seeing him so settled, I thought he'd be happier living permanently in Camp 4 than in a house in Sheffield, even though the city's climbing culture makes it a red-brick industrial version of Camp 4 anyway.

"So when are you guys planning to head up?" Aaron asked.

"Day after tomorrow" Andy was clear, "no time to waste."

"You feeling ready Karen?" Aaron looked at me as he spoke and I could read something in his eyes. A man who'd been scared. A man who was relieved it wasn't him setting off to climb in two days time. A man who was disappointed.

"Not really" I confessed. "Apart from a couple of practices, I haven't climbed properly in fourteen years. I don't know how I'll react up there on my own while Andy climbs up above."

"Yep." He knew what I was talking about. He'd been there.

"I'd feel better if there were more than just the two of us climbing" I went on. "But there's not much chance of that now." I wished we'd thought it through more. I wished that Paul Tattersal or Ian Parnell were there too, like at the Old Man or Kilnsey Crag.

"Well let's go out for dinner tomorrow night. On me. Like a last supper before the wall."

A last supper.

It felt more ominous than ever.

The next day we rushed around preparing for the big climb, buying food for the route, packing and gathering last minute things. I'd seen a picture of Andy's Reticent Wall climb with about a hundred identical plastic water bottles lined up at the base of the route. He said he'd bought them all in Lidl back in

Sheffield. He'd emptied out the lemonade down the drain in the street with his son Ewen, so many litres going down that it had fizzed up through the grates further down the street. I didn't get why he'd flown with a bag full of empty plastic bottles to America and hadn't just got them there but no doubt there was a good reason, like not wasting a day of precious time shopping when he could be climbing, or avoiding the extortionate prices of the Yosemite National Park shops. On the climb retreat would be almost impossible due to the overhanging nature of the rock and our time would be limited by how much water we could haul up. In many ways it was like making a big ocean voyage, with a finite quantity of water meaning as soon as we left the ground it would be rationed and the clock would be ticking. I trusted Andy would take enough but at the same time I knew there would be pressure on us to climb as fast as possible.

It was mid-afternoon and Andy came bounding over, looking somewhat pleased with himself.

"There's these two Aussie girls camping over near the shower" he began. "I got chatting with them and mentioned we might be looking for someone to climb with us. They seem quite interested."

"Really?"

"Yeah, we should go over and meet them. See what we all think."

"Do they know I can't walk?"

"Er, yeah. I think I mentioned that."

"Well what do you think? Would it be better with four?" I asked, though I felt sure it would be if logistically it was possible. Nothing could be worse than sitting on a ledge on my own, hanging in space from a giant cliff with only memories and fear and dread for company.

"Yeah I reckon. They seem really nice. A good laugh. And I was thinking they might be more supportive and stuff than climbing with men."

I hadn't said much about how I felt. I hadn't been able to say 'I'm shit scared.'

"Okay" I replied, still unable to be really honest because I was trying to figure it out how I felt myself. Trying to understand why I'd lost my spark, why I'd been so subdued since arriving in the valley.

Andy was on to me and I was glad of it. He was working on a plan.

We went over to find them by their tent. They introduced themselves as Tash and Gemma and I liked them straight away.

After chatting for a few minutes, Andy asked them if they wanted to climb with us, but it was lost in the jokey, indirect way he said it. When he asked a second time in a serious way, I was sure they'd laugh and politely say no.

"Yeah, alright" they responded and I nearly choked in surprise. Did they know what they were letting themselves in for? Then again, did I?

I felt a tingle shiver down my spine.

This is really happening.

I wondered why they'd agree to climb with these two random strangers but I'd forgotten that Andy wasn't that random when it came to El Cap. Tash and Gemma wanted to climb it – they were just back from an abandoned attempt – and Andy had climbed it twelve times. I wasn't so sure about being part of the thirteenth attempt but whilst I was nervous, I wasn't going to let superstition get the better of me.

Gemma was the louder of the two, with a wide smile and a wiry, athletic build. Her arms looked sinewy and muscular, their veins standing proud from her muscles. She looked like she could climb hard. Tash looked strong too but in a more solid sort of way. She was softer in personality, more reflective and thoughtful before she spoke. They were both positive and smiley and I liked that. We didn't need any more clouds than the one I brought with me and in

Our climbing partners Tash and Gemma. We couldn't have wished for better company, even though they'd never climbed a big wall before either! ANDY KIRKPATRICK

their presence I could feel my darkness break up a little.

It might even be fun.

So Andy had talked Tash and Gemma into it and with them in the equation I'd talked myself into going along too!

The following morning, we practiced in the shade of a big overhanging boulder. We showed them the system I would use to climb and the ins and outs of how it would work. I explained about the risk of pressure sores and why we would put the portaledge up at the end of every pitch so that I could avoid hanging in a harness too long. We decided on the number of ropes we would use – four in total, in different colours to help us communicate. Andy would climb up placing pegs and nuts to protect himself, with one rope to clip in the gear, trailing a second. Tash or Gemma would climb up the rope and take out the gear, while I would climb up the second free hanging rope. Once up the last person would lower out the haul bags and then climb up another rope. Climbing up in rope lengths of fifty metres at a time this would be a slow but steady system – and also one that would prove highly complex.

At the end of each day we'd unfold our two, two-person nylon and alloy tubing portaledges and sleep on the wall, El Cap being almost devoid of ledges. We talked through all the essential aspects of the route ahead and the equipment we'd need, but it still felt to be happening fast. I would have happily delayed but Andy thought there was no time to waste.

"I've picked a route" Andy announced. We would set off the next day. El Cap was waiting.

"Shortest Straw."

"Shortest Straw?" I repeated. "What kind of a route name is that?"

"Yeah, a guy started climbing up it and a few days in he had a bad feeling. He came down and then a big storm hit."

Tash and Gemma laughed, but I didn't like it. It felt like a bad omen.

Shortest Straw was graded A4 5.7, which meant nothing to me except *hard* and that Andy would be climbing slowly. That meant more nights on the wall on a portaledge I'd only sat on once, for a few minutes in summer sunshine at a Peak District crag. In terms of climbing difficulty though, everything would feel the same to me pulling up a rope, but the more overhanging the better so I didn't scrape on the rock. I made up my own grade, PU400+, at least 400 pull-ups per pitch. That's what it would take to get myself up each sixty-metre rope length.

Shortest Straw was over to the right side of the face as you looked at it. Right of 'North America', the crumbling patch of rock in the middle of the wall. At least it would be solid rock.

"We'll head up to the base of the wall tonight" Andy was pushing the pace. "Then we'll be ready for an early start on the wall."

We spent the afternoon packing gear – which seemed endless. It looked

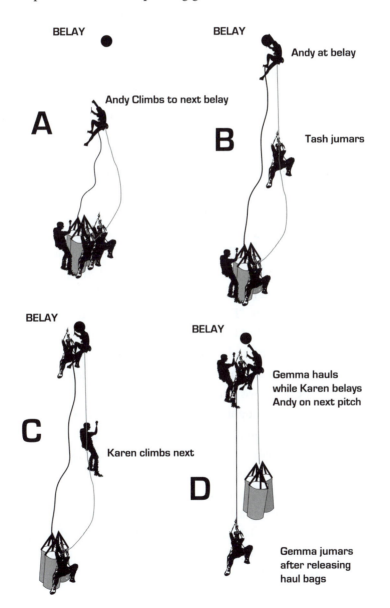

BELAY

BELAY

Andy at belay

Andy Climbs to next belay

A

B

Tash jumars

BELAY

BELAY

Gemma hauls
while Karen belays
Andy on next pitch

C

Karen climbs next

D

Gemma jumars
after releasing
haul bags

far too much to haul up the wall with us and with sixty litres of water added to it, I couldn't believe we'd ever shift it.

"We'll head up with the first load" Tash said. She and Gemma helped each other load the huge sacks onto their backs as the other Camp 4 climbers looked on, the bags towering so high above them it looked like they'd topple over.

"We'll see you on route!" they called back and we watched them teeter off into the distance.

Andy had joked about God being American because he'd put El Cap next to the road. That said, it was still a forty minute hike up a bouldery forest path then a scramble through scree to get to its base. I'd thought about trying to get up there myself, on my bum with a good cushion strapped to it and using my arms to drag myself up. When I'd seen how far it was up through the forest, I'd had to admit it was an unrealistic plan – it would be impossible not to scrape my bum on something and that might mean months in bed nursing pressure sores. Andy said he could piggy-back me and we had an old rucksack with a sleeping bag compartment at its base that I could perch my bum on. If he could hold up in strength, we thought it might just be possible.

I struggled from the car onto Andy's back.

"Lean forward more" I said, "and drop your bum lower so I can get onto the rucksack and my legs around." I grabbed his neck but he leant far forward at the same time and I shot upwards, almost over his head. The people parking their car beside us watched in amusement.

"Excuse me" I called over. "Do you mind tying me to his back?" I knew how ridiculous it sounded, but I didn't want to risk sliding off. Looking very bemused, the couple obliged and came over to us.

"Just tie this strap back around her" Andy instructed, "and back into this hand." A few minutes later we were fully bonded together and I wondered what on earth the couple thought as we began staggering towards the forest.

"I need to rest" Andy puffed, only a hundred metres in.

"There's a giant boulder just over there" I pointed, and he headed for it. With my hands wrapped around his neck I could feel his pulse, his heart beating super fast. Dangerously fast.

"Are you sure about this?" I asked as we rested on the boulder, the rucksack perched on its top and alleviating Andy of my weight. He didn't reply and I knew he was thinking the same as me – there was no way we could do it. You'd need to be superhuman to get up there.

But after a few minutes he nodded and simply said "Yep."

He stood again and took the next steps forward. I watched as he placed each foot in front of the other, praying to I wasn't sure who that his back would be okay, that he wouldn't get hurt, that I wouldn't get dumped on the ground.

It's too much.

It had been too much before, in other relationships. My iron will to keep going, pushing myself and by default pushing other people to the point of breaking.

I didn't want Andy or us to break.

"It's too much Andy. Let's go back down."

"It'll be alright" he muttered between breaths and although I said it again, I knew his will was even stronger than mine. I'd met my match.

"But your heart's going bonkers."

"Just tell me if it stops" he joked and kept on going.

Out of the trees, the sun scorched and we sweated. Andy's hair was sticky, my head pushed into it and my chest stuck to his back, the rucksack straps slicing in, my shoulders burning with the effort of holding on tight. My eyes followed his feet along the path and watched his thigh muscles bulge, imagining the burn of lactic acid he must have in them. As he put each foot forward, I studied the trail just ahead and guessed where he'd put his feet, imagining where I'd put my own feet, searching for ground that looked solid. I liked it when he put his feet where I'd have put mine. It felt safe.

The path steepened and disappeared into Talus, big, angular and awkward to manoeuvre through. I saw in Andy what I hadn't seen since the hardest days in Greenland when he'd searched for routes through the melting ice, stubbornly towing me behind him. Total focus, determination, bloody-mindedness. He wouldn't give up. The tougher the better. He liked it when things were challenging. Maybe that was our attraction.

After almost three hours, we collapsed at the base of the route. Tash and Gemma were waiting having shuttled all the haul bags except one that was left in our car. Almost immediately and with barely a word, Andy set off down to the valley again to get it.

He's a machine.

I wished I could go for it. I hated not being able to help.

A few hours later with dinner wolfed down – a dry bagel with cream cheese

– Andy made a flat space for us to sleep amongst the scree. We lay down in our sleeping bags and held hands as the sun slipped away. We were just metres from the base of the wall, tucked in for safety from falling rocks. I thought back to Alpine bivvies and the nights before big routes. There had always been the sound of rock fall and avalanches sculpting the mountains into the night, yet somehow I'd never been scared and had managed to sleep deeply. Then I'd always woken eager and hungry for the climb but now I lay awake, unable to sleep, my mind churning over what lay in store.

"You awake?" Andy asked.

"Yeah. Can't sleep."

"Imagine tomorrow morning and every little detail of getting ready for the climb" he suggested. "It'll send you to sleep."

I needed not to think about tomorrow so instead we chatted about other things, including bears and how they like toothpaste and beer, until too tired to talk anymore, we just lay and traced the moon lit veins of quartz that crossed the wall like lightning.

"Just tell me if my heart stops" Andy said as he pushed on with me on
his back, up the scree to the base of El Cap. It was a superhuman
effort! NATASHA SEBIRE

Andy weighed down with gear whilst leading the route. NATASHA SEBIRE

28. SHORTEST STRAW

Clonk! Clunk! Clink, clink clink!

The sound of the metal being hammered into the rock rose in tone to a high ping. The sun had barely crept onto the wall and Andy was making his way up the crack line of a curving roof, the first pitch of Shortest Straw. He looked weighed down with the most extensive rack of metalwork I'd ever seen swinging from his waist. Pegs, camming devices, slings, karabiners and bits of climbing gear I'd never even seen let alone knew the names of.

Tash belayed Andy, her eyes trained on him and her forehead creased, attentive, watching his every move. I was glad of that, eager for him to be safe although it was hard to associate the idea of safety with leading a climb like Shortest Straw. It looked steep and terribly overhanging. A memory flashed through me of those moments before I'd fallen from the cliff – my arms pumped with blood, on fire, trying so hard to keep a grip but watching my fingers uncurl and slide from the rock.

He's strong. He's done it twelve times before. He'll be fine.

He would be fine, as long as we played our part and played it well. It wasn't just about his experience or strength. We needed to do things right and be the team that he needed us to be to make it up the route.

"Slack!" he shouted as he lunged upwards, balanced precariously with his foot in a ladder made of nylon tape – an aider – one arm reaching up for the crack above his head.

"Lost arrows!" He called down again. "Small ones! Can you pass some up?!" Gemma leapt about the scree, and Tash looked down at her own rack, searching for what he needed. They found a bunch of metal pegs that looked like arrows and clipped them onto another rope, the 'zip line' for passing stuff up.

Lost arrows, aiders, zip lines…there was so much I didn't know but I soaked up all the jargon like a dry sponge, wishing I'd known it before we'd begun. It was just like starting a new job, bombarded with three letter acronyms and terminology that meant nothing only this time the speed I needed to learn in wasn't optional. It was a matter of life and death.

Whilst the climbing continued, Gemma packed haul bags and I helped as much as I could from my patch amongst the scree. In between packing I poured water down my throat like we had an endless supply and peed into a plastic Coke bottle at almost the same rate. It was a nice white wine in colour instead of dark ale, so at least I was well hydrated. I worried about dehydration. Wee and poo seemed to be the burden of any adventure. If I didn't drink enough my pee would thicken up with sediment and block the catheter and that would mean wetting myself on the wall. Worse than that though, when it came to pooing I could only see messy acrobatics trying to figure out how to get the drop needed to dump in a paper bag, and stuff it in the 'poo tube' issued by the National Park. How could I get a neat turd into a small bag whilst suspended hundreds of metres above the ground, unable to squat and hover and with the complicated logistics of getting it out in the first place?! Embarrassing, messy, grim, and what if it went wrong as it sometimes does? What if I shat myself, got it on ropes, harness, clothes; it would be a test of any relationship. The only bit of kit I had that might help was an inflatable toilet seat. It had worked well on cycling trips, like in the Himalaya where there were no toilets for hundreds of miles, except then I'd dug a pit in the soil to get a drop and now it would only just raise me off the ledge. The inflatable toilet seat had exploded once too, burst open and dropped me down into the contents of the pit. Whichever way I thought of it, I could only see things getting messy and despite having lost most inhibitions after six months in a hospital spinal ward where wee, poo and orgasms are the main topics of conversation, I didn't want the embarrassment. It became another reason not to climb.

Except it was too late for that.

We were packed up and waiting for Andy to finish the first pitch. The sun crept high and my neck muscles hurt from hours of looking up the wall watching his progress. More time passed. We only had the shadow of the haul bags for shelter from burning and we hid in their shade, watching and waiting. It had been a long time since Andy left the ground, but eventually

*Just a few pull-ups into the climb, I wondered how I'd ever make
it up the long stretches of rope above. NATASHA SEBIRE*

he shouted "Safe!" He was at the belay.

It's time to leave the ground.

My inner voice kept on interrupting like a dramatic commentary.

Tash set off next and followed Andy's line, removing all the gear he'd placed as she went. Some routes on the wall were like dot-to-dots between bolts that had been pre-drilled into the rock, but Shortest Straw was fairly clear of bolts. It made Andy's job harder and slower, demanding more thought about where to place pieces of gear to keep him safe as he climbed.

"We're too slow" I thought out loud, and Gemma nodded, the two of us sat on the portaledge.

"We should get quicker as we go."

I liked her optimism and thought as she said it how I was being glass-half-empty instead of half-full about everything so far. It was unlike me.

"The quicker Tash reaches him, the sooner he can start climbing again" Gemma remarked as we both looked upwards, willing Tash to climb fast. Speed was a critical factor – we had enough water and food to last us ten days.

Ten days in vertical hell?!

At least half of day one had gone and Gemma and I still hadn't left the ground. At that speed, it would take at least ten long days to get up the fifteen pitches of Shortest Straw to the top of El Cap. The ten days worth of water and supplies meant the haul bags were full to bursting and with three litres of water each per day, there were 120 kilos solely in water. There was enough gear to sink a ship, or to pull a man off the wall; warm clothes, belay jackets, waterproofs, sleeping bags and mats, bivvy bags, stoves, bagels, cheese, Andy's treats (cans of Coke and 'Beany Weanies'), everyone else's treats, and hanging beneath all of it, the bright yellow 'poo' bag that would carry all our shit out of there. Nice.

Stop delaying. It's time to leave the ground.

I began clipping the rope to my harness, preparing for the moment that had always been inevitable, right since the first mention of El Cap. Gemma helped me fiddle with the straps, pulleys and jumars that made the pull-up system and then I sat in the scree, on the padding of the parapente harness. Waiting.

I thought back to the first time I'd met Andy, to his bin-man meets out-of-shape rugby player meets teddy bear sort of appearance, certainly not that of a typical climber. He'd fired questions at me about how I'd manage an ice-cap crossing, and made a lot of jokes – on the verge of being offensive if I was more sensitive to such things. I hadn't known what to make of him back then let alone imagined that we'd end up in a relationship but his warmth and generosity of spirit had attracted me and our life circumstances had somehow coincided. People say that climbers are selfish but Andy proves that wrong. We'd still barely known each other before he'd suggested we should climb El Cap together. I'd never imagined we really would and now there we were, at the foot of the granite giant.

Some things that happen in life seem like they're not by accident, as if they're planned to challenge and test you; like some sort of game – pass this level and you can progress to the next. There's free choice to take on the challenge or turn away. Either way, things will never be the same. They are life defining events that teach us something. Becoming paralysed. Losing my friend Will. Crossing the Himalaya. Climbing El Cap was another.

I felt the tension go onto the rope and the shoulder straps of the harness digging into my collar bones, the slack of the rope at last taken up. The next time I pulled, my bum lifted and I skimmed the ground. I was airborne.

This is it.
I closed my eyes.
Breathe.
Pull.
Slide jumar up.

With each pull on the yellow bike grips, the centimetres beneath me became metres. Gemma had also started climbing up, and it wasn't long before she drew level with me.

"You alright?" She asked cheerily and I felt glad of her cheery way.

"Only a few thousand more pull-ups to go" I grinned, then looked up and thought what a long, long way it was. I couldn't see the top. Then I looked down and thought what a long, long fall it was.

Sweat trickled into my ears, my collarbones raw with the straps digging in. I was uncomfortable but it didn't matter. It was the least of my worries. I looked up again and could see that Andy had left the belay above, making his way up the second pitch.

If you think this is hard, think of him.

I did and in comparison, my task was nothing. He had all the risk, the exposure, the arm-pumping, head-screwing, tactical battle of leading. All I had to do was pull.

Just keep on pulling.
Breathe.
Pull.
Slide jumar up.
Breathe.
Pull.
Slide jumar up.

It went on for a long time, until finally the purple rope ran out and my body was trapped just beneath the portaledge.

"Hang on" Tash said, as she pushed her feet against the wall and with a massive effort, swung the ledge out enough for me to wrestle up between it and the granite. I heard my body scrape against the sharp crystals in the rock and was glad for all the protection I had, that I was wearing knee and shin guards as well as the protective harness.

"Agghhh!" A noise escaped me as I flopped onto the ledge.

Thank fuck.

Those two words said it all. The portaledge felt a safe haven, something horizontal in the otherwise vertical world. It was a place where bizarrely I found I could relax just a little and get some reprieve from the tension that had wrung me out every pull up the wall so far.

"You okay?" Tash asked as she belayed Andy.

"Yeah, just give me a minute and I'll take over the belaying." I laid back to recover, took a swig of water, closed my eyes and took a deep breath.

Don't think about it. Just do it.

"Ready when you are" I opened my eyes again and took over the belaying from Tash so she could prepare the ropes for the haul bags. It would be a massive physical job to haul the weight of the bags up from the ground.

I lay on my back, the belay rope held tightly in both hands, looking up at Andy slowly unravelling the pitch above. As I looked up, I couldn't help but notice the bolts we were tied to, two small metal ears into which a chunky karabiner was clipped and which held everything. The bolts had been drilled by the first people to climb the route, the bolt itself only as thick as a pencil and as long as your little finger.

I wonder how strong one of those is?

The more I stared at the bolts, the more I wondered what we were tied to; Tash, Andy, Gemma and I and hundreds of kilos of gear. What did I know about these bolts to trust my life to?

This is a mug's game.

My Dad's words came back to haunt me.

"Andy. How strong is one of these bolts?" I shouted up when I saw him rest.

"Errr. Don't worry, they're tested. You could hang a house on them."

"How can you tell if they're decent or not?"

"Errr." He paused. "Sometimes they look a bit bent or rusty, sometimes they break, but never both of them at the same time. As long as you think light thoughts they should hold."

It was a stupid question deserving a stupid answer and just fuelled my worries when I looked around and saw rust dribbles beneath all of the bolts.

Things can rust overnight, I reasoned with my logical brain, remembering a seized and rusty chain on my bike after a night left in the rain. But my brain was running away with questions.

"What's the story with these bits of duct tape stuck around the wall?" I asked but knew that I probably didn't want the answer. I wished I would stop asking questions and imagined he wished I would too.

"You don't want to know" came the answer.

But now I really did.

"What's it for?" I asked, my question coming out a little more panicked.

"It's meant to stop ropes abrading on sharp edges… and snapping" came the reply.

Andy was right – I wished I hadn't asked. Now on every pitch all I could imagine was my rope slowly being sawed through by some sharp duct-tapeless edge.

Stop it. Stop thinking about what could go wrong.

I ran my hand over the rough material of the portaledge only as thick as a deckchair but holding my entire weight above the drop. It felt that at any moment it would give and I'd drop through. I reached up and tightened the strap that held me to the belay one more notch.

It was all a mind game.

I knew from learning about hypnotherapy that the mind is malleable. You can choose your thoughts. You can change your thoughts and I realised as I lay there asking questions that were doing nothing for my anxiety, that's what I needed to do. I tried it out. I told myself to imagine that the portaledge was the ground and that lying there looking up the wall there was only solid earth beneath me. It was total fiction and yet weirdly, even though I knew it was made up, my mind could imagine it. It was like watching a horror film, getting scared, pressing 'stop' on the DVD and changing it out for a better, less scary film. If I told myself 'safe' things, it made me feel safer and if I focused on the job at hand – belaying Andy – instead of on all the big scary things that might happen, then I didn't feel the same fear. It was like my brain was playing a different DVD. Somehow it worked.

Every now and then, I lost focus and forgot to hold down the new 'play' button.

If I allowed myself to think 'Oh my God, it's a long way to fall down', I felt my pulse quicken and my palms get sweaty. When I thought, 'It's okay. The ledge is safe and solid' then I felt myself calm down. Playing with my thoughts became my weapon for survival, my emotions just a response to whatever I thought. I could change how I felt by changing how I thought. It seemed too simple how easily reality could be changed but it somehow seemed to work.

But who are you if you're not your thoughts?

It was a big question. Too profound to consider whilst busy on the wall. I just concentrated on what needed to be done and when I did, there was no past, or future, only the immediacy of the moment. The belay to concentrate on to keep Andy safe, gear to be found and sent up the zip line, ropes like spaghetti to be tidied away, thoughts to be filtered because even if I wasn't them, they created each moment. Choosing what I thought could make me fearful or make me free. They were the difference between smiling and misery.

It was late afternoon. Our progress was slow. The five ropes were a higgledy piggledy rainbow strung around the wall. Andy had reached the end of the second pitch, Tash and I were at the end of the first, and the haul bags were so heavy we couldn't budge them.

"The haul bags are stuck Andy!" Gemma shouted up the wall to him.

"Have you tried using the pulleys?"

"Yeah, we got them moving like that but they've jammed."

"You'll have to go down and sort it out. I can't do anything from up here!"

Gemma abseiled down. Seeing her all the way down there back on the ground was a reminder of how slow we were going. We'd been at it all day and yet still we were only one rope length up.

"Got it!" Gemma called up. "The rope's caught round a boulder in the scree!" She freed up the rope, then jumared back up to join us.

"Okay, together....heave!!!" Tash called as she and Gemma pulled on the ropes.

"They're moving" I reported, watching them lift just slightly off the ground.

"Keep going" I encouraged.

But within five minutes, the haul bags jammed again. We looked down and saw a trunk of wood somehow caught in the rope above them.

"There's a tree caught above the haul bags!" Gemma shouted up to Andy. Exhausted after two hard pitches, frustrated with his under-par team, he snapped. "This is a fucking disaster!", as if we hadn't noticed and abseiled back down to sort out the mess.

By five, the sun hid behind the line of the Nose and the wall fell into shadow.

We were still strung over the two pitches but at least the bags were on the move.

It would soon be dark.

"Two up, two down!" Andy called, after jumaring all the way back up to the high point of the second belay again. We knew what he meant. I would have to jumar – 'jug' for short – up the rope to join him and sleep up there. Tash and Gemma would spend the night at the first belay.

We dug our head-torches out and I made my preparations to climb up in the dark. I wondered if this was just Andy's way of forcing more progress out of me.

Sleeping apart was far from ideal, our gear scattered in different haul bags but such was big wall climbing, always demanding more when you had the least to give. It was a brainteaser working out how to reach each sleeping bag then how to get it to the right ledge. Tash and Gemma sorted out a bag for Andy to haul up, while my job was simply to jug up the green rope towards Andy. I was happy for the dark; it helped me imagine there was no-where to fall.

Breathe.
Pull.

Slide jumar up.
Breathe.
Pull.
Slide jumar up.
On it went.

I fixed my eyes on Andy's head torch, a tiny dot like a bright star and I willed the sky to come to me.

Breathe.
Pull.
Slide jumar up.

Eventually I reached my imaginary star.
And finally we slept.

29. WIDE OCEAN OF FEAR

That's how it went. On and on, on and on. All the next day and the day after that. I felt like a slave to our goal of reaching the top. We were all giving it everything and yet we were going nowhere fast.

When Andy climbed the Reticent Wall, it took him two weeks. Two whole weeks for one kilometre of climbing. That's only about a hundred and fifty metres a day. One of the British newspapers had reported on his climb, the hardest route soloed by a UK climber, with the main comment being 'what took him so long?'. For a non-climber, it's probably hard to comprehend why vertical metres are so slow to cover. I hadn't been able to grasp it either. Until then. This was no place to rush. The combination of steepness, complexity of the climbing and the weight that must be carried up the wall made progress snail like. Not that the days dragged. They flew past.

Three days had flown by. We'd slaved for hour after hour, pushing, pulling, tidying, being so careful not to slip up because that would be fatal, until darkness would fall and finally exhaustion would force us to stop. Andy looked utterly wasted. He was as disheartened as the rest of us by our slow progress. He sat on the portaledge, the climbing over for the day and the 'evening meal' done and dusted. Bean juice dribbled from the corner of his mouth, flecks of dirt filled the apex of his eyes and lines of dried salt were crusted on his face.

"Some fizz for some whizz?" I grinned and passed him a can of Coke, more relaxed now at the third night on the wall. I'd got used to being trussed to the belay bolts, countless lengths of tape attaching me to the tiny metal ears. Most people just tied on to the rope at one or two places but my paranoia had me tied into everything I could. I always had at least six things attaching me to different parts of the wall. It was another mind game – the more things I was tied to the wall with, the safer I felt. At night I slept in a thin harness I wore under my parapente harness, which took a while to get used to sleeping in, along with sharing the sleeping bag with a rope. But it was all okay because it all meant being safe.

We woke early, the morning sun already lighting the Nose, though we were still in shade. I felt claustrophobic and battled my way out of the sleeping bag, frustrated with the tangle of leashes. It was a vertical prison and I felt as bound to the bolts as I sometimes felt to my wheels. The climb wasn't entirely stacking up with the things I enjoyed about being outdoors; freedom, movement, the changing scenery of a journey. The only thing I'd noticed changing was the position of the sun in the sky and the pattern of shadows on the wall. Everything was slow and most of the time I felt hot, sweaty, busy and stressed.

Three days in, we'd only managed three out of twenty pitches. At this rate it would take us two weeks of climbing to reach the top, more than we had in water and food.

With a team you can do more than you can alone. But with a team, you can egg each other on too, get carried into a fantasy. Our group fantasy was climbing El Cap but the reality was that we were doing a bad job.

We're going too slow.

I was so petrified whilst abseiling back down that I distracted myself by taking photos of my shadow on the wall. KAREN DARKE

As I prepared for the day, that's all I could think. But I didn't say a word. Whilst I was in a form of hell, I didn't want to give up.

We prepared breakfast, bagels and spread cheese again but we were all quiet and there was little talk about the day ahead.

"How are you feeling crew?" Andy broke the silence.

"Yeah, good." Gemma said, and Tash and I echoed a similar response.

None of us wanted to say what we really felt and our charade went on for a little while.

"I've been thinking. Maybe I should go down and get more water" Andy braved the topic, "I don't think we've got enough."

Andy didn't want to admit he'd had a nightmare about his son Ewen being run over. He told me later that he'd interpreted it as a reminder of being super vigilant, that even when you are, you don't always get away with it. I didn't want to admit I had a bladder infection and felt rubbish or Gemma that she'd been puking in the night and had a stonking headache. None of us wanted to admit that at the rate we were moving, our water wouldn't last. Because saying any of those things could jeopardise our chances of success. If we admitted the truth it would ruin our fantasy, even though that's clearly what it was.

But Andy had broached the subject.

"If you're going down, so am I." I shared my gut response. When I imagined being alone on the ledge with my skulking fear, I wasn't sure I'd be able to stave it off with mind games.

We were silent again, the magnitude of what we were proposing difficult to get our heads around. I noticed the distant chinking sound of metal, other climbers on the wall.

We knew we should all go down but we didn't want to fail. We talked about it for a long time. Why would it be good to go down? Why would it be good to carry on? We all admitted how we felt, and agreed that we couldn't just carry on as we were.

"We definitely need more water" Andy concluded.

"Why don't we carry on and one of us can abseil down for more water" Gemma suggested. We nodded agreement.

But deep in my gut, I knew what we should do.

I have to back down.

I'd had the feeling before.

No keep going!

I'd ignored it once before.

I lay back and looked up at the sky. Clouds were forming, contaminating the pure blue we were used to.

"Weather looks to be changing." I threw in the comment, on some level hopeful it would change our call.

"What was that?!" Andy asked, ignoring my comment but looking at the girls over on their ledge.

"What was what?" Gemma quizzed.

"That black thing that just fell off your ledge?"

We all peered down and saw something falling. It fell for a long time before finally exploding on the scree far below.

That could be you.

The voice in my head had a life of its own and I didn't want to become it.

"Ah bummer. I think it was all our food." Tash said. We looked at each other, and we all knew the fantasy was over.

It was final.

We were going down.

I want to climb this bloody thing, now we've come this far.

But I knew that voice was only my ego that didn't want to fail.

Lowering off, I took photos of my shadow on the wall. About a hundred photos in fact, Andy lowering me inch by inch on several ropes tied together, my body way out from the rock.

Don't look down. Don't look up. Focus only on your shadow.

It was another mind game that distracted me.

When my bum touched down on the hot talus I allowed my body to flop down. I spend so much of my life wary of hard ground and the risk of pressure sores, but for once feeling the stony earth beneath me – solid ground – was heaven. I rolled onto my side and kissed the rock.

30. BETWEEN A ROCK
AND A HARD FACE

The valley was buzzing as usual, a melee of people and nature – photographers with giant telescopic lenses searching for inspiration, hikers in Stetson hats, climbers weighed down with giant sacks of gear and tourists strolling the paths and looking up in awe. There were more people than usual as the Yosemite Face-lift was in full swing, volunteers from far and wide here to clean up rubbish in the valley.

Our first day back down from the wall we joined the tourists, shuffled around the visitor centre and sat in cafes watching chipmunks scavenge for food. Extra-large America was firmly stamped on the valley's amenities, with the biggest vats of diet coke and the largest, cheesiest pizzas I'd ever seen. We went for pizza too, to celebrate being down in the valley. We were back in the land of abundance, where food and drink weren't rationed and we weren't strung out as if walking a tight rope like it had been all the time on the wall. We got settled in the corner of the restaurant and I sat back in my chair, sipping my cold drink and taking it all in, feeling the days of tension drain from my body and mind. Yet I couldn't quite let go.

Breathe.
Pull.
Slide jumar up.

The repetition and rhythm of climbing was entrenched in me, like a song in your head that you just can't get rid of.

"I'm really sorry I pushed you into the climb" Andy started. "It was a mad idea and I hadn't quite realised how traumatic it would be."

Even at these simple words I felt my throat go thick and a lump form. I fought back tears though I didn't get why – we were down in the valley. I was safe. I should be feeling happy.

"Let's just go on that beach holiday you told your Mum and Dad we were on" he continued. "We'll head down to the Big Sur. Cruise the coastline for our last week or so."

The pizza arrived and I stared down, unable to look at him, not wanting to give away how I felt. Gloops of cheese spilled from the edges of the pizza slice that Andy had put on my plate.

"Yeah that sounds good." I swallowed hard.

Pull yourself together. You're down now, just chill out. No big deal.

"You okay?" Andy asked.

And at that the tears dripped down and stained the red napkin in my lap darker, like blood.

"What?" Andy probed.

We were back on solid ground and in an amazing place, with two whole weeks left to enjoy it. I should be able to smile.

We've tried the climb and now we can leave; make for the coast, enjoy the waves of the Big Sur. Just have a holiday.

But how I 'should' feel wasn't matching up with reality.

What do you want?

Why are you crying?

The questions span around my head.

"What's up?" Andy asked me again softly.

I was quiet.

Being in Yosemite and going climbing again had ripped the scab from a very old wound.

"Let's just go to the coast, forget about it, have that holiday your Mum and Dad think we're on" Andy offered again, looking confused as to why I should be upset.

More tears came at the mention of my Mum and Dad and I knew that their fear about climbing had become my fear too. I felt guilt more intensely than ever. I should have been more careful. I should have listened. I should never have pushed so hard that day.

The big wet lump in my throat grew even bigger and I gasped for air. But it was good. It was therapy. I could feel my guilt lifting, fourteen years after the event that caused it.

"I can't."

"Can't what?" Andy squeezed my hand.

Finally I looked up at him, straightened up from my slump and forced a smile. I looked him in the eyes. I felt his love and smiled for real – because of who he was I could be myself.

"I want to go back up."

He looked shocked.

"Really?"

"Really."

"Are you sure you're on for it?"

For the first time I realised that I'd wanted to climb El Cap all along, since the first moment he'd suggested it.

"I keep thinking of my future self" I tried to explain. "If we leave the valley now and then I imagine looking back at this in a few years time, I know I'll always regret not trying again."

He nodded. He got it. We'd talked before about 'current self' and 'future self' – current self wants to demolish the chocolate bar, future self holds you back because you know you'll feel rubbish afterwards.

"So you really want to go back up there?" he asked but I'm sure he could see I wasn't joking. It wasn't a joking matter. Setting out to climb, backing off, living a drama of fear and guilt was what it had taken for me to realise that climbing it was what deep down I wanted. Now that we could leave, I didn't want to.

So far I'd gone along with things as if none of it was my plan – it was all Andy's idea – as if that was an excuse to avoid the guilt I felt deep down. I'd tried to justify it all by using double ropes, by tying myself to the rock face like I was a sacrificial animal, when the only thing that needed sacrificing was all the internal baggage I'd arrived at the wall with.

"I'm not joking. Let's go climbing again." I nodded in confirmation.

～

"Hey dudes!" Timmy O'Neil grinned at us in the crowded canteen, a wiry climber with a fizzy character, another devotee of El Cap. "What happened up there?" He was referring to our retreat, our failed attempt on Shortest Straw. I'd met Timmy's brother once before. He was paralysed too and they'd climbed El Cap together a couple of times.

"Awww, we were too slow, ran out of water. It wasn't really working" Andy responded. "But we're going back up."

Timmy sat down opposite us and leaned forward over the table.

"Okay, here's the deal" he began, a serious look on his face. "When you're climbing with luggage," he looked at me, raising an eyebrow to indicate that I was the luggage, "you need more help and you need your gimp system to be nailed."

"Gimp?" I interrupted.

"Aw, just slang for one of you guys, you know, handicapped or whatever you call it."

Handicapped, disabled, physically challenged, crips, wobblies, jellies, I thought I'd heard most of the jargon, politically correct or not but gimp topped them all. Didn't it mean some sexual thing involving masks and leather and being tied up? Then again, that wasn't far removed from climbing El Cap.

Timmy continued gushing enthusiasm and advice. He suggested that we pay some people to be 'gimp and bag carriers' or else arrange for some people and donkeys to meet us at the top of the climb and trek out the long way. Suddenly I felt less of a person and more like a problem. He had plenty of good suggestions about how we could improve, like getting loads of practice in the big trees in the valley, more fiddling with the jumaring system and finding a climbing team with bags of big wall experience.

"Why'd you climb with the two Aussie chicks anyway?'"he asked.

"They're great" I defended.

"Yeah but they've never climbed a big wall before. You need a team who've got it nailed."

We chatted for a while, listening to all Timmy's ideas. He was a ball of energy and I guessed an adrenaline junky and his heart was in a good place. The up-shot of his advice though was 'Go home, practice, get a better team, try again another year.' We thanked Timmy for talking about it before he buzzed off to get ready for another climb.

You can prepare and overprepare for anything in life and probably increase your chances of success but then there's reality. Between work and family commitments it had been hard enough to find three weeks to spend in Yosemite. We didn't have all the time in the world and we didn't have a team of expert climbers or pots of money to pay people to carry our gear. We'd practiced a little, not a lot but enough to have a system that worked.

"Good advice d'you reckon?" I asked Andy.

"Well Timmy knows what he's doing. He's climbed El Cap a few times with his brother Sean. They were up there last week."

"Hmmm." I nodded as I listened, inexperienced in the big wall game, willing to go with Andy's verdict. Maybe we would be going on that beach holiday after all.

Then I caught Andy's eyes and saw their mischievous glint.

"But nah, why put off 'til tomorrow what you can do today?" He was grinning like a kid let loose in a sweet shop.

So we set about planning to climb again, totally disregarding Timmy's advice. We were there with an opportunity. We had ten days left and we'd try it again. "Maybe we should try with just the two of us" Andy suggested.

"No Tash and Gemma?"

"Yeah, maybe."

"Do you think it will be simpler?"

"Yeah, maybe."

That evening was the *Yosemite Face-lift* party. The volunteers had collected mini mountains of junk, from plastic bottles to washing machines – it was an impressive amount of rubbish to have collected in a weekend and a surprising amount to have been dumped in a National Park. An eclectic crowd gathered in the hall in the village centre to mark the end of rubbish collecting for another year. The evening line up included a show by Timmy, and the premiere of the Huber Brothers new film, *Am Limit*.

Timmy landed on stage to a psychedelic sound and light show, his wild and entertaining nature hooking the audience instantly. He told the story of climbing El Cap with his brother, of the team of strong men that carried Sean up and down. Sean looked to be half of my weight. I wondered at Andy's apparent strength – his tree trunk legs with calves thicker than most thighs but more important to his strength than that, was the way his head worked. There seemed no such thing as impossible for Andy, just something you had to figure out. At the end of Timmy's talk was a video clip of Sean, slung in ropes arriving back in the valley. Someone asked him how it was to be down, and he just said "I can't wait to get off my arse and see that it's okay."

I laughed, knowing I'd be thinking exactly the same. A tattered backside was always my biggest concern and it reminded me to buy extra foam and pad my harness out even more than the first time.

After Timmy was the story of the Huber brothers, Alex and Thomas and their obsession with climbing El Cap. Every summer they left Germany to spend months in Yosemite, practising religiously to break the speed record for climbing The Nose – the obvious arête of El Cap. The record – set by themselves – was 2 hours 38 minutes. It was an incredible feat. It had taken us longer than that just to leave the ground. Barely anyone takes less than a few days to climb it. Many people take a week. Practice, commitment, obsession – with those qualities anything can be achieved.

After the show we walked back to the camp through the forest, guided by our head torches and the glow from the sliver of moon. My wheels rattled over bumps like a noisy shopping trolley, more noticeable in the quiet of night and sent me into my thoughts. I wondered what was driving me to go back up to climb El Cap. The Huber brothers seemed motivated by speed, risk, adrenaline and record-busting efforts. I didn't want any of those things. I wanted to climb it because it had been a surprise and an ordeal just to get to the point of admitting that I wanted to. I wanted to climb it because I didn't want to turn my back on fear – I wouldn't let it get the better of me. And I wanted to climb it because whilst I value life, I also value what we get when we go closer to the edge of it. I wanted to visit that place that's beyond every day and beyond comfort zones. Once you've been there you want to go again and you search it out because even though it's a little bit risky, going there involves encountering something greater than yourself, and that gives meaning to everything else.

I thought more about the *Face-lift* evening and about Timmy and the Huber brothers talks. They painted a picture of El Cap as a giant fun park, a grown-ups' playground. To the Huber brothers, climbing El Cap was just something they did before breakfast. To me it was Everest – a mountain that seemed near impossible to climb. Like anything in life, the deal is as big as we make it and relative to what we've done before. All those years before when I was first paralysed, sitting up in bed without the use of my stomach muscles had been my Everest but now I could sit up without thinking about it. What seems an arduous challenge to one person is nothing to another. It's not about comparing or holding anyone or thing in awe but about being willing to learn, try, and persevere to the point where the impossible becomes possible. I needed to stop seeing El Cap as this Everest that was sure to kill me. I needed to see it as a do-able challenge and focus on how amazing it was to be there with a team of people willing to climb it with me.

The smell of cooking bacon filled Camp 4 and I wondered why the bears weren't out sniffing for breakfast. They'd broken into some cars a few nights before, ripping open the doors to get to cans of lager. Apparently they had a taste for one particular brand and their senses were finely tuned enough to raid one car over another for their favourite drink.

There was only a day to prepare before our next attempt on El Cap and we began sorting through gear. I practised learning the names of every piece of shiny and beaten metal bit of metal. I needed to know the jargon so that when we got back up there I could speak the language of big wall climbing and be a valuable part of the team.

It felt different from the first time.

The sky looked a clearer blue than ever before and my head felt cloudless. I felt up for it. This time the choice to climb had been my own. I wasn't going along with what Andy or anyone else wanted or thinking of what could or should be. We were going back up because I wanted to.

Tash and Gemma came over and offered their help.

"Guys if there is anything we can do, we'd really like to help. We'd never climbed a big wall before and we feel like we let you down. Is there anything we can do?"

"Errr, yeah" Andy faltered.

I stopped sorting through gear and sat up to chat with them. As I did, Andy and I exchanged glances and it was as if we were reading each other's minds.

"Aw, why don't you come with us?" Andy blurted.

"Yep. It would be great if you'd come back up" I confirmed.

We'd started together, we'd tried and failed together and hopefully learned from it. It seemed a shame not to go back to try again as a team.

"Really?! We'd love to!" Gemma spoke for them.

And so the four of us were on again.

Word spread like fire around Camp 4 and other climbers came and offered their help. Suddenly we had a team of people to help, British and Aussie climbers offered to carry our loads up to the base of the route – water, ropes, kit – and even to meet us to help out with the descent. I dared not even think about the way down – getting up there seemed challenge enough – but I knew that it wouldn't be easy. The descent involved scrambling down steep rocky slabs, some abseils and a lot of forest trail.

We were planning a different route – I was glad to see the back of Shortest Straw. Zodiac seemed a more inspiring route name and being a grade easier would mean that hopefully we'd climb it faster.

"How long do you reckon for this route?" I asked Andy.

"Maybe four days?" Andy answered like a question so I took his answer to be an optimistic guess. It would take us at least four days.

"Do you think I can hold it in for four days?" I spoke aloud. The elephant in my head was how to shit whilst up the wall. I'd somehow avoided it on the last climb. A silver lining of being paralysed is choosing when to go to the toilet – the urgent need to poo doesn't come in the same way – and so you can choose to delay it until a convenient time. It obviously isn't good for you and left long enough inevitably means trouble.

"Can you do that?" Andy was intrigued.

"Well it's not good for you but as a one off, I might get away with it."

"Well if you're not shitting up there, neither am I."

"Can you do that?"

"I dunno but it'll make me climb faster!"

Just in case, I decided to take some stuff up to the bottom of the wall and have a practice that night to test a system on solid ground. One inflatable toilet seat, one bike pump, one eco-design toilet-in-a-bag. If it worked there, it might work on a portaledge.

Tash and Gemma set off to carry kit up to the wall. They would start climbing without us and fix ropes on the first pitch or two. Meanwhile we'd begin extreme piggy-backing all over again. With the early pitches fixed, we should be able to climb the route in four days, six days shorter than last time.

That evening after another epic piggy-back up through the forest and scree slopes, we were back at the base of the wall. It was time to run my toilet experiment. It was a precarious set-up balanced on some rocks amongst the scree.

"We've got to get this on camera!" Andy leapt up with a video camera whilst Tash and Gemma fell about laughing. I knew there'd be no privacy from the most intimate of things for the next four days but I hadn't banked on being a circus act before we even began climbing.

Almost straight away I decided there was no way the system would work on a portaledge.

Four days wait it would be.

Later when it got dark, I lay snuggled in the sleeping bag, staring upwards just like the week before. We chatted for a while but then Andy started snoring, consumed by the exhaustion of piggy-backing me up there again. The moon lit the wall, a shimmering sea of rock and I watched the head torches of benighted climbers twinkling as if the whole thing was studded with diamonds. We would be up higher too before long but the panic I'd felt the week before didn't clutch hold of me this time and my heart beat at an easy pace. From our bed in the scree, El Cap looked more beautiful than ever, not the monster it had looked the week before.

No matter how many times I swung off the portaledge to begin jumaring up the rope, the exposure and knot in my stomach never seemed to lessen. NATASHA SEBIRE

31. ZODIAC

W e started climbing before the sun got up. Andy jugged up the ropes to start leading off while I got my kit on and began again, only this time hoping we wouldn't be coming back down the same way. We were full of new hope that we could pull it together – it was a shorter climb and we had some experience in the bag .

Yet again though we found ourselves out of synch with the wall and its technicalities; stuck haul bags, tangled ropes, shouting and cursing. We were in a mess again. We had five ropes, all different colours in a tangled web with the four of us strung like spiders down the wall.

"Get it together, or we're all going down!" Andy shouted from up high, his frustration obvious. He wasn't used to failing on El Cap and I imagined he was fed up with us. His team – supposedly meaning 'together everyone achieves more' – except I'm sure he thought he'd be better alone.

We tried to focus. I felt out of my depth again, with no time to learn on the job. Climbing El Cap was turning into a terrible exam where failure was not an option but for which the answers were hard to find.

It wasn't helping that I had the most inappropriate nursery rhyme going around my head. It was driving me insane with its negative message.

Humpty Dumpty sat on the wall,
Humpty Dumpty had a great fall,
All the kings horses and all the kings men,
Couldn't put Humpty together again…

I'd tried everything to get rid of it, over-writing it with the only tune I knew every single word to – American Pie – but Humpty just kept sneaking back in. If there was a message in it we were heading for failure.

Don't think like that.

It hadn't helped my head when part-way up the first pitch I'd read the history of Zodiac in the guidebook. A guy called Charlie Porter had made the first ascent over seven days in 1972. At the top of Pitch 3 he'd found a dead bird upside down with its feet in the air but more ominous than that was that he climbed it at the time of the 'Zodiac killer', a serial killer in San Francisco. Every time Porter came back down from a pitch, the Zodiac killer had struck again, as if in time with when he was on the climb. Hence the name.

Great.

It struck me that insanity lies closer than we might think. I'd been talking to myself ever since the climb had begun and had voices in my head – not just one, but two or three, all saying different things and arguing about what to be done. *"This is crazy, you'll never do it."* Then the next would pipe up *"You can do it, just think it through."* Then there'd be a debate. *"You're mad." "This is amazing." "Say you want to abseil back down." "How strong is that bolt?" "Wow this is cool!" "You could be the next victim of the Zodiac killer." "Clip in, clip in, clip in!"* The voices just kept on chattering and making their points. If my hands hadn't been so busy hauling me up, I'd have taken my forehead in them and shaken my head until everything went quiet. Then I really would look insane.

One thing was clear though – we weren't going well. Like a runner who knows his first lap is too slow, it was obvious from the first pitch that we were behind already. A guy walking along the bottom of the wall had watched us for a while, then shouted up, "You guys have got a terrible system!"

As if we needed reminding.

Tash and Gemma were good solid climbers but hadn't spent much time on big walls before. I clearly couldn't be a great climber or I wouldn't be sat in a wheelchair but I knew enough to be doing better than I was. Whilst it felt better being there the second time round, I still needed to stop being caught up in emotional drama so that I could focus totally on the job at hand.

With Andy busy leading the route, the three of us gathered on the portaledge and talked about our system. We tried to figure out what wasn't working and decided that our problem was we didn't really have a system. Sometimes Gemma seconded Andy and sometimes it was Tash. Sometimes the haul bags got released before I began jumaring and sometimes I went first. Because nothing was ever the same we couldn't be slick about what we were doing. We needed to be systematic so that it was clear who was doing what and when.

Figuring out how to make the system work was like an advanced level of Sudoku and I wished we had put pen to paper to work out a logical answer before we'd set off. Gradually though we got a plan together. Gemma was more confident seconding than Tash, so she would follow Andy up the route and remove all the metalwork he'd placed in the rock. Soon after, I would leave the ledge, with Tash lowering me out on a rope in case there was a big swing. Then I'd begin jumaring up the free rope. By the time I got to the portaledge, Andy would already be leading the next pitch and I'd take over from Gemma to belay him. Meanwhile, Tash would have released the haul bags, cleaned up the mass of ropes and knots left at the previous belay and be on her way up the rope to join us. When Tash arrived, she and Gemma would have an almighty effort to pull the haul bags up, using a pulley in the system to reduce the effective weight.

Then we'd start the same thing all over again.

The new system meant that Andy could get on with the job of leading, hopefully without questions and distraction from us. The three of us would be like work horses, belaying, passing gear, pulling bags and generally trying to keep a tidy shop and sort out any mess.

It was late afternoon and the sun dipped behind the Nose. The wall fell into shadow and a nip quickly developed in the air. I pulled my big jacket on, a bulky thing but I was glad of it's warmth.

"Think we'll be climbing in the dark again" Gemma commented.

"Yeah but hopefully we'll all make it up to the top of the pitch instead of being spread across the wall again." I didn't mind climbing in the dark so much – it seemed to be inevitable – but it made things harder setting up and finding gear for the night. At least with our new system we'd started to make better progress. It finally felt like we were going somewhere instead of hanging just above the ground like monkeys in a tree.

∾

"Morning team" Andy woke us with his chirpy way. "How we all feeling?"

"Yeah, good" Gemma responded first and Tash and I echoed her sentiment.

Unlike last time we were being honest. We did feel good. Retreating from the wall hadn't entered our psyche.

I rubbed my eyes and felt the grit in them, flecks of granite, before looking up around the wall. I could see the overnight nests of other climbers, clinging to various parts of the wall as if we were all bats. Each day I watched the other climbers progress as if they were a marker for our own. I was happy when we moved at a similar pace, disappointed if we made less ground. In my imaginary race up the wall, I'd got used to us always being last but that morning I was pleasantly surprised. Our new routine seemed to be paying off. We were level with the Koreans climbing Tangerine Trip.

It was another long, hot day.

Breathe.
Pull.
Slide jumar up.
Breathe.
Pull.
Slide jumar up.

We began before the sun warmed the wall. We finished long after it set.

"Two days down. Two to go." I mumbled as we lay on the portaledge again, exhausted and searching for the energy to eat dinner and set up for the night.

"You reckon we're on track Andy?" Gemma asked.

"Maybe" he replied, his stock answer for "I don't know." You couldn't know on El Cap. Anything could happen to slow you down.

"You see that Korean guy fall off?" Andy asked.

"Luckily no." I spooned cold ravioli into his mouth, watched him lying exhausted on the ledge. I'd never seen him look so wasted, his eyes deadened by effort, hollowed, his hair gelled with sweat.

Hanging from the rock face in the dark, the chill of the night sending shivers down my spine, I forgot about the height, the distance to fall, the drama. The darkness somehow numbed it out. Bats squealed just above our heads and a mouse poked its head out from behind a flake but it didn't bother me like it did before and I relaxed enough to chat.

"The Korean, he got up it in the end. He was on the crux. Iron Hawk. It's a hard route." He swigged his end-of-day Coke-treat, said the fizz helped him revive. Tomato stains seeped from the corners of his mouth, making red blotches on his drained pale face. I thought about the Korean falling off and the terror of hurtling down the wall. Would there be time to register you were falling? Would there be time to wonder if the rope would hold? I thought about Andy and the falls he'd taken on El Cap, the roulette of it all. Some fell without even a bruise but for others it took their life.

I looked again at Andy, at the grit and salt that clung to his forehead, his matted hair and dribbled stains. Something told me he was mad for liking this, that we were all mad for being there but mostly I understood how he liked to push himself to this state of exhaustion, to simplify life to this game of staying alive. I saw in him what I had in myself.

The next morning we began as we meant to carry on – quickly, Andy climbing out of bed and straight onto the next pitch as the rest of us packed away. It was no holiday.

At the end of his pitch Andy exclaimed how exciting the next pitch would be – the Nipple, the crux of the route – but I thought how it was all the same to me. We were just somewhere, way up high, lost on the wall. I noticed other things instead, like the lightning white forks of quartz splitting the face, the shadow line that crept across the wall with the day, the faint but acrid aroma of old urine that painted dark streaks, the swifts that cliff-dived and swooped by my ears, fast black jets of colour. I noticed how everything was miniature in the valley below.

The Nipple was a shapely bulge of rock. As we approached it I could see why it was the crux – it had an overhanging groove leading to a point of rock. I belayed Andy as he made his way up to it. An overhanging crack line led to a protrusion of rock, hence the name, with nothing between it and the ground hundreds of metres below. I tensed up as I watched Andy picking his way towards the point, his legs dangling in space, pedalling for the security of the aider that he'd just clipped in. It looked horrible.

"Talk about a head for heights" I whispered as I watched Andy glide by the Nipple like it wasn't hard at all. I quietly admired his skill but there was no way I'd want to be in such an exposed position. I wished though that I could feel the rock like he did and get the tactile essence of climbing instead of the monotony of jumaring up a long rope.

As we climbed that day I was aware of so many things and surprised at the sensory overload of hanging from the rock face. I'd never have thought there'd be so much to notice. The biggest thing I noticed though was the space. Between all the rock and climbers and trees in the valley below, there was an awful lot of space. Our pee fell into it everyday, litres of strong yellow stuff, and it would disperse into a fine mist before it reached the ground. There were times when I laid on the portaledge, a momentary pause in the business of climbing and I'd look up and out and if I dared, down. Besides feeling my stomach lurch and a flash of fear, I felt awe.

Awe at the space, at the vastness of it, at how the space, the air, whatever it was, held everything in place even though it was nothing. It felt quite profound to be aware of the space and aware of being aware. We were hung delicately in a great nothingness that seemed to hold everything.

In those moments, being on the wall was a kind of spiritual experience though I could still feel the knot in my stomach and the drunken rush of adrenaline as I prepared to leave the portaledge.

"You day-dreaming?" Tash called across to me. "It's your turn to go."

It was time again. The sickening lurch of my tummy as I swung from the illusionary safety of the portaledge came about three times a day. I clipped my jumaring equipment into the rope and unclipped myself from the belay. I asked Tash to double-check that I'd set everything up right, still not trusting myself. Then I shimmied across to the edge of the ledge, ready for launch. I looked at Tash with a cross between a grimace and a smile, then shoved myself off. Whilst she lowered me out to stop me from taking a big swing, there was still a moment when my weight transferred onto the rope when I'd lurch down and my heart leapt into my head. I knew to expect it now and held Tash's eyes as if they could save me from falling.

"You're good" she re-assured me.

Once I was out I didn't look up or down, just straight in front. I took my attention to each small movement, concentrated on the precision of what I needed to do to jumar up the rope.

Breathe.
Pull.
Slide jumar up.
Breathe.

Pull.
Slide jumar up.

It was late afternoon again. A gentle breeze had worked up – nothing much but enough to set my rope swaying gently. I wanted to feel like a child on a swing but instead felt like an apprehensive adult clutching at a rope.

"You okay?" Gemma shouted down from above.

"Yeah, thanks!" I called back, and felt relieved because I actually was okay.

Breathe.
Pull.
Slide jumar up.

I was keeping my head under control. The voices had gone quiet. I'd got off the emotional roller-coaster.

Breathe.
Pull.
Slide jumar up.
I dared for a moment to look down.
You're doing it.
We were doing it. We were a long way up.

It was the third evening and the third sunset had gone. Climbing parties were everywhere, their head-torch beams like fairy lights strung across the wall, frantic late evening efforts to settle down for the night. I liked knowing we weren't alone. The day had been hot again and tiny grains of rock stuck to the sweat and salt that covered our faces. When I wiped my forehead it felt like sandpaper and my eyes were grittier than ever to rub. We clipped smelly boots, helmets and damp clothes up to dry, a jumble of gear, and dug deep into the haul bags, always aware that one clumsy move could mean dropping something vital. We didn't cook, in fact we didn't even have a stove, though Tash and Gemma had a tiny one for boiling water and making foil bags of porridge and stew. We just had bagels and cream cheese, an apple and some peanuts, Andy's choice, and though the bagels were stale and the cheese runny, I didn't mind. I didn't have an appetite anyway. The wall was taking its toll.

Water and sleep were enough and my head couldn't have hit the makeshift pillow too soon.

I slept long and deep.

It felt special to watch the sun creep across the face each morning, snuggled warm in billows of sleeping bag, so tight against Andy that my blinking eyelashes would tickle him. At not much more than a metre wide, that's the nature of a portaledge, barely enough space for two sets of shoulders. Since the first night, I'd insisted on having the wall side of the bed. Being able to touch the rock and feel it solid against my shoulder was a comfort that I needed to help me sleep.

On the morning of our fourth day on the wall, the sky hadn't cleared to its usual yawn of blue. The orange streaks of early morning lingered and the the sky was fish-scaled red and grey towards the horizon.

"We'd better get a shimmy on today" Gemma suggested, also noticing the sky. "The weather's changing."

"Red at night, shepherd's delight. Red in the morning, sailor's warning." I couldn't help but remember the saying from childhood.

I didn't fancy being on a big wall in bad weather any more than I'd taken to being there in good weather. The rain would tumble in waterfalls through the overhangs of rock. Our only shelter was a flimsy nylon tarp so we'd get drenched and cold quickly.

"How can we speed up?" I asked. There seemed little we could do to move faster. We had a system that worked but with four people things took more time and there was more equipment, food and water to haul up the face. Even if we tried our very hardest, we'd take a while longer to reach the top. There were five pitches left – so far we'd only averaged three or four a day – but at least the crux was done.

We moved at a reasonable pace but by mid-afternoon the wind was lifting the long loops of rope that dangled below us, and they snaked around the wall like giant lassoes.

"We need to watch those ropes don't snag on anything below!" Andy reminded us from up above. We didn't want a repeat of our first attempt when the rope had snagged on a block of scree and then there'd been the tree.

"There are more rope bags in the big grey haul bag!" He shouted down again. We searched them out and the climbing became even more of an operation than it had been. I packed loose rope into the rope bags like I had a severe case of obsessive compulsive tidiness, knowing one snag could mean much worse. When I jumared, there were always two ropes dangling below, so I carried two rope bags clipped to my waist and stuffed any loose loops into them. Concentrating so hard on the ropes and not getting them tangled, my brain felt like it had only felt after tackling horrendous pure maths equations in 'special' level maths and the downside was that everything took much longer.

The wind nagged at my ears and I felt the stress rise inside me.

"Mother fucking ropes!" I screamed into space.

The wind ripped at my hair. My hair whipped my face.

I was spinning.

Dizzy. Disoriented.

Above, all I could see were twisted ropes, purple, green, pink.

I slid my jumar up but it jammed.

I was dangling, in a void beneath a massive overhang, the wind roaring up the face, a storm front coming our way.

"Fucking haulbags!" I heard myself shout, my voice weak with anguish, as I saw the ropes connected to the bags had become wound tight around my own.

I hung there trapped, the others now above me looking down, helpless.

Andy had stopped climbing – a bad sign.

I must be in even more trouble than I thought.

I closed my eyes and tried to fight the fear as the wind whipped me around on the wall. Backwards and forwards like some terrible ride, a ride I just wanted to get off.

I thought about the ropes rubbing across the lip of the overhang. The razor sharp granite gnawing slowly through ten millimetres of nylon rope.

What's the point. Panicking isn't gonna help you. The voice in my head reasoned and watched me lose it but couldn't stop the eruption. I was seven hundred meters above the ground, way out from the illusionary comfort of its face, spinning, stuck, wrapped around the haul bag line.

"Unclip your safety line!" Andy shouted from way above.

I hated him for saying it because I knew it was what I had to do but I didn't want to do it. It would be the first step to untangling the mess.

Just do it Karen.

The wind roared in my ears.

I froze. I couldn't do it. I let the tears spill sweat and dirt down my face, sending a salty suncream taste into my mouth. I felt ashamed to be crying, to be losing it, to be weak. I was aware of the others looking down, willing me to get it together.

This is it Karen – this is all your nightmares come true.

I was stuck, no way to go up, and no way to go down. Panic gripped me – but there was something else – this other weird patient part of me that I was suddenly aware of, watching me with crystal clear perception as I spilled my fear out into the space. It was waiting for the panicked bit of me to calm down so it could softly encourage me to do what I needed to do.

I thought I saw my Mum and Dad.

Just breathe deep.

I saw Simon.

Just breathe deep.

I saw the faces of all the people I loved who wanted me to make it through.

Just breathe.

"It looks really difficult down there" Andy shouted down, his voice fighting against the wind.

"Yeah, we're just saying we're glad we're not you right now!" Gemma joined in.

They think this is funny!

No – they're as scared as me.

Suddenly I didn't feel so stupid for losing it.

If they all thought it looked hard, it must be.

Maybe fifteen minutes passed, and finally I began to move. I reached out and watched my fingers grab the silver karabiner, the blue rope sliding from its clasp and into the grip of my other hand.

You're doing it.

Take you're time.

There's no need to rush.

There – told you so.

I unclipped the safety line. I tried not to think about my life hanging on one rope, one skinny bundle of threads, a few strands of nylon.

You're safe – keep going.

I started myself spinning to untangle the ropes.

It was quiet above. I knew that they knew just to leave me alone.

Nearly there.

I felt dizzy from spinning but at last the jumar was free to slide upwards again. I focused on it, saw my blistered fingers, torn cuticles and white knuckles gripped tight on yellow rubber. I noticed every movement.

Breathe.

Pull.

Slide jumar up.

The world of El Cap had centrifuged into my dizzy fingers.

It felt like an eternity when at last my head came level with the others feet and they grabbed beneath my armpits and hauled me onto a stance called Peanut Ledge. They said encouraging things in soft voices, said they'd have felt the same if they'd been spinning out in space too. I was grateful for their kindness, for the people they were and for being there with them.

"Chocolate?" With a sympathetic expression, Andy extended his hand with a Snickers bar towards me.

Peanut Ledge was just about large enough to take us all without needing to set the portaledge up. So I sat perched, legs dangling into the void, no barrier this time between me and the ground. It forced me to look down and notice what a long, long way we'd climbed. The trees were tiny below, like matchsticks. I thought how, to the people looking up from the meadow, we were the colourful specks of climbers now and I wondered if anyone had been watching through binoculars at me stuck beneath the overhang, if they were relieved that I'd got out of my predicament. Of course not, nobody would be watching. We were nothing in this vast place but another dot on an ocean of rock.

I just wanted to crawl into my sleeping bag and escape the void.

"We need to really push it" said Andy looking suddenly serious. "A big storm's coming and we have to reach the top. We've got three pitches to go, but we have to do them even if we climb all night." My heart sank, then rose with the thought of the summit. We all nodded, aware how close to the edge we were but also confident that we could pull it off.

The wind died with the sun, the salmon and slate sky turning to jet as night fell and the cold bit into the tender skin of my fingers. It was silent on our ledge except for us breathing and fidgeting for warmth, waiting for Andy to finish running the last two pitches together. Far, far below the traffic hummed like electric interference in the otherwise quiet night.

A shooting star fell.

"Safe!" echoed through the blackness. This time it was almost true.

Andy had made it to the top of the wall.

We all screamed.

"Ropes fixed!" he shouted next, his voice sounding very far away.

It was time for me to climb one more time.

My stomach did a sickly lurch as I slipped over the lip of the ledge, and swung into space for the last time. I began to pull. The final pitch of PU4000+. It wasn't so scary in the dark. There was no up, no down, no yesterday, no tomorrow. There was just a yellow pull-up bar and the Perlon pattern of the rope passing through the jumar. The purple rope ran forever upwards, chasing Andy's voice into the heavens. Grit fell into my eyes. I closed them and kept pulling. My arms were exhausted and bloody, grating against the rock with each pull-up but not as tired as my mind. Fine threads of tension suspended in every synapse, tearing, ready to break. I needed Zodiac to end.

> *Breathe.*
> *Pull.*
> *Slide jumar up.*
> *Breathe.*
> *Pull.*
> *Sore fingers.*
> *Too hot.*
> *Slide jumar up.*
> *Gritty eyes.*
> *I hung, slowly spinning.*
> *It felt as if I had been pulling up all night.*
> *How much further?*

Gradually I fell into the routine, the discomfort of it all lost to the rhythm, to the silence, to my awareness that this was the last pitch, the last set of pull-ups, the last chance to appreciate being there and all the madness that went with it.

> *Just one more pull-up.*
> *Than the one after that.*
> *Pull; too hot, gritty eyes.*
> *Again.*

Pull; sore fingers, burning muscles.
Again.
Pull; grimace, just keep going.
Again.
Pull; trickling sweat, flicker of head-torches.
Again.
Pull; silent night, starry sky.
Again. Again. Again. Again. Again. Again. Again. Again. Again.
Again. Again. Again. Again. Again. Again. Again. Again. Again.
Again. Again. Again. Again. Again. Again...

My head banged against a overhang, and beyond it were only stars.

I was hanging below the final rim of El Cap.

I said Andy's name but got no reply.

I pulled hard, my jumars jamming and scraping as I forced them over the lip, measuring my progress by inches as I tried to cross the threshold between the wall and the flat world. My head popped over the edge and I saw three rusty bolts a foot away, the ropes clipped to them with big bulky knots. There was no sign of Andy and I suddenly felt very alone and very, very tired.

You're not there yet Karen.

I gritted my teeth and pulled and pushed hard, my body scraping across the rock, closing the gap on the bolts until my jumar slammed into them.

I could go no further. The only problem was my legs and bum were still left dangling.

El Capitan would not let me go.

I was bound in ropes and whichever way I rolled, my hips or knees were caught beneath the summit lip. I rested my cheek on the cold coarse granite, belly-flopped over the cusp of the prize. I didn't cry. I didn't shout. I didn't even kiss the top. I just hugged the edge and closed my eyes.

There was no 'up' anymore.

I noticed the rich smell of earth, of Manzanita bushes mingled with pine. I opened my eyes to take in the beautiful flatness before me but instead my eyes met with Andy's and we smiled.

"I can't pull you up until the others get here – so just enjoy hanging there a bit longer"

And that's what I did until I could hear Tash and Gemma just below and knew we'd made it. I knew that in a few minutes they would help pull me over the edge. In half an hour I'd be in my sleeping bag on the flat hard granite. I had no idea what time it was but knew there would be no group photograph at the summit, no gung-ho thumbs-up pose like on the Matterhorn. I just felt lucky to be alive, privileged, humbled by our passage.

I put my head back against the rock and felt the cold of the granite against my cheek and noticed that I felt absolutely calm inside. Completely still.

All of the fear, stress and guilt that I'd been recycling for weeks – maybe even years – had gone.

El Cap had brought me to surrender.

It began to snow.

32. GROUND

I shivered inside the billow of my sleeping bag, Andy snoring beside me. A damp grey tarp was wrapped around us like a shroud, the snow making a deeper and deeper blanket. When the daylight came there would be a mammoth piggy-back down to the valley but for now it was good just to sleep without a harness. I wiggled deeper into my bag, the cold seeping through me and put my hands in my armpits to cuddle myself warm.

We woke to a thick mist but it cleared quickly and opened up a fairytale view of peaks and towers and other big walls, everything black and white, coated in snow. I wished I could frame the view and keep it forever but it was nothing a camera could capture.

A cloudy morning with snow in the air, packing up to set off down from the top of El Cap. NATASHA SEBIRE

We'd thought about easier ways to descend, like by donkey or a hand-pedalled mountain bike via the gradual track through the forests over the back of El Cap but the logistics were complicated and it was a long way out. We'd thought about phoning Yosemite search & rescue. Andy had joked about the imaginary phone call.

"Excuse me, we're on top of El Cap and my girlfriend can't walk."

"Okay we'll be right there."

When the helicopter came they'd be sure to ask, "When did this happen?"

"Fourteen years ago" I'd answer. They'd probably throw us off.

Andy had told me about a rescue he'd once witnessed on El Cap. A climber had fallen and broken a leg. The rescue helicopter had flown in and called to the climber with a megaphone.

"Climber on El Cap! Climber on El Cap! We're here to help. If you've broken your leg, raise your arm; if you've broken your arm, raise your leg."

The climber had raised his arm, then the rescue team had shouted back. "Okay. We're sorry but it's too dark now, so get a good nights sleep, and we'll see you in the morning." I thought of the poor guy, the hope then the disappointment as he watched them fly off into the sunset. It wasn't dissimilar from getting to the top then realising the drama wasn't over yet because there was still a long, long way to go down.

It would be the mother of all piggy-backs.

If I was a slither of a woman with a waif-like build then a piggy-back of such proportions might not be so surprising but I'm five feet eleven, the same height as Andy, with big bones. I was tall enough that even on Andy's back my feet still scraped the ground and with two-thirds of me paralysed, I was a significant 'dead weight'. Getting to the top of El Cap was the sexy bit we'd all focused on but getting down again was just a dull essential.

Andy went on a reconnaissance, unsure despite all his previous descents as to the best route down. When he returned, his expression was stern and there was none of the lightness of his usual nature.

"Lets get going" he pressed, as fresh flakes of snow fell. The descent would be tough I knew, scrambling down an area called the Eastern Ledges. There would be rocky slabs and some abseils down to the forest trails. It was a route that took most climbers two or three hours but we'd be lucky to reach the valley before the moon was up.

We hurried, stuffing the last strewn-around items into the already overloaded sacks. We would leave two rucksacks at the top as there was too much to carry down all at once. I filled the base of the piggy-back rucksack with soft clothes that would support my bum and bum-shuffled onto higher ground ready to climb on.

For a brief moment the clouds swirled away and I could see the ravines that cut into the valley between the towers of rock. The trees in them were golden instead of green. Autumn had arrived and was creeping down towards the valley floor.

"Come on" Andy pushed, uncharacteristically agitated to get a move on. I manoeuvred forward, grabbed his shoulders and pulled myself onto the stuffed base of the rucksack that was tied to his back. Tash and Gemma grabbed hold of me and pulled the straps and slings tight, binding me to Andy for the long slog down.

As we set out for the valley I remembered my wheelchair. I missed it, just a welded bunch of metal but it gave me so much. It's funny that people talk about being 'wheelchair-bound' when it's a device that gives so much freedom and independence. Like my hand-bike. It was easy to see why I cycle for miles and miles, why I can never turn around until I've reached the end of the road, why I push myself past the day's end into the darkness. As long as I'm moving under my own steam I don't feel broken or diminished by the fact I can't walk.

The first few hundred metres we were slow and I could feel Andy strain under my weight. I worried about his back.

"We're never doing this again" I said to him.

"Damn right."

Quite quickly though we were moving at a pace, the sturdy red branches of the Manzanita bushes flicking Andy's legs as we hurried down. The path was sandy with grains like ball-bearings that snatched his feet away and added to our fear about falling down.

The snow was falling again.

We layered up in hats, gloves and jackets so we felt clumsier than we should. The waterproof fabric meant I slipped from Andy's shoulders and it was hard to hold tight.

The snow fell thick.

There were slabs of wet rock and the slopes were slippery to descend, protected only by makeshift belays with the rope slung around pine trees.

I didn't realise I was gripping Andy's neck tight enough to strangle him until the fraught moments were punctuated by the relief of easier terrain.

"This is where the abseils start" Andy informed me. It looked horrible. Our nerves were as frayed as the old bits of rope I could see hanging from the abseil. Somehow we kept going but I refused to abseil down on the fixed ropes that were in place. I wouldn't trust them, not now we'd come safely so far.

The hours ticked by as we slowly picked our way down. Tash and Gemma were always there, positive and encouraging, belaying us when they could. I was amazed at what a team we'd become considering we were strangers only a week or so before.

Finally the snow turned to sleet, and eventually to rain. The valley was getting closer.

Descending the last stretch, the air smelt somehow denser and sweeter, heavy with autumn. It was a smell as comforting as a home roast and the sight of green meadows looked as cosy as a giant feather duvet. I felt like I couldn't keep gripping on much longer so could only imagine how Andy's thighs must feel. I wished we could hurry to the end but Andy seemed to be slowing down and relaxing now the worst was over. He kept sitting on fallen logs, chatting randomly with passing climbers and hikers. I didn't want to chat. I just wanted to be down so that I could check my skin and see that my bum was free of any pressure sores.

Andy was immersed in conversation with a freelance photographer who walked up the trail, taking about cameras. Looking back I know he was just exhausted but wanting to get down I squeezed his shoulder – a silent message to say 'Stop talking, lets get going' – and I realised as I did it that we weren't brand-new together anymore. He stood up and carried on.

After ten minutes more the trees got thinner. We entered a grassy clearing with El Cap's white mass soaring high above. We could hear car engines and like he'd finally lost it, Andy started jogging. We practically sprinted into the car park.

Hitting the tarmac Andy squatted and fell backwards to the ground so we lay flat on our backs, Andy on top of me. Tash and Gemma let their haul bags drop to the ground and stood over us grinning in exhaustion, all of us relieved that we had made it down.

Laid in the car park, tourists looked at as we looked up at the sky, at El Cap looking down on us. We laughed at the madness of what we had done.

The descent took everything out of us, with nine hours of piggy-backing interrupted by this section of abseiling. NATASHA SEBIRE

33. BROKEN

My leg is like a Giant Sequoia trunk, patterned with bruises too swollen to fit into my shoe. I think it might be broken, not that I feel pain, but it looks bad, and my heart palpates and I'm sweating in strange places that tell me something's wrong; but I'll wait to find out until I get home. My shoulder feels rusted, like it needs a good oil. My fingers are swollen and bruised, throbbing blisters trying hard to heal; they keep splitting open when I push my wheels through the dry Californian dirt.

We're on the California coast, the Big Sur, a few days to hang out before we fly home. The sky is so flawless and blue it almost irritates me with its perfection but the sun warms my back, comforting. I feel utterly drained, all tanks empty, my body stiff and sore like an old arthritic woman. Four thousand or so pull-ups have done something to me. Climbing El Cap pushed me to a psychological limit and now I feel completely wasted, so that holding this pen is an effort, struggling to move it, to connect to my brain.

We're at Randolph Hurst's mansion – a long drive. All I want to do is lay in my sleeping bag, but being here takes my mind off my leg.

The woman at the counter tells me I can't go into the mansion. "There are too many stairs I'm sorry." Ironic. Andy goes and I wait.

I'm drinking a small diet Pepsi that must be at least a litre large, so big I feel bloated after a few tiny slurps; maybe its fizz will sparkle me up, out of this stagnant, empty feeling. I've no energy, no enthusiasm, no imagination for the future, though Andy's been bouncing around excited about 'what next'. I just feel a void, a giant El Cap vacuum. I have no idea what next, feel barely able to get to the next moment. In my mind I see a big junction, road signs pointing all over the place, people busy, everyone with a direction, knowing where they're going but I'm just in this weird space where I can't even be bothered to read the signs, let alone work out where to go.

'It will pass', the words echo within me and I know that I have to let this be, that it is temporary, as is everything. 'It will pass' swirls around my mind and now I hear the meaning in the words and a small space opens up around the stagnant, broken thing that I feel. It's like I can watch myself sitting here, in this exhausted state and know that it will be okay. Nothing lasts forever. My zing will return. El Cap has done something to me, something big; it was a journey through my brain, through my past and I'm left feeling broken. But it will pass.

A very large American has just sat beside me, a friendly guy. He told me stories of how he used to surf in Hawaii, the good old days in 'The Pipe'. Now he drips over the edge of his seat, drinking diet Pepsi and I suddenly wish I wasn't drinking it too and I wonder what happened, how he got that large, that unfit, that attached to his memories of how it used to be that he'd recount them to a stranger within seconds of meeting. I suddenly felt glad for climbing El Cap. Whatever it had done to me that I didn't understand, it had at least made me feel alive.

≈

Back home, I catch a taxi from the airport straight to Aberdeen Royal Infirmary, my leg now black and purple – the rest of me equally as wrecked, along with my mind. I think of the staff that had looked after me so well here all those years before, of the painting that was hung in a corridor in intensive care given by my parents in thanks for them saving my life. Fourteen years later and I'm back again. I'm embarrassed to admit I've been climbing again.

Queues. X-rays. A predictable verdict. Broken. The tibia, luckily just a simple fracture and not displaced.

"How do you think it happened?" The doctor asks, and I lower my eyes and mutter something about a forest, a piggy-back and a stumble. In truth I didn't know for sure how it happened, but thought it was probably in the car park at the end when Andy had fallen backwards. My ankle had twisted beneath his weight but it seemed too much to explain.

"Where? Why were you piggy-backing in the forest?" The doctor gently questions me and I can't really lie. I mention the climb. Those two little words that have devoured me – El Cap. He disappears for a while, then returns –

eyebrows raised.

"I've just googled El Cap – I think you're lucky that a fractured tibia is all you've got."

I lay in bed. In hospital. Two nights. Leg raised up, wrapped in a gadget to reduce the swelling. I live through every moment of El Cap. Then Corsica. Then Greenland. Japan. The Himalaya. Back and back over fourteen years to my last visit – waking from a coma – every bone broken. At the time it had felt worse than dying.

I don't sleep at night, not since the wall. Intense tingles and muscle spasms wrench me from sleep whenever I get close. I wake confused. I grab at the bed and the blankets. A nightmare that I'm falling from the portaledge high on El Cap.
Falling.
Falling.
Falling.
I'm falling, legs hanging over the edge of the bed, pulling me out, dead legs pulling me down. Strip lights glaring. Panic in plastic clammy sheets, an old lady mumbling, half-asleep, about David Ike and a conspiracy theory.

Mum calls. I haven't called for weeks. She's worried. The instant I speak she knows I am broken. I tell her where I am. Back there. And where I had been.
She's quiet for a while, listening.
"I've never told you this – but when you were ten, and we were working in America, we took you to Yosemite."
"Yeah I remember going."
"Below El Cap we pointed out the tiny dots that were climbers and you said 'One day I'm going to climb El Cap too.'"

Hand-biking to the hills. MARTE LUNDBY REKAA

34. FIZZ

I pedalled slowly up the hill behind my house, the pain in my shoulders almost gone and my fingers no longer sausage like. My waterproof trousers were tight over the plaster on my leg – it wasn't due off for a few weeks yet. The calmness I'd felt on top of El Cap had returned. Now I could sleep again, savour being able to turn on a tap for water, enjoy eating fresh food, having a toilet, talking to friends and re-building a sense of normality. I was happy for the simplicity of the inconsequential but precious things about everyday life.

The road snaked on and on up the remote valley, the Highlands opening up before me, the sky ominous. Snow was on the way.

Andy was back down in Sheffield with his kids. I hadn't seen him for weeks since El Cap. Maybe life would never be simple but knowing we were in each other's lives felt good. I didn't know if we would last the passage of time, or even if we should – together we'd get into trouble.

But the trouble with trouble is it can be so much fun.

My bike ran smoothly, well oiled and well tinkered with by my friend Ian, a gruff bearded Scotsman.

"Have you ever wondered how good you might be if you just stuck to one thing" he'd said to me that week after I'd told him about Corsica and El Cap and about plans to kayak along the coast of Sweden and maybe ski to the South Pole. "If you just stuck to cycling – who knows – you might be good enough for the Paralympics or something." I laughed at the thought of it, thinking myself too old for dreams like that or maybe too fearful of the focus it would take.

At the head of the glen, I glanced at my leg, the plaster wrapped in a carrier bag for extra protection and paused to breathe in the damp October air. The sky was big and dramatic and Scottish, painted over warm autumn mountains, their slopes glowing with the hues of heather. Serene. Beautiful. I cycled towards it all.

There wasn't enough time to make it all the way to the end of the road, where the tarmac ended at a rough track. Darkness would catch me out and I'd left my lights at home. I thought that maybe it would snow on the way back as well, ice already skinning over the puddles at the side of the road.

Going on was asking for trouble.
The road didn't go anywhere.
What was the point?
It would only end in an epic.
The sensible thing was to turn around.
That was the sensible thing.
For the first time since El Cap, I felt a fizz of excitement inside.

THANKS

Without you none of this would have happened...

There are too many people I need to thank for making this book happen, and for making the 'impossible possible'. It's hard to know where to start and how not to miss anyone out.

My Mum and Dad have been endlessly supportive and encouraging, albeit scared for my life many times and appropriately cautious because of it – but they have never let that stand in the way. My brother Simon has always been there for me as well as sharing a few adventures together, and we plan to again – when his three small boys allow. It's a privilege to share these special times with him, and hopefully with my nephews Archie, Bertie and Milo as they grow older.

If one person has opened my mind up to being or doing more than we might ever imagine, it's my partner Andy Kirkpatrick. Andy has a unique ability to see the way to success – whether that is forging ahead and sidelining all doubt, or listening carefully and backing off when necessary. Thank you Andy, for showing me a way of living and thinking that opens up so much. And thank you to his kids, Ella and Ewen, for the times you've wished your dad was by your side instead of on an adventure, and for your love and fun in the things we've shared (and the time you nearly drowned in a canoe on Loch Ness)!

Years and distance have separated me from friends Anna and Pasi, but for their inspired idea of crossing Greenland together, the commitment and effort and friendship that went with all of that, I am eternally grateful. I hope we share adventures and saunas together again. A great thanks to Harvey

Goodwin and Jacek for sharing in the Greenland adventure too.

When life gets difficult, friendship is so very important. This was never more true than with Jon, Carol and Barry on the adventure we shared kayaking around Corsica. Here's to the French autoroute, the van, the tunes, the miles of coastline, but most of all, to your friendship. Thank you.

Climbing is an act of trust in so many ways, not least in your climbing partner. Ian and Paul – thank you for helping me through my second initiation into climbing. Why two people would ever agree to climb with two strangers – one of them paralysed – is beyond me, but I'm so very happy Tash and Gemma that you did. What we shared together on El Cap is forever unbelievable and special. I am still amazed that we did it.

There are friends that have been there for years, our lives inter-twined forever, even if we haven't shared so many 'big' adventures. Thank you to you all (you know who you are). You are my constant source of love, support, inspiration, encouragement, and without you, life would be so much less.

Some people who have been part of the journey, I'm embarrassed not to remember everyone's names, but I remember strongly your spirits – encouraging, supportive, generous and great companions.

Of course there are the friends and acquaintances that have helped make this book happen. I'm very thankful for the Banff Centre Mountain Writing program and editors Tony Whittome, Marni Jackson, the sponsors at Mount Engadine Lodge and my companions on the course. More recently I owe thanks to Andy Kirkpatrick, Rob Sanders, Rebecca Varley, Gini Chappell and Wilma Machray for reading, editing and encouraging me to write.

GETTING FIT

Info to Help You

"When I feel stressed or want to shake off the busy-ness of the day, I ride my bike. Staying physically healthy seems to keep me healthy in other departments too. A blast of fresh air and a surge of exercise-induced blood to the brain seem to bring a fresh and positive perspective to so many things."

This is a recent comment I wrote for Sports Psychologist Donald MacNaughton's book "From Super Spud to Super Star." Staying active keeps you healthy in more ways than just physically, but it can be a challenge when you use a wheelchair due to the lack of access to suitable equipment, the expense of buying it yourself, or the general difficulty of trying to find a way to make something work for you.

So, I've written a bit of 'beta' on the sports I take part in, equipment I use and links that might be useful. This is available on my website.

www.karendarke.com